Early Praise for *Getting Clojure: Build Your Functional Skills One Idea at a Time*

At long last, Russ Olsen brings his engaging and encouraging style to the Clojure landscape. I wish *Getting Clojure* had been available when I was learning the language. If you're looking for a smooth transition into Clojure, this is it.

➤ **Ben Vandgrift**
   Chief Architect, Oryx Systems Inc.

The book was a joy to read and is highly recommended due to its comprehensive scope and brilliant writing. It also showcases the spirit of the Clojure community: a deeply knowledgeable but also informal, exploratory, no-nonsense approach to thinking about software.

➤ **Tibor Simic**
   Software Developer, Inge-mark

My favorite sections in the book: "In the Wild"—code that is live and used today. Seeing real code immensely propelled my understanding of the materials, far beyond any contrived examples. I wish I had this book five years ago!

➤ **Nola Stowe**
   Software Engineer, Condé Nast

Let Russ Olsen's destructuring of Clojure map mind-twisting concepts into a promise of your bright future as a capable functional coder.

➤ **Stefan Turalski**
   Software Developer, BNP Paribas

The perfect initiation into the world of Clojure.

➤ **Scott Downie**
   VP Support and Services, Illumio

Getting Clojure

Build Your Functional Skills One Idea at a Time

Russ Olsen

The Pragmatic Bookshelf

Raleigh, North Carolina

Many of the designations used by manufacturers and sellers to distinguish their products are claimed as trademarks. Where those designations appear in this book, and The Pragmatic Programmers, LLC was aware of a trademark claim, the designations have been printed in initial capital letters or in all capitals. The Pragmatic Starter Kit, The Pragmatic Programmer, Pragmatic Programming, Pragmatic Bookshelf, PragProg and the linking *g* device are trademarks of The Pragmatic Programmers, LLC.

Every precaution was taken in the preparation of this book. However, the publisher assumes no responsibility for errors or omissions, or for damages that may result from the use of information (including program listings) contained herein.

Our Pragmatic books, screencasts, and audio books can help you and your team create better software and have more fun. Visit us at *https://pragprog.com*.

The team that produced this book includes:

Publisher: Andy Hunt
VP of Operations: Janet Furlow
Managing Editor: Brian MacDonald
Supervising Editor: Jacquelyn Carter
Development Editor: Michael Swaine
Copy Editor: Candace Cunningham
Indexing: Potomac Indexing, LLC
Layout: Gilson Graphics

For sales, volume licensing, and support, please contact *support@pragprog.com*.

For international rights, please contact *rights@pragprog.com*.

Printed in the United States of America.
ISBN-13: 978-1-68050-300-5

Book version: P1.0—May 2018

To

Mikey

Felicia

Jackson

Charlie & Jennifer

Tim & Emily & Evan

Nicholas & Jonathan

Meg & Alex & Zachary

and

Scott Downie

The future is in your hands.

Contents

Part II — Intermediate

Part III — Advanced

Acknowledgments

If it takes a village to raise a child, it takes a community to build a programming language. I'd like to thank Rich Hickey for creating Clojure and everyone who has ever contributed even a little to Clojure for making my professional life just a bit better.

I'd also like to offer my warm thanks to everyone at Cognitect, especially Justin Gehtland and Mike Nygard for their generous support of this book.

In the same spirit, while authors get most of the credit, behind every book stands a village of people who contributed in some way. So I'd like to say thanks to Jamie Kite, Alex Miller, Ben Vandgrift, Nola Stowe, and Karen Cross for suffering through the early drafts of this book and suggesting ways that I could turn a confused mess into something people might read.

Special thanks to Jay Martin for his insightful comments and to Paul deGrandis for pointing out the MAL project.

I'm grateful to Jeb Beich for his patience with my amazingly stupid questions.

I'd also like to thank Scott Downie, Jackson Olsen, Alex Redington, Tibor Simic, Nola Stowe, Stefan Turalski, and Ben Vandgrift for providing technical feedback as this book went to press.

I'm also grateful to all the folks at The Pragmatic Bookshelf (especially Michael Swaine) for their help in pushing this book out the door.

Last and certainly not least I'd like to thank my lifelong partner Karen Cross for her constant love and support and encouragement. And thanks to my son Jackson Olsen for the same and for forgiving me for making fun of *The Wheel of Time*. Well, *mostly* forgiving me.

Preface

I have been writing this book—at least in my head—for decades. As a professional programmer who has used everything from assembly language and FORTRAN to C and Python and Java and Ruby, I've spent much of my career longing to get my hands on a better programming language. In my mind's eye I could see exactly what I wanted: I wanted a language that had the stripped-down syntax of Lisp. I wanted a language that embraced the power of functional programming. I wanted a language that was fast enough to run the real-world applications that I was writing. Most of all I wanted a language that had all the above *and* ran on the computing platforms I worked with. For years my imaginary programming language remained just that—imaginary. I spent a lot of that time mentally composing a book that would lay out the case for my dream programming language.

Then in 2009 I found the programming language of my dreams. It was a Lisp with macros and S-expressions and it was adamantly functional. It was as fast as I needed it to be and, because it was compiled, it held out the prospect of getting still faster. Best of all, it lived where I lived, in the practical if messy world of Java and JAR files and JVMs. Ironically, the language I'd been waiting for all this time was called *Clojure*.

So I began to learn Clojure and the book in my head got longer and longer. And then I started typing.

Who Is This Book For?

This book is for people with some programming experience—perhaps in Java or JavaScript or Ruby or Python—who want to learn Clojure. Notice I didn't say *learn to program in Clojure*. Certainly by the time you get to Chapter 21 you will be able to write functions and map vectors and quote lists and do all the other things that come with being able to sling Clojure code. But behind every programming language lies a vision: a vision of how programs should be built. The vision behind Clojure is of a radically simple language framework holding together a sophisticated collection of programming features. Thus learning Clojure—really understanding the language—involves much more than just working out where the parentheses and quotes go and knowing which library to use when parsing a URL. To really get Clojure you need to understand the framework and how it pulls together the major chunks of the language. So in the pages that follow we'll focus on the ideas behind Clojure. Each chapter will take a feature (or two or three) from the language, and explain the syntax and the mechanics behind that feature so that you know how to use it. Then we turn to the important questions:

- *What is the thinking behind this feature?*
- *How do Clojure programmers use this feature in real life?*
- *What are the dangers, the things to watch for, as you use this feature?*

As I say, I'll assume that you have some programming background. And, since most programmers find that learning Clojure is an exhilarating intellectual experience, you're definitely going to need an open mind.

How Is This Book Organized?

Generally we're going to start small and work toward the bigger ideas:

- The first chapter is a quick *this is what Clojure code looks like and how you make it go.*

- Next we look at Clojure's pair of sequential data structures: the list and the vector. Then we move on to maps, a data structure that lets you associate a key with a value. Along the way we'll run into yet another data type, the keyword, which is like a string with an attitude; and we'll explore sets, which are like maps without the values.

- Rounding out the fundamentals of Clojure we take a long look at Clojure's riff on if statements and Boolean logic.

- With the very basics out of the way we move on to a couple of chapters about functions. We discover just how to build a more fully featured (dare I say functional?) function and then discover that in Clojure functions are values akin to numbers and strings.

- From there we move on to names and namespaces, Clojure's answer to the twin questions of *How do I associate a name with a value?* and *How do I avoid name collision–induced insanity?*

- Next we turn to Clojure sequences, both the garden variety and the lazy kind. We'll see how Clojure programmers frequently use sequences as an elegant replacement for the loops that you find in more traditional programming languages.

- Then we look at destructuring, a feature you can use to dig your data back out of all those data structures.

- Next we look at building more sophisticated data containers and adding to them the behavior we need.

- At this point you'll know more than enough Clojure to be dangerous, so we'll move on to talking about how to ensure your code actually works.

- From there we turn to some of the knottier questions of writing real-world programs, including *How do I interact with Java?* as well as *How do I manage mutable state?*—not to mention *How do I write programs that can live with more than one thread?*

- Finally we take a long look at Clojure's syntax, which will lead us to think about how Clojure expressions get evaluated. This will get us to macros and how they enable you to extend the syntax of the language without taking your hands off the keyboard.

As I say, I'm not going to tell you everything about Clojure. Instead, the goal is to get you to the point where you can figure the rest out on your own.

About the Code Examples

As I write this, there are two industrial-strength Clojure implementations in wide use: First there's the original Java VM–based Clojure. Then there's ClojureScript, which compiles to JavaScript and runs anywhere JavaScript runs, including on your favorite browser. To keep things simple, I'll stick to discussing the original Java-based Clojure implementation. Mostly it doesn't matter: the differences between Clojure and ClojureScript are almost all related to the environments in which they run. In every way that matters, Clojure and ClojureScript are the same language.

The pages that follow include excerpts from various open source projects. Obviously the code for these projects is covered by the open source licenses under which they were released. In particular, the Clojure source code is copyrighted by Rich Hickey, who generously released it under the terms of the Eclipse Public License.

Online Resources

This book is overflowing with examples of Clojure in action—examples that you can download from the Pragmatic Bookshelf website.[1] You will also find a community forum there that you can use to ask questions, report any mistakes you find in the book, and generally connect with other readers.

Russ Olsen

russ@russolsen.com

May 2018

---

1. https://pragprog.com/book/roclojure/getting-clojure

Part I

Basics

CHAPTER 1

Hello, Clojure

This is where the fun starts: In this chapter I'm going to take you through the basic elements of Clojure, at the *just enough knowledge to be dangerous* level. By the time you get to the end of this chapter you'll be familiar with Clojure's very simple syntax and you'll know about many of the basic Clojure data types. Most importantly, you will be able to create and use the fundamental unit of Clojure code, the function. A couple of things to keep in mind as you read:

First, I can't actually teach you Clojure. All I can do is to serve as your guide, to take you around, show you the sights, point out the cool bits, and warn you about the occasional pothole. It's up to you, armed with patience and a keyboard, to do the real work of exploring the land of Clojure.

Second, know that Clojure is worth the effort. Clojure enables you to write clean, compact code that does what you want it to do. In fact, as we go along you'll discover that the Clojure way of programming provides enormous power wrapped up in lovely, elegant code. Let's get started.

The Very Basics

To get started you need to install some development tools. There's a wide selection of Clojure development environments and build tools available—everything from the clj tool that comes packaged with Clojure starting with version 1.9 to the IntelliJ-based Cursive to Emacs and Cider and boot.[1] [2] [3] [4] [5] [6] But

---

1. https://clojure.org/guides/deps_and_cli
2. https://www.jetbrains.com/idea
3. https://cursive-ide.com
4. https://www.gnu.org/software/emacs
5. https://github.com/clojure-emacs/cider
6. https://github.com/boot-clj/boot

in this book we're mostly going to stick to the popular Clojure development tool *Leiningen*. So if you haven't already, head over to the Leiningen website and follow the installation instructions for your operating system.[7] While you're there, you might also note that it's pronounced LINE-ing-en.

By tradition, the first program you write when learning a programming language simply prints a greeting. Here's the Clojure version:

hello/examples.clj
```
(println "Hello, world!")   ; Say hi.
```

To keep things simple, we'll take our first stab at Hello, World in the Clojure *REPL*, a handy utility that lets you type in code and see it evaluated right here, right now. The command to start a REPL with Leiningen is as follows:

```
$ lein repl
```

And once you have the REPL running you can type in this code:

```
user=> (println "Hello, world!")   ; Say hi.
```

And see the familiar greeting:

```
Hello, world!
nil
```

Don't fret about the nil; that's just the value returned by println after it does its thing, which the REPL helpfully printed for us.

REPL Who?

 The REPL is one of the few programs whose name is its algorithm. All the REPL does is read some code—the code you type in—evaluate the code, print the result, and then loop back to read some more code: *Read. Evaluate. Print. Loop.*

One of the things that has made Hello, World such a popular first program is just how much we can learn from that single line of code. Looking at our Clojure Hello, World, we can work out that in Clojure strings come "wrapped in double quotes".

We can also see that comments start with a semicolon and run to the end of the line. Typically Clojure programmers will use a single semicolon when they add a comment to the end of a line with some code—as we did in the example—but will double up on the semicolons if the comment is all alone on its own line:

---

7. https://leiningen.org

```
hello/examples.clj
;; Do two semicolons add up to a whole colon?

(println "Hello, world!")    ; Say hi
```

More subtly, we can deduce that Clojure treats simple, unadorned names like println as identifying things that get looked up. Thus our little program only worked because println is the name of a predefined function, one that comes to us courtesy of Clojure itself. As you might expect, Clojure predefines a whole range of other handy functions. There is, for example, str, which takes any number of values, converts them to strings, and concatenates the whole thing together:

```
(str "Clo" "jure")              ; Returns "Clojure".

(str "Hello," " " "world" "!")       ; Returns the string "Hello, world!"

(str 3 " " 2 " " 1 " Blast off!")  ; Fly me to the Moon!
```

There is also count, which will tell you how long your string is:

```
(count "Hello, world") ; Returns 12.

(count "Hello")          ; Returns 5.

(count "")               ; Returns 0.
```

Clojure also comes with a number of predefined constants. For example, we have the Boolean siblings true and false:

```
(println true)      ; Prints true...

(println false)     ; ...and prints false.
```

There is also nil, which is Clojure's version of the "nobody's home" value, known in some languages as null or None:

```
(println "Nobody's home:" nil)    ; Prints Nobody's home: nil
```

Note that println will print just about anything you throw at it, so that if we run this:

```
(println "We can print many things:" true false nil)
```

we'll see

```
We can print many things: true false nil
```

You've probably noticed something odd about the parentheses in a Clojure function call: they are on the outside. It's

```
(println "Hello, world!")
```

not

```
println("Hello, world!")
```

If you're coming to Clojure from a more traditional programming language, those parentheses will look out of place. There is a method to the Clojure syntax madness, which we'll return to in *Read and Eval*. For now let's just note that the Clojure syntax for making something happen—such as calling a function— is to wrap the something in round parentheses, and move on.

Arithmetic

Another thing that usually comes early in learning a programming language is figuring out how to do basic arithmetic. Clojure's approach to doing math is refreshingly—and perhaps a little disconcertingly—simple. To see what this means, let's add a couple of numbers together:

```
(+ 1900 84)
```

Run the expression in that example through the REPL and you will get back 1984. You do multiplication, subtraction, and division in the same way:

```
(* 16 124)   ; Gives you 1984.
(- 2000 16)  ; 1984 again.
(/ 25792 13) ; 1984 yet again!
```

As you might expect, you can assemble these basic math operations into arbitrarily complex expressions. Thus you can get the average of 1984 and 2010 with this:

```
(/ (+ 1984 2010) 2)
```

Arithmetic in Clojure can be a bit disorienting at first, a disorientation that can be summed up by the question *Why is the + first?* or perhaps *What happened to my nice infix operators?* The answer is that Clojure is trading some convenience, in the form of the familiar infix operators, for simplicity. By treating the arithmetic operators like ordinary functions, Clojure manages to keep the syntax of the language uniform. In Clojure, no matter what you are doing, you do it by saying

```
(verb argument argument argument...)
```

This means that in the same way we print the string "hello" with (println "hello"), we add two numbers with (+ 1982 2) and we divide them with (/ 25792 13). It's always the thing we want to do, followed by any arguments, all wrapped in round parentheses.

Conveniently, the basic math operators/functions take a variable number of arguments. Thus we can add up a bunch of numbers with this:

```
(+ 1000 500 500 1)  ; Evaluates to 2001.
```

or do a running subtraction with this:

```
(- 2000 10 4 2)      ; Evaluates to 1984;
```

There is one other twist lurking in the math functions, specifically in the / (division) function. Many programming languages, when asked to divide one integer by another, will give you back a truncated integer result. For example, in Ruby or Java when you divide 8 by 3 you get 2. Not so in Clojure, where (/ 8 3) will give you 8/3, which is a *ratio*, one of Clojure's built-in data types.

To get the familiar integer truncating behavior, you need to use the quot—short for quotient—function. So one way to get 2 is to write (quot 8 3).

By default, Clojure turns unadorned numeric literals like 8 and 3 and 4976 into integers. If you are interested in numbers with decimal points, Clojure also offers the familiar floating-point notation. Here's our averaging expression again, this time using floating-point numbers:

```
(/ (+ 1984.0 2010.0) 2.0)
```

Clojure also provides a sensible set of numeric promotions, so that if you add an integer to a floating-point number, perhaps (+ 1984 2010.0), you will get back a floating-point number—in this case 3994.0—for your trouble.

Not Variable Assignment, but Close

Once you get beyond the *add a few numbers together* stage you naturally start looking for a way to hang a name on the result. The most straightforward way to do that in Clojure is with def:

```
(def first-name "Russ")
```

There are very few surprises in using def. You give it an identifier—Clojure calls this a *symbol*—and a value, and def will associate, or *bind*, the symbol to the value. In this example the symbol is first-name and the value is the string "Russ". The value that you supply to def gets evaluated, so it can be any expression. So evaluating this

```
(def the-average (/ (+ 20 40.0) 2.0))
```

Will bind 30.0 to the-average.

One thing that you might find surprising is that it's the-average and not theAverage or the_average or even TheAverage. While the Clojure language is gloriously easygoing when it comes to the characters you can use in a symbol—this&that|other and

Much=M*re! are both fine—Clojure programmers have adopted the all-lower-case-with-words-separated-by-dashes convention—also known as *kebab case*—when picking symbols, so it's first-name and the-average.

A note of caution: def is great when you're just playing around or debugging in the REPL, but it's not the direct analog of traditional variable assignment that it seems. We'll get back to the distinction in *Def, Symbols, and Vars*, but for now we'll put that aside and continue to def things with wild abandon.

Symbolic Rules?

As I say, there are very few rules about the characters that can go into a symbol. But there are some: You can't, for example include parentheses, square brackets, or braces in your symbols since these all have a special meaning to Clojure. For the same reason, you can't use the @ and ^ characters in your symbols.

There are also some special rules for the *first* character of your symbols: you can't kick your symbol off with a digit—it would be too easily confused with a number—and symbols that start with a colon are not actually symbols but rather *keywords*, which we'll talk about in *Maps, Keywords, and Sets*.

A Function of Your Own

Let's return to our Hello, World example and see if we can turn our one-liner into something more worthy of the name *program*. We can do this by wrapping it with the fundamental unit of Clojure code, the function:

```
(defn hello-world [] (println "Hello, world!"))
```

Once you have hello-world defined you can call it just like any other Clojure function, so that if you run

```
(hello-world)
```

You will see Hello, world! printed.

As with the original, you can learn a lot from this new version of Hello, World. For example, you can see that the function definition kicks off with defn instead of def and is wrapped in its own set of parentheses *on the outside*. Inside the defn we have the function parameters, set off with square brackets, []. Since our hello-world function doesn't have any parameters, there is nothing inside of its brackets.

While we wrote the original version of Hello, World entirely on one line, we could have spread the defn over a couple of lines:

```
(defn hello-world []
  (println "Hello, world!"))
```

It's all the same to the compiler because Clojure mostly ignores whitespace.

Clojure programmers do, however, have opinions about whitespace. By convention, you can either write a short function on a single line or spread it out over a couple of lines as we did in the last example. Longer functions should take up as many lines as they need. Clojure programmers also have a strong opinion about indentation, one that we followed in the example: each level of indentation is done with two spaces. There are exceptions to the two-space rule, mostly around lining up function arguments and the like. But for the moment we'll stick to two spaces. And note it's always *spaces*, no tabs allowed.

Sans Tabs?

 Why no tabs? Because one of the great mysteries of programming is the exchange rate between tabs and spaces. Is it four spaces to a tab? Eight? Three? It's safer to stick to spaces.

Writing a function with a parameter or two is also straightforward: just put the parameter names in the brackets and then use them inside the function body. Here's a greeting function that takes a single parameter:

```
(defn say-welcome [what]
  (println "Welcome to" what))
```

The say-welcome function takes one parameter, called what, and prints an appropriate greeting. Calling your new function is like calling the println function, so that if you do this:

```
(say-welcome "Clojure")
```

you should see a friendly greeting:

```
Welcome to Clojure
```

Happily, we can rely on println to supply the spaces around the values that it prints so that we see "Welcome to Clojure" and not "Welcome toClojure."

Now that we have the basic function-building mechanics down, let's see if we can create a function that does something useful:

```
;; Define the average function.
(defn average [a b]
  (/ (+ a b) 2.0))
;; Call average to find the mean of 5.0 & 10.0.
(average 5.0 10.0)      ; Returns 7.5
```

The average function takes a couple of numbers and returns their arithmetic mean. There are three things to note about the average function. The first is the comma between the two parameters: it's not there. In contrast to many programming languages, Clojure never requires you to sprinkle commas in when you're writing a sequence of items such as the parameter list of a function. A bit of whitespace between the items is plenty. But if you really miss the commas, you can put them in: Clojure treats commas *as whitespace*. Clojure programmers mostly dispense with commas.

The second thing to note about average is that there is no explicit return statement. Clojure functions just return whatever they compute. More precisely, they return the *last* thing computed by the function. We need the qualifier because you can have more than one expression inside of your function body. Here, for example, is a variation on average that has a four-expression body:

```
(defn chatty-average [a b]
  (println "chatty-average function called")
  (println "** first argument:" a)
  (println "** second argument:" b)
  (/ (+ a b) 2.0))
```

You can probably guess what happens when you evaluate chatty-average:

```
(chatty-average 10 20)
```

Each expression inside the body gets evaluated in turn, so that you would see this:

```
chatty-average function called
** first argument: 10
** second argument: 20
```

Since the last expression supplies the return value, the function returns 15.0.

The final thing to note about average is that there are no type declarations, nothing stating explicitly that a and b must now and forever be numbers. Nor is there anything declaring what the function returns. In the great "static versus dynamic typing" trade-off, Clojure has chosen the flexibility and terseness of dynamic typing.

In the Wild

While the REPL-based Hello, World is wonderful for getting a feel for writing Clojure, it doesn't quite capture the whole spirit of the Hello, World exercise. Along with giving you a feel for the language, Hello, World is supposed to get you to work out the details of going from source code stored in a file to a running program. Happily, we're exactly one command away from getting a real Clojure project set up on disk. All we need is lein new app followed by the name of the application. So if we were creating a book store–related application for Blotts Books (Ms. Flourish has retired) we might say this:

```
$ lein new app blottsbooks
```

Feed that command into your operating system's command line, and Leiningen will respond with this:

```
Generating a project called blottsbooks...
```

And you will have a newly minted—albeit skeletal—Clojure project in a directory called blottsbooks. Look around inside of the new blottsbooks directory and you will find a collection of files—CHANGELOG.md and README.md among them—as well as a number of subdirectories, with src and test chief among them:

```
$ cd blottsbooks
$ ls
README.md doc/ project.clj resources/ src/ test/ ...
```

For our purposes we're mostly interested in the file src/blottsbooks/core.clj, which contains the Clojure source code for our project. It'll look like this:

```
hello/blottsbooks-1/src/blottsbooks/core.clj
(ns blottsbooks.core
  (:gen-class))

(defn -main
  "I don't do a whole lot ... yet."
  [& args]
  (println "Hello, World!"))
```

Note that the file starts off with an ns (short for *namespace*) expression, which sets up a new namespace and requests—with the :gen-class—that the namespace be compiled. We'll have a lot more to say about namespaces in Chapter 9, *Namespaces*, on page 95, but for the moment let's move on.

The second expression in core.clj obviously defines a function, but this defn clearly has some optional accessories that we haven't encountered. There is, for example, a mysterious string just before the parameters, and then there is an ampersand in the parameter list. We could stop here and talk about supplying a handy description of your function or about functions that take a variable number of arguments, but let's leave that to Chapter 5, *More Capable Functions*, on page 49, and instead focus on the thing that makes this function special: its name. The main function in a Clojure program, the one that gets run to kick off the program, is always called -main.

To see this in action, we can replace the -main with our book store greeting code. Here is our modified core.clj in its entirety:

hello/blottsbooks-2/src/blottsbooks/core.clj
```
(ns blottsbooks.core
  (:gen-class))

(defn say-welcome [what]
  (println "Welcome to" what "!"))

(defn -main []
  (say-welcome "Blotts Books"))
```

We can get our Clojure application to run like this:

```
$ lein run
```

Do that, and you should see

```
Welcome to Blotts Books !
```

Aside from the technical thrill of seeing the code run, we can learn something subtle from our little Clojure application. Did you notice how we defined say-welcome *before* we used it in -main? This underlines a basic Clojure rule: you need to define your functions before you use them. This means Clojure code tends to read from the bottom up, with the lower-level functions defined first.

Declaration First?

There is a way to get around the *you gotta define it before you use it* rule: you can use declare, as in (declare say-welcome), to do a sort of predefinition of a function.

Mostly Clojurists stick to defining their functions before they use them, and reserve declare for sticky situations like mutually recursive functions.

Finally, be aware that both def and defn draw from the same well of names. This means that

```
(def author "Dickens")

(defn author [name]
  (println "Hey," name "is writing a book!"))
```

will leave you with a function called author. Reverse the order of the def and defn, and author will be a string. The rule is that the last def or defn in wins.

Staying Out of Trouble

The irony of picking up a new programming language is that while the goal is to write perfect code, a key skill is to learn how to deal with the myriad of mistakes you're going to make along the way. To that end, let's make some mistakes and look at Clojure's reaction to them.

For example, what happens if we make the classic *divide by zero* blunder?

```
(/ 100 0)
```

What you will see when you divide by zero depends on the environment in which you are executing your Clojure code. You might see a brief

```
ArithmeticException Divide by zero
  clojure.lang.Numbers.divide (Numbers.java:156)
```

Or you might see this much more extensive message:

```
java.lang.ArithmeticException: Divide by zero
Numbers.java:156 clojure.lang.Numbers.divide
Numbers.java:3731 clojure.lang.Numbers.divide
/Users/russolsen/projects/clojure/quill1/foo.clj:3 user/eval6197
Compiler.java:6703 clojure.lang.Compiler.eval
Compiler.java:6666 clojure.lang.Compiler.eval
core.clj:2927 clojure.core/eval
eval.clj:77 lighttable.nrepl.eval/->result
AFn.java:156 clojure.lang.AFn.applyToHelper
```

```
<<and on and on and on>>
```

```
ThreadPoolExecutor.java:1145
  java.util.concurrent.ThreadPoolExecutor.runWorker
ThreadPoolExecutor.java:615
  java.util.concurrent.ThreadPoolExecutor$Worker.run
Thread.java:745 java.lang.Thread.run
```

Yes, it can be a bit overwhelming, but it is well intentioned: the idea of this huge stack trace is to give you the fullest explanation of what went wrong and especially *where* it all went bad. But don't be intimidated. Just focus on the first line of this field of computing debris, which is where the most important bit of information is hiding:

```
java.lang.ArithmeticException: Divide by zero
```

You also shouldn't be intimidated by the java part of that exception. Clojure—at least the version we're working with here—is built on top of Java, and now and then, especially when the exceptions go flying, you will see the Java leaking through. Don't panic: knowing Java is not a prerequisite for being a Clojure programmer.

Moving on, let's see what happens if you misspell a symbol, perhaps typing catty-average instead of chatty-average:

```
CompilerException java.lang.RuntimeException:
  Unable to resolve symbol: catty-average in this context,
  compiling:(NO_SOURCE_PATH:0:0)
```

Or you might get its 80-line big brother. Either way, you just need to fix the name of the function.

Clojure beginners also tend to have a hard time with the parentheses. The easiest parentheses problem to diagnose is adding one too many to the end. If you do something like this:

```
(+ (* 2 2) 10))
```

you will get a straightforward message back:

```
RuntimeException Unmatched delimiter: )
  clojure.lang.Util.runtimeException (Util.java:221)
```

On the other hand, if you happen to forget a closing parenthesis like this:

```
(+ (* 2 2) 10
```

and you are using Clojure interactively via the REPL, then, well, nothing. The REPL will wait patiently for you to complete the thought by supplying that final parenthesis. So the rule of thumb is that if you're sitting in the REPL and nothing is happening, consider that you need to add a closing parenthesis. Or perhaps six closing parentheses.

One other thing to remember as you stick your toe into Clojure coding is that Clojure functions are themselves values. So, in exactly the same way that you might type first-name into the REPL and get back "Russ", you can also get the value of a function by typing in the function name sans parentheses. Do this:

```
chatty-average
```

and you will see the value of the function, which gets printed something like this:

```
#object[user$chatty_average 0x39fcbef6 "user$chatty_average@39fcbef6"]
```

There is actually a fairly deep reason for this behavior (which we'll talk about in Chapter 6, *Functional Things*, on page 63), but it does tend to confuse beginners when they forget a parenthesis. The bottom line is that if you see unexpected values that look like #object[user$chatty_average... coming out of your program you probably missed an opening parenthesis somewhere. If you do get frustrated with all the parentheses, just be patient. Yes, Clojure's syntax is a little odd. But it's also simple: before you know it, all those parentheses will seem like old friends and you will wonder how you ever got along without them.

Wrapping Up

In this chapter we looked at the basics of Clojure. We saw what the language looks like, and we've printed some strings, done some arithmetic, and defined some functions. We also had a quick look at setting up a new project with Leiningen. Along the way we ran into the Clojure rule about defining functions before we use them and learned a bit about formatting Clojure code and dealing with those pervasive parentheses.

As we continue our tour of Clojure we're going to return to the topics we only managed to touch on in this chapter. For example, Chapter 5, *More Capable Functions*, on page 49, and Chapter 6, *Functional Things*, on page 63, are devoted to getting more out of your functions, while Chapter 8, *Def, Symbols, and Vars*, on page 85, will look into the mechanism behind def, and Chapter 19, *Read and Eval*, on page 229, will take a long look at Clojure's syntax and how it got that way. But for the moment we're going turn to the practicalities of handling data in quantities larger than a single string or number.

CHAPTER 2

Vectors and Lists

Now that you have a few basic Clojure concepts under your intellectual belt, it's time to think bigger. Life is full of complicated things, things that can't be represented by a single number or a lone string. So in this chapter we're going to look at a couple of the collections that Clojure has to offer, namely vectors and lists. We'll see just how easy it is to create these two sequential data structures and explore some of the functions that Clojure supplies for doing interesting things with them. Finally, we'll look at some real-world code to discover that a little Clojure knowledge goes a long way.

One Thing After Another

The vector is one of Clojure's most widely used—and useful—data structures. It's just an ordered collection of items. Here, for example, is a vector of four numbers:

vector/examples.clj
```
[1 2 3 4]
```

Syntactically, our little four-element vector could not be simpler: it's just four values surrounded by a pair of square brackets, sans commas. While our first vector contained only numbers, there is no requirement that all the items in a vector be of the same type. You can, for example, mix in strings:

```
[1 "two" 3 "four"]
```

Or Booleans:

```
[true 3 "four" 5]
```

You can even nest vectors within vectors:

```
[1 [true 3 "four" 5] 6]
```

And then do it again:

```
[0 [1 [true 3 "four" 5] 6] 7]
```

You can, in fact, embed any Clojure value in a vector.

A Toolkit of Functions

Along with the literal syntax there is also a function that manufactures vectors, called, appropriately enough, vector. The vector function takes any number of any kind of argument and wraps a vector around those arguments:

```
;; The same as [true 3 "four" 5]
(vector true 3 "four" 5)
;; The same as []
(vector)
```

However you conjure it up, once you have a vector you'll want to do stuff with it. Fortunately, Clojure provides all sorts of useful functions to go with your vectors. For example, if you're interested in how many items are hiding inside your vector you can use our old friend count:

```
(def novels ["Emma" "Coma" "War and Peace"])
(count novels)        ; Returns 3.
```

You can get at the first item of your vector with the first function:

```
(first novels)
```

Run the preceding code and you will get "Emma" back for your trouble.

The rest function is a sort of negative doppelgänger of first; rest will give you back everything *but* the first item, so that this:

```
(rest novels)
```

will return a collection that starts with "Coma" and ends with "War and Peace". You may notice something odd about the results that come back from rest: the collection returned from rest prints with round parentheses instead of the square brackets that you are probably expecting. Instead of (rest novels) returning this:

```
["Coma" "War and Peace"]
```

you will in fact see this:

```
("Coma" "War and Peace")
```

The short explanation of this mystery is that instead of returning a vector, rest actually returns a sort of generic collection, called a *sequence*. You can find the longer answer in Chapter 10, *Sequences*, on page 111. Note that you can drop as many items off the front of your vector as you have patience for by nesting calls to rest, so that this:

```
(rest (rest novels))
```

will give you a collection containing all but the first two elements, or just ("War and Peace"). Note that calling rest on a one-element vector, like this:

```
(rest ["Ready Player One"])     ; Returns an empty collection.
```

will give you back an empty collection, as will calling rest on an empty vector:

```
(rest [])                       ; Also an empty collection.
```

With a bit of effort you can use a combination of rest and first to get at any element in your vector. Need the third item? No problem; all you need is two calls to rest and one to first:

```
(def year-books ["1491" "April 1865", "1984", "2001"])
(def third-book (first (rest (rest year-books))))     ; "1984".
```

This is doable but not very convenient, and happily there is an easier way: you can turn to nth, which takes a vector and a (zero-based) index:

```
(nth year-books 2)     ; Returns "1984".
```

Alternatively, you can call the vector like a function, supplying the index as an argument:

```
(year-books 2)         ; Also returns "1984".
```

Keep in mind none of these operations change the original vector in any way. While first and nth both return a value from the vector, that value stays firmly in place in the original vector. Similarly, rest returns a *new* (shorter) vector without changing the original. This is our first glimpse of something very fundamental to Clojure: with a few exceptions, Clojure is built on a mountain of immutability. Generally, once you create a Clojure data structure such as a vector, *there is no way to modify it*. The closest you can come is to use a function like rest to make a new data structure, one that is a only a little different from the original.

Immutable Exceptions?

 There are some exceptions to the Clojure *everything is immutable* rule. For example, consider that something must change when we say (def n 99). To find out what, see *Def, Symbols, and Vars*.

Growing Your Vectors

Now that we've seen how to get things out of a vector let's move on to putting new things in. Again, you can't actually change an existing vector, but you can make a new, slightly longer vector. One way to get a bigger vector is with the conj—short for *conjunction*—function:

```
(conj novels "Carrie")  ; Adds "Carrie" to our list of novels.
```

Evaluate the preceding code and you will get back a new four-element vector:

```
["Emma" "Coma" "War and Peace" "Carrie"]
```

Note that Stephen King's guide to dealing with high-school conflict has landed at the *end* of the new vector. If you want to add an item to the front of your vector you can turn to the cons—as in *construct*—function:

```
(cons "Carrie" novels)
```

Evaluate the preceding code and you will get this:

```
("Carrie" "Emma" "Coma" "War and Peace")
```

Note that unlike conj, cons returns one of those round-parentheses sequence things. Again, let's leave that until we're ready to talk about sequences.

Lists

Clojure has a second data type that—at least at first blush—seems a lot like the vector: the list. Like a vector, a list is an ordered collection of items. To make a list, you surround your items with round parentheses instead of the square brackets you would use for a vector:

```
'(1 2 3)
```

If you look closely at the list in that code example, you will see a second syntactic twist: the list is preceded by a single-quote character. We need that quote for a very prosaic reason: lists, with their round parentheses, look just like Clojure code. Syntactically it's hard to tell the difference between (1 2 3) and (def x 99). The quote's job is to stand there in front of the list and shout, *Hey! The thing that comes next is data. Don't try to execute it!*

Happily, since the single quote applies to the whole of the thing that comes next, you only need one quote no matter how deeply your lists are nested. The only exception to the *quote that list!* rule is when you have an empty list: since there is no way that () can be mistaken for anything other than an empty list, you can write it sans quote.

And yes, it's hard to the tell the difference between a list and those sequence things we discussed earlier, since they both are surrounded by round parentheses. Again, I'll have more to say about sequences in Chapter 10, *Sequences*, on page 111.

Like vectors, lists can hold whatever data you care to throw at them, so that all of the following are perfectly good lists:

```
'(1 2 3 "four" 5 "six")
'(1 2.0 2.9999 "four" 5.001 "six")
'([1 2 ("a" "list" "inside a" "vector")] "inside" "a" "list")
```

And as with vectors there is also a function that will create a list from the arguments you pass in:

```
;; More or less the same as '(1 2 3 "four" 5 "six")

(list 1 2 3 "four" 5 "six")
```

And you can do many of the same things with a list that you can with a vector:

```
(def poems '("Iliad" "Odyssey" "Now We Are Six"))

(count poems)     ; Returns 3.
(first poems)     ; "Iliad".
(rest poems)      ; ("Odyssey" "Now We Are Six")
(nth poems 2)     ; "Now We Are Six".
```

As you can see, count, first, rest, and nth do exactly what you expect.

Lists versus Vectors

So if vectors and lists are both ordered, sequential data structures, why have both? The reason Clojure includes both vectors and lists is that while they are similar on the outside, internally these two data structures are very different. As shown in the next figure, you can think of a vector as similar to an array, a big chunk of continuous memory. Just put the first item in the first slot of your block of memory, the second item in the second, and so on.

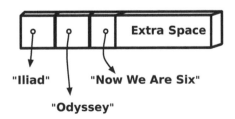

Lists, by contrast, are implemented as linked lists—hence the name. As illustrated in the figure on page 22, you can think of a list as a series of two-slot objects.

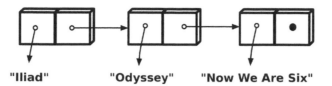

"Iliad"   **"Odyssey"**   **"Now We Are Six"**

One slot contains a reference to some data item while the second slot points at the next object in the list.

These two ways of organizing a single-file line of items have very different strengths. For example, getting to the 654th item of a vector is quick—behind the scenes Clojure does a little address arithmetic and there is the 654th item. In contrast, getting to the 654th item on a list involves running down the chain of all the previous items one at a time.

How Many Slots?

Those two-slot list objects actually have three slots. The third slot is a count of the number of items in the list. This enables the count function do its thing without having to run down the whole list saying, *One item, two items, three items* .... We can get away with caching the count because lists are immutable.

However, the advantage does not lay entirely with the vectors. It's much easier—and quicker—to tack a new item to the front of a list than a vector: with a list you just allocate a new two-slot thingie, then point the one slot at your item and the other slot at the original list. Since vectors rely on more or less continuous chunks of memory, adding a new item to the front is a lot more involved and might require allocating more memory and copying items from here to there. On the other hand, adding a new item to the end of a vector can be quick if there happens to be room at the end of the block of memory.

The implementation difference between lists and vectors bubbles to the surface very clearly with the conj function. Recall that conj takes a collection and an item and returns a new collection with all of the stuff from the original, plus the new item. Significantly, conj is aware of the differing strengths of vectors and lists and acts accordingly: it efficiently tacks the new item to the *front* of lists but to the *end* of vectors, so that

```
(def poems '("Iliad" "Odyssey" "Now We Are Six"))
(conj poems "Jabberwocky")
```

will give you

```
("Jabberwocky" "Iliad" "Odyssey" "Now We Are Six")
```

On the other hand, adding a new item to a vector with conj puts the item at the end, so that

```
(def vector-poems ["Iliad" "Odyssey" "Now We Are Six"])
```

```
(conj vector-poems "Jabberwocky")
```

will return

```
["Iliad" "Odyssey" "Now We Are Six" "Jabberwocky"]
```

Staying Out of Trouble

The main way to trip up with Clojure's vectors and lists is to forget just how immutable they are. For example, if you start with this:

```
(def novels ["Emma" "Coma" "War and Peace"])
```

and then add a new book like this:

```
(conj novels "Jaws")
```

you have done nothing. Well, not precisely nothing: you started with the three-element novels vector. Then you created a new vector with four elements. Then *you threw that new vector away*, leaving the universe pretty much as you found it. To do something useful you need to grab the new, four-element vector, perhaps by binding it to a new symbol:

```
(def more-novels (conj novels "Jaws"))
```

Exactly the same logic applies to most other Clojure data structures, including lists:

```
;; Create a list.
(def novels '("Emma" "Coma" "War and Peace"))
;; Just making the room warmer!
(conj novels "Jaws")
```

A downside of immutable lists and vectors is that it tends to cause disquiet in the hearts of new Clojure programmers, a disquiet centered on performance. The fretting generally runs like this: *What if I have a 50,000-element vector and I need to add a series of values to it? Won't that require a lot of useless copying as conj manufactures one same-except-for-one-element result after another?*

In a word, *no*. Under the hood, vectors store their data in chunks, organized in a shallow tree. Breaking the data up into chunks means that when it comes time to make an almost-the-same copy, Clojure can minimize the amount of copying by reusing most of the chunks as is.

This scheme is surprisingly efficient: some CPU cycles and memory do go into managing the chunks, but not a lot. Accessing an element of a vector—which involves traversing the tree—is not quite as fast as getting at an element of a simple array, but it's still fast. And you can make modified copies without much actual copying. And it's not just vectors: under the hood, all of Clojure's data structures are carefully designed to support fast creation of *almost-the-same* copies.

Conversely, the payoff from immutability is huge. In Clojure, once your code gets hold of a data structure, you don't have to worry that some other bit of code will unexpectedly change it. In Clojure your data structures always have the values that they were born with.

There is one other nontechnical danger lurking in Clojure data structures: the terminology. The computer-science term for immutable data structures that support the manufacture of very fast almost-the-same copies is *persistent*, as in *persistent data structures*. This is a very different use of the word *persistent* than most professional programmers are used to. Keep in mind that in Clojure, a persistent data structure is immutable and efficient and is not necessarily destined to be stored in a database or a file or anywhere else.

In the Wild

If you look at real-world code you will discover that Clojure programmers overwhelmingly choose the vector over the list for their sequential-data-structure needs. Thus, finding real-world uses of the vector brings new meaning to the word *easy*. Vectors are found at the heart of just about every Clojure program. Take, for example, this bit of real-world code:

```
(defn escape-html [string]
  (replace-all string [["&" "&amp;"]
                       ["\"" "&quot;"]
                       ["<" "&lt;"]
                       [">" "&gt;"]]))
```

Clearly the preceding function—which I adopted from the Clostache HTML templating library[1]—defines a function called escape-html. Equally clear is that the escape-html function takes a single parameter with the less-than-enlightening name of string. The body of escape-html consists of a single call to the function replace-all, which takes the string and a vector of vectors.

Step back a bit and it's obvious what escape-html is all about—obvious, at least, to anyone who has ever tripped over an ampersand in the middle of a web

---

1.   https://github.com/fhd/clostache

page. The escape-html function is in the business of foiling those attempts to embed actual HTML in innocent-looking text. And it's all done with vectors.

You can find a similar use of vectors in this bit of code, lifted from the Pedestal application framework examples:[2]

```
(defroutes routes
  [[["/" {:get home-page} ^:interceptors [bootstrap/html-body]
    ["/hiccup" {:get hiccup-page}]
    ["/enlive"  {:get enlive-page}]
    ["/mustache"  {:get mustache-page}]
    ["/stringtemplate"  {:get stringtemplate-page}]
    ["/comb" {:get comb-page}]]]])
```

This bit of code contains Clojure features we haven't covered yet: what, you might wonder, is this defroutes thing? (It's a macro. See Chapter 20, *Macros*, on page 241.) And what is this ^:interceptors weirdness? (It's metadata. See Chapter 19, *Read and Eval*, on page 229.) Not to mention all the curly brackets. (Those are maps. See Chapter 3, *Maps, Keywords, and Sets*, on page 27.)

But skip over all that and focus on the vectors and, again, if you are at all familiar with web applications, it's probably clear what is going on: the code is using the vectors to specify what the application should do when a *get* request comes on various URL paths: do *this* if someone points their browser at "/hiccup" and *that* if they hit "/enlive". The lesson here is that even at this very early phase of our adventures in Clojure, we can look at some advanced code and glean a bit of what it's up to. And that there are vectors everywhere.

While Clojure programmers mostly rely on vectors, lists do get a fair bit of use, especially in those situations where you want to build your sequence by appending new items to the front as opposed to the back. Certainly it is no great leap to imagine defroutes with lists instead of vectors. But when there aren't great algorithmic issues at stake, Clojure programmers generally reach for square brackets.

There is one giant exception to the *mostly use vectors* rule. Earlier we saw that you need the quote in front of your list to prevent it from being confused with Clojure code, specifically a function call. Clearly we don't want to confuse '("Emma" "Coma" "War and Peace") which is data, with (println "Emma" "Coma" "War and Peace"), which is code. But as we'll see in Chapter 19, *Read and Eval*, on page 229, the similarity between lists and code is neither accidental nor skin-deep. In fact we'll discover that every time you write Clojure *code* you are really creating lists, lots of lists. Stay tuned.

---

2. https://github.com/pedestal/samples/blob/master/template-server/src/template_server/service.clj

Wrapping Up

We kicked off this chapter by talking about vectors, Clojure's *almost an array* sequential data structure. We then moved on to lists, which are Clojure's other sequential data structure. We also explored some of the functions that can help you turn a data structure into useful information, and then on to how Clojure data structures are immutable. We discovered that you can make a vector or a list and fill it with whatever you want, but once it exists you ain't changing it. We also looked at how you can get into trouble by forgetting just how immutable Clojure's data structures are and at how the word *persistent* may not mean exactly what you think it means. Finally we had a look some real-world code to see vectors in action.

We are now ready to round out our toolkit of basic Clojure data structures with maps.

CHAPTER 3

Maps, Keywords, and Sets

As we saw in the last chapter, when a Clojure programmer wants to store some values one after the other, single file, they tend to reach for a vector or perhaps a list. But *one thing after the other* is not the only way to organize the data in your programs. Sometimes you want to take a hodgepodge of values, give each one a name, and roll them all into a single value. Perhaps you have the author's name and the title and the date of publication and you want to pull them all together into a single bookish thing. In this chapter we're going to look at maps, the Clojure data structure that allows you to do exactly that. Along the way we'll run into another Clojure data structure, the set, as well as a new primitive type, the keyword. Let's get started.

This Goes with That

Virtually all modern programming languages include some kind of data structure that lets you associate arbitrary keys with equally arbitrary values, and Clojure is no exception. Appropriately enough, Clojure calls its arbitrary mapping data structure a *map*. In keeping with Clojure's barebones philosophy, the map literal syntax only requires a pair of curly braces and some key/value pairs. For instance, this:

map/examples.clj
```
{"title" "Oliver Twist" "author" "Dickens" "published" 1838}
```

creates a map that associates the string "title" with "Oliver Twist", "author" with "Dickens", and "published" with 1838.

You can also cook up a new map with the hash-map function:

```
(hash-map "title" "Oliver Twist"
          "author" "Dickens"
          "published" 1838)
```

Why Not Just map?

Yes, the name of the function that manufactures new maps is hash-map, not map. There is a map function, which we'll meet presently, but it does something different.

Once you have a map, there are a surprising number of ways to look up a value. The most obvious is to call the get function. For example, if we have this:

```
(def book {"title" "Oliver Twist"
           "author" "Dickens"
           "published" 1838})
```

then we can get the date our book was published with this:

```
(get book "published")     ; Returns 1838.
```

An alternative—and more common—way to pull a value out of a map is to call the map itself like a function, supplying the key as an argument, so this:

```
(book "published")
```

will also give you back 1838, while (book "title") will return "Oliver Twist". If you happen to reach for a key that's not there, as in (book "copyright"), you will get a nil.

Keywords

While a map will let you use virtually anything for a key, Clojure programmers commonly use *keywords* as keys. Like strings, numbers, and Booleans, keywords are a basic data type that comes packaged with Clojure. Syntactically, a keyword literal starts with a colon and then follows the same rules as symbols. Thus any of the following are fine keywords:

```
:title
:author
:published
:word-count
:preface&introduction
:chapter-1-and-2
```

You can look at keywords as a sort of subspecies of a string: both are just a sequence of characters. The reason we have both keywords and strings is that, like vectors and lists, they are good at different things. Strings are data. If you read an author's name or title from a file, you'll probably store that information in a string. Keywords are part of the program itself and meaningful to the people who read code. If you need a label to represent something in your code, perhaps the state of your finite state machine or whether you want to your logger to include the :debug information, use a keyword.

Keywords Behind the Scenes

 Technically, keywords are interned strings, similar to symbols in Ruby and distant cousins to the individual items that go into enumerated types in other languages.

Maps underline the contrast between keywords and strings brilliantly: they bring together the data—which could be the string "Oliver Twist"—with its programmatic marker, :title. Thus a more idiomatic version of our novel would be:

```
(def book
  {:title "Oliver Twist" :author "Dickens" :published 1838})

(println "Title:" (book :title))
(println "By:" (book :author))
(println "Published:" (book :published))
```

Using keywords as the keys of your map gives you yet another way to look up values in your map: if you call the keyword like a function and pass in a map, the keyword will look itself up in the map. In plain English this means that you can reverse this:

```
(book :title)
```

to this:

```
(:title book)
```

and still get back "Oliver Twist". In fact, the second form, the one that uses a keyword as the function, is probably the most common way to extract a value from a map.

Changing Your Map Without Changing It

The rule for modifying maps is pretty simple: you can't. In exactly the same way that lists and vectors are immutable, maps are stubbornly resistant to change. But like lists and vectors, you can create a new map that is a modified copy of an existing map. One way you can make a modified copy is to add a key to a value, which you can do with assoc:

```
(assoc book :page-count 362)
```

Which will give you this:

```
{:page-count 362
 :title "Oliver Twist"
 :author "Dickens"
 :published 1838}
```

Using assoc is easy. You supply the original map, along with a key and a value, and you will get back a new map, just like the old one but with the key set to the new value. You can also feed more than one key/value pair into assoc, so if we wanted to change the title at the same time we add a page count, we could write this:

```
(assoc book :page-count 362 :title "War & Peace")
```

which would give us a historically incorrect 362-page Russian novel by Dickens.

The assoc function's natural partner in crime is dissoc. Where assoc adds a new key or changes the value associated with an existing key, dissoc removes a key and its associated value. Using dissoc is also straightforward: give it a map and a key and you will get back a new map, just like the old one, sans the key. Thus if you wanted to remove the publication date from Oliver Twist, you could do this:

```
(dissoc book :published)
```

You can also throw multiple keys at dissoc, so that this:

```
(dissoc book :title :author :published)
```

will leave you with a completely empty map. Keep in mind that dissoc will quietly ignore any keys that aren't actually in the map, so that this:

```
(dissoc book :paperback :illustrator :favorite-zoo-animal)
```

will return book untouched.

Associative Vectors

Vectors and maps have a lot in common. They both associate keys with values, the difference being that with vectors the keys are limited to integers while in maps the keys can be more or less anything.

That is, in fact, how Clojure looks at vectors—which means that many of the functions that work with maps will also work with vectors. For example, assoc and dissoc work fine on vectors. Thus (assoc [:title :by :published] 1 :author) will give you [:title :author :published].

Other Handy Map Functions

If you need to get hold of all the keys in a map—well, you can guess the function name:

```
(keys book)
```

Evaluate that expression and you will end up with a collection of the keys of your map, something like this:

```
(:title :author :published)
```

Or it might be (:published :title :author) or (:author :published :title); the maps that you create with the literal {} or the hash-map function make no promises about the order of their keys.

Sorted Maps

 There is a second flavor of map that keeps its keys sorted. You can make one of these sorted maps with the aptly named function sorted-map.

In much the same way that you can get all the keys from a map with keys, you can get all the values out of the map with the vals function, so that this:

```
(vals book)
```

will give you all of the values in the map. Again, the order of values returned from vals is arbitrary, but it's guaranteed to match the order of the keys returned by the keys function.

One final note on map literals: earlier I made a big deal out of how Clojure doesn't require all of those annoying commas between items in lists and vectors and, as you can see from the preceding example, the elements of a map. Except that sometimes commas can be helpful:

```
{:title "Oliver Twist", :author "Dickens", :published 1838}
```

Since Clojure treats commas as whitespace, this last example is perfectly valid code. Clojure programmers seem a bit torn on the question of commas in maps. They are widely but not universally used. So here is an area where the convention seems to be *use them if they help.*

Sets

Along with maps, Clojure also sports a built-in *set* data type. The literal syntax for a set borrows the braces from maps but adds a # to the front:

```
(def genres #{:sci-fi :romance :mystery})
```

```
(def authors #{"Dickens" "Austen" "King"})
```

Like their mathematical namesakes, Clojure sets are all about membership: a value either is or is not a member of a set. Since a value can only be in a set once, if you repeat a value in a set literal, you'll get an error. Thus, this:

```
#{"Dickens" "Austen" "Dickens"}
```

is one "Dickens" too many:

```
IllegalArgumentException Duplicate key: Dickens...
```

Like maps, sets have their own ideas about the order of their elements. The set that you wrote as #{:sci-fi :romance :mystery} is liable to come back to you as #{:sci-fi :mystery :romance}.

Since sets are all about membership, the main thing you can do with them is discover if this or that value is in the set. You can check set membership with the contains? function, which will return either true or false:

```
(contains? authors "Austen")    ; => true
(contains? genres "Austen")     ; => false
```

Or you can use the set like a function, in which case it will return either the value or nil:

```
(authors "Austen")     ; => "Austen"
(genres :historical)   ; => nil
```

If you happen to be looking for a keyword in your set, you can switch things around and use the keyword as a function:

```
(:sci-fi genres)       ; => :sci-fi
(:historical genres)   ; => nil
```

You can create a larger set from an existing set with our old friend conj:

```
;; A four element set.
(def more-authors (conj authors "Clarke"))
```

It's not an error to conj a value into a set a second time:

```
(conj more-authors "Clarke")
```

But it is a bit of a waste, since a value can be in a set only once.

Finally, you can remove elements with disj:

```
;; A set without "King".
(disj more-authors "King")
```

In this context, the word *remove* means *make a second, smaller set.*

In the Wild

Maps are the Swiss Army knives of Clojure programming: any time you need to bundle together some related data items into a unified whole, one of your first thoughts should be, *Hey, I'll use a map.* You can see this thinking at work in the clojure.java.jdbc library, which provides an easy-to-use Clojure interface to a wide variety of relational databases. The functions supplied by clojure.java.jdbc need several pieces of configuration information to find your database, which you supply with a map:

```
(require 'clojure.java.jdbc)

(def db {:dbtype "derby" :dbname "books"})

(clojure.java.jdbc/query db ["select * from books"])
```

In the example, the map bound to db contains the database connection information. Don't worry about the require expression—it simply ensures that the clojure.java.jdbc library is loaded. I'll have much more to say about this in *Namespaces*. For now focus on how using a map for this kind of configuration data means you're free to vary the contents depending on circumstances. Thus, if you want to connect to a different kind of database, you just cook up a different map:

```
(def db {:dbtype "MySQL"
         :dbname "books"
         :user "russ"
         :password "noneofyourbeeswax"})
```

Along with the connection information, clojure.java.jdbc also returns query results in maps. So, if you had a simple-minded table called books in your database, you would see something like this come back from the query function:

```
({:id 10, :title "Oliver Twist", :author "Dickens"}
 {:id 20, :title "Emma", :author "Austen"})
```

In this way clojure.java.jdbc is a typical bit of Clojure software: maps go in and maps come out.

Sets are not nearly as common as maps in real-world Clojure code, but neither are they rare. For example, clojure.java.jdbc also contains this expression:

```
(#{"derby" "h2" "hsqldb" "sqlite"} subprotocol)
```

It may look odd, but it's not complicated: this is a set—in this case a set literal—used as a function, which will return the value only if subprotocol is one of the elements in the set. Otherwise it will return nil. In essence this is a test to see if the value bound to subprotocol is the name of a database that we recognize.

But the clear popularity winner is the keyword: it's hard to write any significant Clojure code without sprinkling in some keywords. For example, if you browse through the source of the Clojure build tool and Leiningen competitor boot,[1] you will come across this:

```
(defn resolve-dependencies
  [{:keys [checkouts] :as env}]
  (let [checkouts (set (map first checkouts))]
    (->> [:dependencies :repositories :local-repo :offline? :mirrors :proxy]
         (select-keys env)
         resolve-dependencies-memoized*
         ksort/topo-sort
         (keep
           (fn [[p :as x]] (when-not (checkouts p)
             {:dep x :jar (dep->path x)})))))))
```

For those who are counting, that's 11 keywords in 10 lines of code. Keywords are everywhere in Clojure code.

Staying Out of Trouble

Like everything else in programming maps, sets and keywords have their pitfalls. The good news about keywords is that they're so simple it's hard to go wrong with them. Mainly you just have to keep in mind that keywords are not strings. The keyword :title is not, for example, the same as the string "title". Thus with a keyword-based map like this:

```
(def book
  {:title "Oliver Twist"
   :author "Dickens"
   :published 1838})
```

doing this:

```
(book "title")
```

will return you exactly nothing (well, a nil), whereas doing this:

```
(assoc book "title" "Pride and Prejudice")
```

will return a *four*-entry map:

```
{:title "Oliver Twist"
 :author "Dickens"
 :published 1838
 "title" "Pride and Prejudice"}
```

There are also some map-specific pitfalls to watch out for. For example, while it's true that maps and sets both return nil if you go searching for a nonexistent key like this:

---

1. https://github.com/boot-clj/boot

```
(book :some-key-that-is-clearly-not-there)    ; Gives you nil.
```

be careful depending on this behavior to deduce whether a key is present. After all, someone may have written this:

```
(def anonymous-book {:title "The Arabian Nights" :author nil})
```

The anonymous-book map is still a two-entry map, even if one of the values is nil. If you need to know if some key exists in a map, reach for contains?:

```
(contains? anonymous-book  :title)           ; True!
(contains? anonymous-book  :author)          ; Also true!
(contains? anonymous-book  :favorite-color)  ; False!
```

Exactly the same logic—and solution—applies to sets. If you're worried that you may have a set with nil as a member, use contains? to check for membership:

```
;; Our books may be anonymous.

(def possible-authors #{"Austen" "Dickens" nil})

(contains? possible-authors  "Austen")       ; True!
(contains? possible-authors  "King")         ; False!
(contains? possible-authors  nil)            ; True!
```

Another feature—and it really is a feature—of maps that sometimes trips up the new Clojure programmer is that the language is happy to treat maps like ordinary sequences of values, such as lists or vectors. We'll talk more about this in *Sequences*, but for now remember that functions like first, rest, and count see maps as collections of two-element vectors:

```
(def book {:title "Hard Times"
           :author "Dickens"
           :published 1838})

(first book) ; Might return [:published 1838].
(rest book)  ; Maybe ([:title "Hard Times] [:author "Dickens"]).
(count book) ; Will definitely return 3.
```

Also be aware that since Clojure makes no promises about the order of maps, exactly which key/value pair you get from first is anybody's guess. One thing you can rely on is that for any given map the results of first and rest will be consistent.

Finally, keep in mind that in expressions like (:author book) or (:sci-fi genres), the keywords :author and :sci-fi aren't just pretending to be functions. They *are* functions—functions that look themselves up in a map or a set. It is very common, if a bit confusing to beginners, to see a keyword like :title in a context where a function is clearly called for. In those situations you can bet that there is either a map or a set involved.

Wrapping Up

In this chapter we looked at the Swiss Army knife of Clojure data structures, the map. We saw that Clojure maps let you associate arbitrary keys with equally arbitrary values. Along the way we discovered that Clojure keywords make great map keys. We also looked at several ways you can look up a value in your map, and at how you can create new maps with additional—or fewer—keys. We also had a look at the map's close cousin, the set. We saw how you can test set membership in much the same way that you look up values in a map. Then we looked at the real-world use of maps, sets, and keywords in the clojure.java.jdbc library. We also saw why you want to keep in mind that while keywords have a lot in common with strings, they are indeed different. Finally we looked at the philosophical slipperiness of having a nil value in your map or set.

Having completed our look at maps and sets, we're done with the basic Clojure data structures. So now it's time to turn our attention back to code—specifically to writing conditional logic in Clojure.

CHAPTER 4

Logic

There comes a time in the life of virtually every program when decisions need to made. If the bank account is overdrawn, then send a nasty email. If the denominator is zero, then best not to do that division. If this is a preferred customer, then give them a break on the shipping charge. Programs are so full of these kinds of decisions that it's not surprising that we sometimes refer to them as *logic*.

In this chapter we'll look at how you make decisions in Clojure programs. We're going to start with the logic hammer suitable for most coding nails—the if expression—and then move on to the slightly more general cond expression. Along the way we'll discover that Clojure has its own ideas of what is true, what is false, and what things are equal, ideas that may surprise you.

The Fundamental If

Clojure includes an if expression, and the good news is that there isn't a lot to say about it: Clojure's if is about as boring a programming-language feature as you are likely to come across. An if expression starts with the word if, which is followed by two other expressions: first a condition, then an expression to evaluate if the condition is true. The whole if expression is wrapped in round parentheses:

logic/examples.clj
```
(defn print-greeting [preferred-customer]
  (if preferred-customer
    (println "Welcome back to Blotts Books!")))
```

Call the function in that example with true, and you will get a warm greeting printed. Call it with false, and you will get silence. You can also add an optional third expression inside of your if, giving you the classic if/then/else expression, sans the else keyword:

```
(defn print-greeting [preferred-customer]
 (if preferred-customer
   (println "Welcome back to Blotts Books!")
   (println "Welcome to Blotts Books!")))
```

Notice that I keep talking about if *expressions*. I do this because a Clojure if, like everything else in the language, is a value-returning expression. Thus if preferred customers get free shipping while every one else pays 10 percent, we might come up with something like this:

```
(defn shipping-charge [preferred-customer order-amount]
  (if preferred-customer
    0.00
    (* order-amount 0.10)))
```

The value returned from an if is the value returned from the last expression evaluated in the if. If you have a one-legged if—one with no else expression—and the condition is false, then the whole if expression will evaluate to nil. Thus this:

```
(if preferred-customer
  "So nice to have you back!")
```

will return either the string or nil, depending on the value of preferred-customer.

You should also note that Clojure programmers usually write short if expressions like the last example on a single line, so that this:

```
(if preferred-customer "So nice to have you back!")
```

is perfectly good Clojure.

Asking Questions

Being able to branch on an explicit true or false is only half of what makes if the programming workhorse that it is. The other half is being able to ask the questions that evaluate to a Boolean. Probably the most common question we ask in programs is *Does this thing equal this other thing?* Happily, the Clojure equality-testing function has a very obvious name.

It's just a single equals sign:

```
(= 1 1)                          ; True!

(= 2 (+ 1 1))                    ; True again!

(= "Anna Karenina" "Jane Eyre")  ; Nope.

(= "Emma" "Emma")                ; Yes!
```

Like + and *, the = function looks like an operator but is really just a function. And like + and *, the = function will take any number of arguments:

```
(= (+ 2 2) 4 (/ 40 10) (* 2 2) (- 5 1))  ; True!
(= 2 2 2 2 3 2 2 2 2 2) ; False! There's a 3 in there.
```

Equality

Note that the = function is built on the idea of structural equality: roughly, two values are equal according to = if they have the same value. Under the hood, = is identical to the Java equals method.

You can check if two things are *not* equal:

```
(not= "Anna Karenina" "Jane Eyre")       ; Yes!
(not= "Anna Karenina" "Anna Karenina") ; No!
```

As you might expect, Clojure has a wide range of other Boolean-returning functions—or predicates—besides =. You can, for example, find out which of two numbers is bigger with > and <:

```
(if (> a b)
  (println "a is bigger than b"))
(if (< b c)
  (println "b is smaller than c"))
```

If you have trouble mentally parsing the > and < expressions, start by thinking about the infix version: (a > b) or (b < c) and then move the operator to the front, giving you (> a b) and (< b c). Accompanying < and > are <= and >=, which do exactly what you expect.

There is also a variety of *is this a that?* functions:

```
(number? 1984)              ; Yes!
(number? "Anna Karenina")  ; "Anna Karenina" isn't a number.
(string? "Anna Karenina")  ; Yes, it is a string.
(keyword? "Anna Karenina") ; Not a keyword.
(keyword? :anna-karenina)  ; Yes a keyword.
(map? :anna-karenina)      ; Not a map.
(map? {:title 1984})       ; Yes!
(vector? 1984)             ; Nope.
(vector? [1984])           ; Yes!
```

These will tell you if a value is a number, a string, a keyword, a map, or a vector.

Clojure also features the usual cast of characters for doing more complicated Boolean logic. There is, for example, the not function, so that (not true) is false and (not false) is, unsurprisingly, true. There are also and and or for assembling larger Boolean expressions:

```
;; Charge extra if it's an express order or oversized
;; and they are not a preferred customer.
(defn shipping-surcharge? [preferred-customer express oversized]
  (and (not preferred-customer) (or express oversized)))
```

It's important to note that and and or do short-circuit evaluation: they evaluate just enough of their arguments to come up with a result. Thus in the last example, if we're dealing with a preferred customer the function won't even consider whether the order is being shipped express or is oversized.

Truthy and Falsy

One notable aspect of Clojure's handling of Booleans is that the language is willing to treat any value as a Boolean. This, for example is a perfectly good if:

```
(if 1
  "I like science fiction!"
  "I like mysteries!")
```

As is this:

```
(if "hello"
  "I like science fiction!"
  "I like mysteries!")
```

And even this:

```
(if [1 2 3]
  "I like science fiction!"
  "I like mysteries!")
```

Not only are these good if statements, but in all three cases the winner is science fiction. The rule is simple: in an if statement and any other Boolean context, only false and nil get treated as false. Everything else is treated as true. Thus this expression will announce a love of mysteries:

```
(if false "I like scifi!" "I like mysteries!")  ; Mysteries!
```

And so will this one:

```
(if nil "I like scifi!" "I like mysteries!")    ; Mysteries!
```

Since everything other than false and nil—and I do mean *everything*—gets treated as true, Clojure treats all strings, all numbers, and all keywords as true. Consequently, all of the following expressions will evaluate to "yes":

```
(if 0 "yes" "no")       ; Zero's not nil or false so "yes".
(if 1 "yes" "no")       ; 1 isn't nil or false so "yes".
(if 1.0 "yes" "no")     ; 1.0 isn't false nor nil: "yes".
(if :russ "yes" "no")   ; Keywords aren't false or nil so "yes".
(if "Russ" "yes" "no")  ; "yes" again.
(if "true" "yes" "no")  ; String contents don't matter: "yes".
(if "false" "yes" "no") ; The string "false" isn't false: "yes".
(if "nil" "yes" "no")   ; And the string "nil" ain't nil: "yes".
```

The *anything else is true* rule also applies to collections. Thus, since no vector is equal to false nor is any vector equal to nil, all vectors—even empty ones—are treated as true:

```
(if [] (println "An empty vector is true!"))
(if [1 2 3] (println "So is a populated vector!"))

(if {} (println "An empty map is true!"))
(if {:title "Make Room! Make Room!" }
  (println "So is a full map!"))

(if () (println "An empty list is true!"))
(if '(:full :list) (println "So is a full list!"))
```

All the if expressions in the preceding examples will produce some output.

One issue with having a more or less infinite collection of true things along with two different false things is the terminology. When we say something is true, do we mean the specific value true or just true in the sense of not being false or nil? To avoid confusion, Clojurists sometimes refer to the values that are treated as true in the more general sense as being *truthy*. Thus, while only true is really true, "hello", 1.0, and "Russ" are all truthy. Similarly, we can use *falsy* to describe the metaphysical quality shared by nil and false. In Clojure there are exactly two falsy things—false and nil—and an infinite number of truthy things.

Falsy

 Some Clojure programmers believe the proper spelling is *falsey*. This belief is false.

Do and When

One wrinkle with Clojure's if is that you are limited to one expression for the truthy leg and one for the falsy leg. But what happens if you want to do several things when the condition is truthy? Or several when the condition is falsy? The key word here is *do* because that is what Clojure calls its *group a bunch of expressions into a single expression* construct. Thus, this:

```
(do
  (println "This is four expressions.")
  (println "All grouped together as one")
  (println "That prints some stuff and then evaluates to 44")
  44)
```

is a single expression that returns 44. Armed with do, we can flesh out a simple if with multipart true and false legs:

```
(defn shipping-charge[preferred-customer order-amount]
  (if preferred-customer
    (do
      (println "Preferred customer, free shipping!")
      0.0)
    (do
      (println "Regular customer, charge them for shipping.")
      (* order-amount 0.10))))
```

Clojure also sports a variant of if called when, which doesn't have an else (or falsy) leg but which supports multiple statements without needing the do:

```
(when preferred-customer
  (println "Hello returning customer!")
  (println "Welcome back to Blotts Books!"))
```

As you might expect, when returns nil when the condition is not truthy.

Dealing with Multiple Conditions

Technically, no matter how complicated the decision you need to make, the plain old if is all you ever need. Choosing between three alternatives? Just nest a couple of ifs. Say, for example, our shipping charges were free to preferred customers and otherwise $5 for orders under $50, $10 for orders between $50 and $100, and 10% of the purchase price for bigger orders, we could write something like this:

```
(defn shipping-charge [preferred-customer order-amount]
  (if preferred-customer
    0.0
    (if (< order-amount 50.0)
      5.0
      (if (< order-amount 100.0)
        10.0
        (* 0.1 order-amount)))))
```

Have another alternative? Then just nest another if—and at some point drive yourself crazy. While your CPU may be fine with deeply nested if expressions, the mushy computer between your ears probably prefers to look at this sort of situation as a series of alternatives: *Is it this? No? Well, is it that?* ...

Fortunately Clojure has an expression for just such occasions: cond. Here's a partial implementation of our shipping-cost function using cond:

```
(defn shipping-charge [preferred-customer order-amount]
  (cond
    preferred-customer 0.0
    (< order-amount 50.0) 5.0
    (< order-amount 100.0) 10.0)))
```

As you can see in the example, cond takes pairs of expressions, each pair made up of a predicate expression and a value expression. In the example, the predicates are preferred-customer, (< order-amount 50), and (< order-amount 100). When it's evaluated, cond evaluates each predicate in order. If the predicate is falsy—that is, either nil or false—cond goes on to the next pair. If the predicate is truthy, then cond will evaluate the value expression and return that, leaving the remaining pairs unevaluated.

One problem with our cond-based shipping-charge function is that it doesn't handle orders of $100 or more properly. If you evaluated (shipping-charge 200) you would get a nil back for your trouble, since that's what cond returns if none of the predicates come back truthy.

We have a couple of options for fixing shipping-charge. We could certainly add a predicate to explicitly cover the "$100 or more" case:

```
(defn shipping-charge [preferred-customer order-amount]
  (cond
    preferred-customer 0.0
    (< order-amount 50.0) 5.0
    (< order-amount 100.0) 10.0
    (>= order-amount 100.0) (* 0.1 order-amount)))
```

Alternatively, we could add in a catch-all :else clause:

```
(defn shipping-charge [preferred-customer order-amount]
  (cond
    preferred-customer 0.0
    (< order-amount 50.0) 5.0
    (< order-amount 100.0) 10.0
    :else (* 0.1 order-amount)))
```

Note that the :else clause is not special new cond syntax. It's just another predicate/expression pair. Think about it: if none of the other predicates are truthy, cond will arrive at the last predicate/expression pair, decide that since :else is neither false nor nil it must be truthy, and return 10% of the order amount. In principle we could have used any truthy value instead of :else. :default, true, and "whatever" would all work. We use :else because that's the Clojure convention for the *everything else* clause of a cond.

Along the lines of cond we have the somewhat less powerful but still useful case, which lets your code turn this way or that based on a single value. Here is how we might use case to come up with a welcome message:

```
(defn customer-greeting [status]
  (case status
    :gold        "Welcome, welcome, welcome back!!!"
    :preferred   "Welcome back!"
                 "Welcome to Blotts Books"))
```

The idea is that your value—status in the example—should match one of the constants in the case statement—:gold or :preferred in the example. If it does match, then the whole case evaluates to the expression paired with the constant. If nothing matches, then the expression evaluates to the last, unpaired expression—in this case "Welcome to Blotts Books".

A couple of things to keep in mind about case: First, the last catch-all expression is optional, but if you do leave it out the case will generate an error if none of the constants match. Second, the constants need to be just that: constant. The constants in case expressions are one of the few places where an expression does not get evaluated.

Throwing and Catching

Although we've spent most of this chapter talking about how you can use if and cond and case to control the flow of execution through your code, sometimes the flow of execution reaches out and takes control of its own accord. I'm talking, of course, about exceptions. Exceptions are your program's way of telling the world that something is *very, very wrong*:

```
user=> (/ 0 0)

ArithmeticException Divide by zero clojure.lang.Numbers.divide
(Numbers.java:158)
```

By default, an exception will terminate your program immediately. If that's not what you want, you can include some exception-handling code by wrapping your suspect expression in a try:

```
(try
  (publish-book book)
  (catch ArithmeticException e (println "Math problem."))
  (catch StackOverflowError e (println "Unable to publish..")))
```

Any code after the try but before the first catch gets run as normal, and if there are no exceptions the try will have no effect.

But if your code does trigger an exception, the try will act as a sort of case expression, and attempt to match the exception type to one of the catch clauses. In the example, if the exception is of type ArithmeticException, then it will get handled by the first catch and your program is saved. If the exception isn't an ArithmeticException but is a StackOverflowError, it gets handled by the second catch clause and again your program will live to compute another day. If the exception thrown doesn't match any of the catch clauses, then it will continue to wreak havoc on your program.

Exceptions arise from doing dumb things like dividing by zero, but you can also throw an exception manually. For that you will need two things: a throw expression and an exception value to use in the throw expression. And the easiest way to get hold of an exception value is to use the built-in ex-info function:

```
(defn publish-book [book]
  (when (not (:title book))
    (throw
      (ex-info "A book needs a title!" {:book book}))))
  ;; Lots of publishing stuff...
  )
```

The ex-info function takes a string describing the problem and a (possibly empty) map containing any other pertinent information. And to complete the circle, if you want to catch an exception generated by ex-info you will need to look for exceptions of type clojure.lang.ExceptionInfo.

In the Wild

As you might expect, it's easy to find very familiar-looking examples of if, when, cond, and case. Here, for instance, are a few lines pulled from Leiningen:

```
(when (real-directory? f)
  (doseq [child (.listFiles f)]
    (delete-file-recursively child silently)))
```

We may not follow the details, but the general idea of this code is not hard to work out: when f is a real directory—that is, not a file or a symbolic link—then delete it and all of its contents.

Here's another snippet, also from Leiningen:

```
(if (.isDirectory entry)
  (.mkdirs f)
  (do (.mkdirs (.getParentFile f))
      (io/copy (.getInputStream jar entry) f)))
```

If entry is a directory, then do *this*; otherwise do something else.

Dot What?

The reason for the funny un-Clojurelike function names such as
.isDirectory and .mkdirs is that this code is calling into lower-level Java
libraries. More on this in Chapter 16, *Interoperating with Java*, on
page 189.

Surprisingly, the *if (or when) this, then do that* use case of if is not all that
common in Clojure. What you find instead is if, when, and cond used to compute
a value. Take this bit of code, again lifted from Leiningen:

```
(if (vector? task) task [task])
```

The interesting thing about this expression is that it doesn't *do* anything.
Instead it *evaluates* to a value, specifically the original task, or task wrapped
in a vector. Thus we might bind the result to a symbol:

```
(def task-vector (if (vector? task) task [task]))
```

or maybe embed it in a function:

```
(defn ensure-task-is-a-vector [task]
  (if (vector? task) task [task]))
```

When used this way—which it commonly is—Clojure's if is a lot like the ternary
expressions that you find in Java or C++: If this is truthy I want this value;
otherwise I want this other value.

You can find a great example of cond in the open source library Korma.[1] Korma
(tagline: "Tasty SQL for Clojure"; you've got to give them points for wit) tries
to help Clojure programmers deal with vagaries of SQL and contains the following bit of code:

```
(defn str-value [v]
  (cond
    (map? v) (map-val v)
    (keyword? v) (field-str v)
    (nil? v) "NULL"
    (coll? v) (coll-str v)
    :else (parameterize v)))
```

The job of str-value is to take a Clojure value and turn it into a string that is
acceptable to SQL. The function goes about its duties by asking what kind
of value it has: Is it a map? Well, then hand it off to map-val. Is it a keyword?
Then off to field-str, and so on.

---

1.   https://github.com/korma/Korma

Notice that Korma uses a cond and not a case since this is not a test for specific values but for whole classes of values. On the other hand, elsewhere in Korma we find this case expression:

```
(case (:type query)
  :insert (update-in query [:values] #(map prep-fn %))
  :update (update-in query [:set-fields] prep-fn)
  query)
```

Here we're testing against a pair of known values: If the query type is :insert, then return this. If the type is :update, return something else. Otherwise just return the query unchanged.

Staying Out of Trouble

Depending on your programming background, the truthy/falsy approach to logic will seem either completely mundane or like an outrage to all that is right and moral. If you lean toward the outrage school of thought, please keep in mind that the *false and nil are false and everything else is true* rule is not a minor aberration that only pops up when some programmer isn't careful. There is a lot of code in Clojure that takes advantage of this behavior. For an example of this, look no further than and. While (and true true) does indeed evaluate to true and (and false false) is comfortably false, the and function can and will return some decidedly un-Boolean values:

```
(and true 1984)        ; Evaluates to 1984, which is truthy.
(and 2001 "Emma")      ; Evaluates to "Emma", again truthy.
(and 2001 nil "Emma")  ; Evaluates to nil, which is falsy.
```

The point is that the behavior of and only makes sense if you look at it from the truthy/falsy point of view. Given this, you should avoid testing for true or false explicitly. For example, the condition part of this if:

```
(if (= (some-predicate? some-argument) true)
  (some-other-function))
```

isn't just extra wordy; it's *wrong*. The author of some-predicate?—like the author of and—may have decided to return something other than true to indicate truthyness. If it does, then this if will miss it.

There's also a stylist pothole that you should avoid: As you build functions that contain if and cond and do a bit of nesting, you're going to find yourself needing to close off a lot of open parentheses as you get to the end. The convention is to close off the parentheses on the last line of your expression, the way we did with the three parentheses at the end of shipping-charge:

```clojure
(defn shipping-charge [preferred-customer order-amount]
  (cond
    preferred-customer 0.0
    (< order-amount 50.0) 5.0
    (< order-amount 100.0) 10.0
    :else (* 0.1 order-amount)))  ; Close, close, close.
```

What you should *not* do is grant each closing parenthesis its own line, like this:

```clojure
(defn shipping-charge [preferred-customer order-amount]
  (cond
    preferred-customer 0.0
    (< order-amount 50.0) 5.0
    (< order-amount 100.0) 10.0
    :else (* 0.1 order-amount)    ; No.
  )                               ; No.
)                                 ; No!
```

As you get used to Clojure's parentheses-based syntax, all those closing parentheses will begin to fade into the psychological background. Don't draw attention to them while you wait for that to happen.

Wrapping Up

In this chapter we looked at decision-making in Clojure. We saw how Clojure sports a straightforward family of logical expressions: everything from the generic if and when to the multiway cond and case. We also explored the some-times-less-voluntary changes in the flow of your program with try, catch, and throw. But mostly we looked at Clojure's take on Boolean logic, which counts false and nil as falsy and everything else as truthy.

Now that you've tamed the if and plumbed the depths of truth, it's time to revisit functions and discover that there is much more to them than we've seen so far.

CHAPTER 5

More Capable Functions

One of the interesting things about Clojure—at least compared to more mainstream programming languages like Java or Python—is just how uniform Clojure code is. Look at a typical Java or Python program and you will find packages and classes and methods and annotations along with a menagerie of field declarations. Certainly Clojure sports analogs to many of these programming-language features, but real-world Clojure code consists mainly of one thing: functions. Lots of functions. There's a simple reason for this: Clojure programs—and the entire Clojure programming language—is built around functions.

If you're going to construct a whole language around functions, then those functions had better have some serious talents. So in this chapter we'll have a look at some features of Clojure that will enable you to supercharge your functions.

One Function, Different Parameters

Because Clojure—and Clojure programmers—do rely so heavily on functions, it's not surprising that the language provides some extras to help you craft just the function that you want. For example, all the functions we've written so far have taken a fixed number of arguments. Sometimes it's convenient to build functions that take a less doctrinaire view of how many arguments they are willing to accept. For example, we might want to create a *Hello, World*–style function that will let you supply a greeting or default to a plain old "Hello". This is not hard:

capable/examples.clj
```
(defn greet
  ([to-whom] (println "Welcome to Blotts Books" to-whom))
  ([message to-whom] (println message to-whom)))
```

The greet function as defined here will accept either one or two parameters. The single-argument version works like our original say-welcome, while the two-argument rendition takes a message along with the recipient. Notice how greet is essentially two function definitions in one, each with its own parameter list and body, each one wrapped in yet another set of round parentheses.

Armed with the preceding code, we can call greet with one argument, like this:

```
(greet "Dolly")            ; Welcomes Dolly to Blotts Books.
```

or with two, like this:

```
(greet "Howdy" "Stranger") ; Prints Howdy Stranger.
```

The technical term for the number of arguments a function takes is *arity*, and so functions like greet are called *multi-arity* functions. A Clojure function can have as many arities as you like, but in practice people tend to limit themselves to three or four.

One problem with greet is that the two function bodies are reasonably redundant: both variations of greet print a message and a name. This is a fairly common occurrence in multi-arity functions. After all, each arity of the function should be doing more or less the same thing or we probably should have written two separate functions.

The way to get rid of this redundancy is simple and equally common: just call one arity from the other:

```
(defn greet
  ([to-whom] (greet "Welcome to Blotts Books" to-whom))
  ([message to-whom] (println message to-whom)))
```

The idea of this *filling in the defaults* technique is that you have one arity—usually the one with the most arguments—that really does something. All the other arities, the ones that take fewer arguments, call that main version, filling in the missing parameters as they go.

Arguments with Wild Abandon

Multi-arity functions are fine for functions like greet, functions that might take one or two or some other definite number of arguments. But what if you want to write a function that can deal with a completely arbitrary number of arguments? The good news is that you can get this done with the strategic placement of an & in your argument list.

Here, for example, is a function that will take any number of arguments and print them all out:

```
(defn print-any-args [& args]
  (println "My arguments are:" args))
```

When someone calls print-any-args, the arguments show up in the args parameter—the one after the ampersand—*as a collection*. So if you call print-any-args like this:

```
(print-any-args 7 true nil)
```

you will see this:

```
My arguments are as follows: (7 true nil)
```

In the same spirit, here's a function that returns its first argument:

```
(defn first-argument [& args]
  (first args))
```

Even better, you can have ordinary arguments before the &, so that we can rewrite first-argument like this:

```
(defn new-first-argument [x & args] x)
```

Functions that take advantage of the magic of the & are called *varargs* or *variadic* functions. Note the key syntactical difference between variadic functions and the multi-arity functions that we looked at earlier: multi-arity functions devote a separate body to each argument set while variadic functions (the ones with the &) have a single function body.

Multimethods

Multi-arity and variadic functions are great for those situations where you want to build functions that are less picky about the number of arguments they will accept. Sometimes what you want is to be able to vary your function's behavior based on some other aspect of the values that get passed to it.

For example, imagine that our system was getting book data from various sources, in different formats. Some books still look like the maps we've been using:

```
{:title "War and Peace" :author "Tolstoy"}
```

While others come in maps with different keys:

```
{:book "Emma" :by "Austen"}
```

And still others are encoded in vectors:

```
["1984" "Orwell"]
```

Clearly we could handle all of this by writing a function to convert the odd-ball formats into our standard map, complete with :title and author keys:

```
;; Normalize book data to {:title ? :author ?}
(defn normalize-book [book]
  (if (vector? book)
    {:title (first book) :author (second book)}
    (if (contains? book :title)
      book
      {:title (:book book) :author (:by book)})))
```

There's nothing wrong with this kind of *just do it* approach, but what if we suddenly had to deal with a whole blizzard of book formats, everything from lists to XML and JSON encoded strings. Our simple normalize-book function is likely to get very ugly very rapidly.

One way to deal with this kind of situation is to build a multimethod. Like functions with multiple arities, multimethods let you have a single function with multiple implementations. But unlike multi-arity functions, which pick the implementation based on the number of arguments, multimethods allow you to pick the implementation based on any—and I do mean *any*—characteristic of its arguments.

Writing a multimethod is an exercise in splitting the problem apart. First we need a function to do the splitting by categorizing the different sets of arguments. In our example this would be a function that can distinguish the different formats of book data:

```
(defn dispatch-book-format [book]
  (cond
    (vector? book) :vector-book
    (contains? book :title) :standard-map
    (contains? book :book) :alternative-map))
```

Pass a book value to dispatch-book-format, and it will tell you which format you have—:vector-book, :standard-map, or :alternative-map.

Next, we declare a multimethod that uses our function to categorize its arguments:

```
(defmulti normalize-book dispatch-book-format)
```

That code example defines a new multimethod—essentially a function—that picks its implementation based on what it gets back from its *dispatch function*, in this case dispatch-book-format. All that is left is to define the implementations, one for each possible value returned from the dispatch function. We do this with defmethod:

```clojure
(defmethod normalize-book :vector-book [book]
  {:title (first book) :author (second book)})

(defmethod normalize-book :standard-map [book]
  book)

(defmethod normalize-book :alternative-map [book]
  {:title (:book book) :author (:by book)})
```

We end up with a single argument function called normalize-book that will first run its argument through dispatch-book-format and, based on the result, pick an implementation:

```clojure
;; Just returns the same (standard) book map.
(normalize-book {:title "War and Peace" :author "Tolstoy"})

;; Returns {:title "Emma" :author "Austen"}
(normalize-book {:book "Emma" :by "Austen"})

;; Returns {:title "1984" :author "Orwell"}
(normalize-book ["1984" "Orwell"])
```

And thus we can bring harmony to our books.

Multi Who?

 The careful reader will have noticed that normalize-book doesn't contain any code to handle bad input. The good news is that if the dispatch function produces a value for which there is no corresponding defmethod, Clojure will generate an exception, which is probably what you want. Alternatively, you can supply a method for the value :default that will cover the *everything else* case.

The cool thing about multimethods is that in writing the dispatch function you can choose any criteria that you want. For example, in the United States the copyright period is different depending on when a book was published. If our book maps include a :published key, then we could write a multimethod that decides what to do based on the year of publication:

```clojure
(defn dispatch-published [book]
  (cond
    (< (:published book) 1928) :public-domain
    (< (:published book) 1978) :old-copyright
    :else :new-copyright))

(defmulti compute-royalties dispatch-published)
```

```
(defmethod compute-royalties :public-domain [book] 0)

(defmethod compute-royalties :old-copyright [book]
  ;; Compute royalties based on old copyright law.
  )

(defmethod compute-royalties :new-copyright [book]
  ;; Compute royalties based on new copyright law.
  )
```

In a sense multimethods are a generalization of the kind of type-based polymorphism that you find in most object-oriented programming languages. Multimethods are more general in the sense that *you* get to decide which criteria to use to pick the implementation. You can always change the guts of dispatch-book-format to pick your implementation a different way. Or create a different multimethod that categorizes its arguments in some other way.

Even better, there's no requirement that all the bits of a single multimethod be defined in the same file or at the same time. If, for example, our books contained a :genre key, like this:

```
(def books [{:title "Pride and Prejudice" :author "Austen" :genre :romance}
            {:title "World War Z" :author "Brooks" :genre :zombie}])
```

we could certainly create a multimethod based on the genre:

```
;; Remember you can use keys like :genre like functions on maps.

(defmulti book-description :genre)

(defmethod book-description :romance [book]
  (str "The heart warming new romance by " (:author book)))

(defmethod book-description :zombie [book]
  (str "The heart consuming new zombie adventure by " (:author book)))
```

But what if much later someone comes up with a new genre?

```
(def ppz {:title "Pride and Prejudice and Zombies"
          :author "Grahame-Smith"
          :genre :zombie-romance})
```

No problem! Just define a new method:

```
(defmethod book-description :zombie-romance [book]
  (str "The heart warming and consuming new romance by " (:author book)))
```

As I say, this sort of multimethod addition does not have to appear in the same file or be written by the same programmer as the originals. And this means multimethods provide a great extension point for your code.

Deeply Recursive

Along with letting you do interesting things with your function arguments, Clojure also provides specialized support for writing recursive functions. A recursive function is, of course, a function that calls itself. For example, suppose we had this collection of book maps:

```
(def books
  [{:title "Jaws"  :copies-sold 2000000}
   {:title "Emma"  :copies-sold 3000000}
   {:title "2001"  :copies-sold 4000000}])
```

and we wanted to know the total number of books sold. We could write a recursive function to run through all the elements of the vector:

```
(defn sum-copies
  ([books] (sum-copies books 0))
  ([books total]
   (if (empty? books)
     total
     (sum-copies
       (rest books)
       (+ total (:copies-sold (first books)))))))
```

Notice that sum-copies uses the *filling in the defaults* trick we discussed earlier. The second arity—the one that does all the work—takes two arguments: the vector and the current total. The first arity kicks things off by supplying a zero for the count so that you can call sum-copies with just the vector. Other than that, the operation of sum-copies is simple: it starts by using the Clojure-supplied empty? function to check if the vector is empty. If it is, then sum-copies returns total and we're done. Otherwise sum-copies recursively calls itself with all but the first book and a new total.

Unfortunately there is serious problem with sum-copies. Every time sum-copies recursively calls itself, it eats up some stack space. That means sum-copies will work for a modestly sized collection of books, but make the books vector a little too long and you will run out of stack space:

```
StackOverflowError   clojure.walk/walk (walk.clj:44)
```

On my machine, *too long* is around 4,000 books. Not small, but well within the realm of the possible.

This is where the specialized support for recursive functions comes in. Notice how making the recursive call to sum-copies is pretty much the last thing the function does? And how the only data flowing from one invocation of the function to the next flows through the function parameters? Given this, there's no reason to accumulate all those stack frames. We can take advantage of *tail call optimization* by replacing the recursive call to sum-to-n with recur:

```
(defn sum-copies
  ([books] (sum-copies books 0))
  ([books total]
    (if (empty? books)
      total
      (recur
        (rest books)
        (+ total (:copies-sold (first books)))))))
```

It appears that recur is making the same recursive call that we had in the first version of sum-copies. But recur knows how to take advantage of being the last expression in a function to avoid accumulating all those stack frames. And that means that this second version of sum-copies will work no matter how many books you're dealing with.

One apparent downside of recur is that we need to build a new function—or, in the example, a new function arity—to use it, something that will get old quickly. Fortunately we can dispense with the function with loop. Here's our sum-copies one more time, this time recast as a loop expression:

```
(defn sum-copies [books]
  (loop [books books total 0]
    (if (empty? books)
      total
      (recur
        (rest books)
        (+ total (:copies-sold (first books)))))))
```

The way to understand loop is to think of it as a blend of a phantom function and a call to that function. In our example, the "function" has two parameters, books and total, which initially get bound to the original book collection and 0. With books and total bound, we evaluate the body, in this case the if expression. The trick is that loop works with recur. When it hits a recur inside the body of a loop, Clojure will reset the values bound to the symbols to values passed into recur and then recursively reevaluate the loop body.

There are a couple of things to keep in mind about recur. The first is that recur, either with or without loop, is the Clojure way of writing a completely general-purpose loop. Think about it: recur lets you execute the same block of code over and over, each time with slightly different data, and break out just when you are ready. That is a loop. The second thing is that recur is a reasonably low-level tool. Chances are there is a better—and easier—way to get your task done. If, for example, you need to add up all those book sales, you would probably say something like this:

```
(defn sum-copies [books] (apply + (map :copies-sold books)))
```

Well, that's what you'll say after you read a bit further. As we'll see in the next few chapters, the map bit converts the collection of books into a collection of numbers—the copies sold—while the apply + sums up the copies. Details aside, the beauty of this last rendition of sum-copies is that it enables us to rise above the item-by-item processing of loop and recur and instead deal with the collection as a whole. While loop and recur are great tools to have as a last resort, there is usually a better way to solve most programming problems.

Docstrings

One of the challenges of programming is that code has two audiences, one electronic and the other human. On one hand, code is the medium that we use to order the computer around, and we have to do that ordering with explicit, sometimes painful, precision. But code is also literature. It needs to communicate its intent and workings to the humans who maintain and enhance it.

The traditional way you help the people understand code is via comments. A comment is always as close as the semicolon key. Thus, if we wanted to add a bit of explanation to our average function we might do something like this:

```
;; Return the average of the two parameters.
(defn average [a b]
  (/ (+ a b) 2.0))
```

As every programmer knows, the beauty of comments is that they disappear early on in parsing. Thus you can gab away inside a comment, confident that whatever you say will be forgotten by the time the compiler gets down to business. But the early demise of comments has a downside. We don't write comments for decorative purposes; we write them because we're trying to say something helpful about the code. Wouldn't it be nice if we could somehow hang those helpful descriptions on the function?

Helpful indeed, which is why Clojure provides documentation strings. A documentation string—or *docstring* for short—is a regular string that you can insert just after the function name in your defn:

```
(defn average
  "Return the average of a and b."
  [a b]
  (/ (+ a b) 2.0))
```

Clojure will store the string along with the function. You can get at the docstring for any function with the built-in doc macro. To get at the docstring in the REPL, you just use doc:

```
user=> (doc average)
------------------------
user/average
([a b])
  Return the average of a and b.
```

Note that Clojure even added the argument list to the documentation for free.

Docstrings for the House!

Docstrings are not just for functions. Other members of the Clojure menagerie, creatures like macros and records—which we'll meet in later chapters—also support docstrings.

So you can also supply a docstring in a plain old def: (def ISBN-LENGTH "Length of an ISBN code." 13).

Adding docstrings to multi-arity functions is also easy. We could, for example, implement a well-documented number-averaging function that can average two or three numbers, like this:

```
(defn multi-average
  "Return the average of 2 or 3 numbers."
  ([a b]
  (/ (+ a b ) 2.0))
  ([a b c]
  (/ (+ a b c) 3.0)))
```

Just remember that the docstring always comes after the function name.

Pre and Post Conditions

Aside from being convenient units of code, functions provide natural choke points where you can improve the reliability of your code by checking that the values passed to your function are what you expect. For example, if we had a function to publish a book and we wanted to make sure our book had a title before we did any publishing, we might write this:

```
;; Publish a book using the (unseen) print-book
;; and ship-book functions.

(defn publish-book [book]
  (when-not (contains? book :title)
    (throw (ex-info "Books must contain :title" {:book book})))
  (print-book book)
  (ship-book book))
```

Happily, Clojure provides a shortcut for this sort of thing in the form of the :pre condition:

```
(defn publish-book [book]
  {:pre [(:title book)]}
  (print-book book)
  (ship-book book))
```

To set up a :pre condition just add a map after the arguments—a map with a :pre key. The value should be a vector of expressions. You will get a runtime exception if any of the expressions turn out to be falsy when the function is called. So if we wanted to ensure that our books had both authors and titles, we could write this:

```
(defn publish-book [book]
  {:pre [(:title book) (:author book)]}
  (print-book book)
  (ship-book book))
```

You can even take the checking one step further by specifying a :post condition, which lets you check on the value returned from the function. Thus we could write

```
(defn publish-book [book]
  {:pre  [(:title book) (:author book)]
   :post [(boolean? %)]}
  (print-book book)
  (ship-book book))
```

to ensure that the return value (which is ultimately going to come from ship-book) is a Boolean. Note that we use % to stand in for the return value in the :post conditions.

Staying Out of Trouble

One of the surprising things about Clojure functions is that you can mix and match the variadic & into a multi-arity function *if you are careful*. Here's us being careful:

```
(defn one-two-or-more
  ([a] (println "One arg:" a))
  ([a b] (println "Two args:" a b))
  ([a b & more] (println "More than two:" a b more)))
```

We just need to keep in mind that Clojure is sharp enough not to let us define a multi-arity function with overlapping arguments. For example, if we had written that last function as

```
;; Oh no!
(defn one-two-or-more
  ([a] (println "One arg:" a))
  ([a b] (println "Two args:" a b))
  ([& more] (println "More than two:" more)))
```

then we wouldn't get past the Clojure compiler. The problem is that it's unclear which arity should get evaluated when you call the function with two parameters.

You should also be careful not to confuse a *more than one expression in the body* function, like this:

```
(defn chatty-average
  ([a b]
    (println "chatty-average function called with 2 arguments")
    (println "** first argument:" a)
    (println "** second argument:" b)
    (/ (+ a b) 2.0)))
```

with a multi-arity function:

```
(defn chatty-multi-average
  ([a b]
    (println "chatty-average function called with 2 arguments")
    (/ (+ a b) 2.0))
  ([a b c]
    (println "chatty-average function called with 3 arguments")
    (/ (+ a b c) 3.0)))
```

The key is to look for the parameters, which will tell you which flavor of function you have.

Finally, keep in mind when you're defining variadic functions that & is just an ordinary one-character symbol that happens to have a special meaning in the context of defining function arguments. That means this:

```
(defn print-any-args [& args]
  (println "My arguments are:" args))
```

is a function that will take any number of arguments, while this:

```
(defn print-any-args [&args]
  (println "My arguments are:" args))
```

will not compile. Why? Look again and note the lack of whitespace between the & and the args, which means we're trying to define a function with a single argument called &args. Our function then tries to use the unbound symbol args and *blam!*—we have a compiler error. What we meant to write was an &, then some space, then the catchall argument: [& args].

In the Wild

Our old friend the built-in = function is a great example of the function-related goodies we've been looking at in this chapter:

```
;; Code edited a bit for clarity.

(defn =
  "Equality. Returns true if x equals y, false if not. Same as
  Java x.equals(y) except it also works for nil, and compares
  numbers and collections in a type-independent manner.
  Clojure's immutable data structures define equals()
  (and thus =) as a value, not an identity, comparison."
  ([x] true)
  ([x y] (clojure.lang.Util/equiv x y))
  ([x y & more]
   (if (clojure.lang.Util/equiv x y)
     (if (next more)
       (recur y (first more) (next more))
       (clojure.lang.Util/equiv y (first more)))
     false)))
```

The = function takes any number of arguments and returns true if they are all equal. Fortunately, = can turn to the lower-level clojure.lang.Util/equiv function to do most of the work. The catch is that equiv can only compare two values at a time.

Notice how the code breaks the job up into three arities. The single-argument arity is easy enough: evaluate (= anything) and you will always get back true. The two-argument arity is also pretty straightforward: just call clojure.lang.Util/equiv.

It's the third arity, the one that deals with more than two arguments, where things get interesting. In this case the basic flow is to compare the first two or three arguments with clojure.lang.Util/equiv and to resort to recur if there are arguments left over.

Simple Equality?

 This whole two- or three-argument dance in = appears to be there to improve performance. We *could* build a perfectly rational version of = that simply compares the first two arguments and resorts to recur if there are more than two.

The ClojureScript source code contains a lovely example of a multimethod in to-url. Here's a somewhat simplified version of to-url:

```
(defmulti to-url class)
(defmethod to-url File [f] (.toURL (.toURI f)))
(defmethod to-url URL [url] url)
(defmethod to-url String [s] (to-url (io/file s)))
```

Like our normalize-book example, to-url is trying to bring order to a chaotic world by converting various URL-like things into a single data structure. Unlike the book example, to-url uses the built-in class function, which will return the underlying type of the value as its dispatch function. Essentially what we have here is a rough approximation of the class-based polymorphism that you find in many object-oriented programming languages, implemented in a handful of lines of code.

Wrapping Up

In this chapter we took a look at how flexible a Clojure function can be. We've seen how you can define functions that take a variable number of arguments and at how you can hang a bit of documentation on your function. We also looked at multimethods, which enable you to define functions that execute different code depending on the arguments they are passed. We've seen how to write functions that take advantage of tail recursion and we've had a tour of pre and post conditions, which enable you to validate the data entering and leaving your functions.

Now that we've taken a good look at what a Clojure function is capable of, it's time to address a bigger question: *Why are functions so central to Clojure programming that we call Clojure a functional language?*

CHAPTER 6

Functional Things

Even people who don't know very much about Clojure tend to know one thing about it: Clojure is a functional programming language. But what does it mean for a programming language to be functional? After all, no matter if they call it a function or a method or a subroutine, all mainstream programming languages come equipped with some kind of *call it with arguments and get back a result* thing. What makes functional languages like Clojure different?

In this chapter we're going to take a hard look at the thing that makes Clojure a functional programming language: the idea that functions are first-class values, values that you can manipulate with the language. Along the way we'll discover that much of the power of Clojure comes not from writing functions that do things, but in writing functions that create functions that do things. If all this sounds a bit like science fiction, well, prepare for light speed.

Functions Are Values

Let's start our adventures in functional programming by imagining that we have decided to add price and genre to the maps we've been using to keep track of our books, like this:

functional/examples.clj
```
(def dracula {:title "Dracula"
              :author "Stoker"
              :price 1.99
              :genre :horror})
```

Further, let's imagine that we need to write some code to distinguish the books based on an arbitrary price:

```
(defn cheap? [book]
  (when (<= (:price book) 9.99)
    book))
```

```
(defn pricey? [book]
  (when (> (:price book) 9.99)
    book))
```

```
(cheap? dracula)        ; Yes!
(pricey? dracula)       ; No!
```

or the genre:

```
(defn horror? [book]
  (when (= (:genre book) :horror)
    book))
```

```
(defn adventure? [book]
  (when (= (:genre book) :adventure)
    book))
```

```
(horror? dracula)       ; Yes!
(adventure? dracula)    ; Nope!
```

The only halfway interesting thing about these functions is that they take advantage of Clojure's truthy logic and return nil when the book fails the test, and the book map itself—which is truthy—when it passes.

We might also be interested in combinations of price and genre:

```
(defn cheap-horror? [book]
  (when (and (cheap? book)
             (horror? book))
    book))
```

```
(defn pricy-adventure? [book]
  (when (and (pricey? book)
             (adventure? book))
    book))
```

We could write functions like this all day. What about cheap books by some author or the expensive books entitled *Possession*?

Possession

 It turns out there's a remarkable number of novels called *Possession*, with at least a dozen in print as I write this.

The key—and unfortunate—word here is *write*. When you are building real systems you don't want to spend your time writing these kinds of combinations by hand. What you want is to code the basic operations and then create the combinations dynamically. Fortunately, all you need to get out of the hand-coding business is to realize that in Clojure functions have something in common with numbers and strings and Booleans and vectors. Like these more mundane things, *functions are values*.

This means that when you evaluate the name of a function you've defined with defn, perhaps like this:

```
cheap?
```

you will see something like this:

```
#object[user$cheap_QMARK_ 0x71454b9d "user$cheap_QMARK_@71454b9d"]
```

The #object[user$cheap_QMARK_..."] is the semi-intelligible string that gets output when Clojure tries to print the function that knows a cheap book from an expensive one. You can also bind that function value to another symbol:

```
(def reasonably-priced? cheap?)
```

Do that, and reasonably-priced? is now an alternate name for our thrifty function:

```
(reasonably-priced? dracula)        ; Yes!
```

You can also pass function values to other functions. To take a silly example, we could do this:

```
(defn run-with-dracula [f]
  (f dracula))
```

run-with-dracula does exactly what the name suggests: it evaluates a function with the dracula value as an argument. Which function? The one that you pass to run-with-dracula:

```
(run-with-dracula pricey?)     ; Nope.
(run-with-dracula horror?)     ; Yes!
```

More practically, this idea of functions as values gives us an easy way of combining our predicates:

```
(defn both? [first-predicate-f second-predicate-f book]
  (when (and (first-predicate-f book)
             (second-predicate-f book))
    book))
(both? cheap? horror? dracula)      ; Yup!
(both? pricey? adventure? dracula) ; Nope!
```

The only difference between the more general-purpose both? function and the very specific cheap-horror? is that both? lets you pass in your pair of predicate functions, which means you can use it to run your books by any two predicates you can cook up.

Functions on the Fly

There's something else you can do with functional values: you can manufacture new ones, on the fly. In much the same way you can make a new number with (+ 2 3) or (* 5 x), you can use fn to create new functions. Here, for example, we manufacture a new function with fn, one that doubles its argument:

```
(fn [n] (* 2 n))
```

As you can see from the example, using fn is a lot like using defn, except that you leave out the name. Like defn, fn creates a new function, essentially a packaged bit of code. The difference between fn and defn is that fn doesn't bind its newborn bundle of code to a name; you just get the function value. So what can you do with a function value? Anything you can do with any other value. You can, for example, print it:

```
(println "A function:" (fn [n] (* 2 n)))
```

or bind it to a symbol:

```
(def double-it (fn [n] (* 2 n)))
```

and, most importantly, call it:

```
(double-it 10)          ; Gives you 20.
((fn [n] (* 2 n)) 10)   ; Also gives you 20.
```

Returning to our book example, here is a nameless function that does the same thing as cheap?:

```
(fn [book]
  (when (<= (:price book) 9.99)
    book))
```

Armed with fn, we can write functions that produce functions:

```
(defn cheaper-f [max-price]
  (fn [book]
    (when (<= (:price book) max-price)
      book)))
```

It's important to understand just how meta we've gone here: cheaper-f is a function that produces a whole family of bargain-spotting functions, each with its own idea of what constitutes a bargain.

```
;; Define some helpful functions.

(def real-cheap? (cheaper-f 1.00))
(def kind-of-cheap? (cheaper-f 1.99))
(def marginally-cheap? (cheaper-f 5.99))
```

```
;; And use them.

(real-cheap? dracula)        ; Nope.
(kind-of-cheap? dracula)     ; Yes.
(marginally-cheap? dracula)  ; Indeed.
```

If this all looks less than spectacular, look again. The thing to note is that a function produced by fn picks up and remembers the parameters around when the fn was run. So in the last example, the function produced when you call (cheaper-f 1.00) will remember that max-price is 1.00 while the function produced by (cheaper-f 5.99) will remember max-price as 5.99.

Going a step further, we can write a function that manufactures both?-like functions:

```
(defn both-f [predicate-f-1 predicate-f-2]
  (fn [book]
    (when (and (predicate-f-1 book) (predicate-f-2 book))
      book)))
```

With both-f we can then build a whole family of book-discriminating functions:

```
(def cheap-horror? (both-f cheap? horror?))
```

```
(def real-cheap-adventure? (both-f real-cheap? adventure?))
```

```
(def real-cheap-horror? (both-f real-cheap? horror?))
```

And then go up yet another level of meta:

```
(def cheap-horror-possession?
  (both-f cheap-horror?
    (fn [book] (= (:title book) "Possession"))))
```

This idea of a function grabbing and remembering the bindings that existed when the function was born is called a *closure*. We say that the function *closes* over the scope in which it was defined. More than anything else, the twin ideas of functions as values and *closure* are at the heart of what makes Clojure the programming language it is, and might explain the name as well.

A Functional Toolkit

Since so much of Clojure programming revolves around creating, combining, and using functions, it's unsurprising that the language provides a fair number of functions aimed at easing the job.

Take, for example, the apply function. It tackles the surprisingly common situation where you have a function and the arguments that you want to call that function with *in a collection*. In other words, instead of having this:

```
(+ 1 2 3 4)        ; Gives you 10.
```

what if you had the function (+ in this case) and the arguments, like this:

```
(def the-function +)
(def args [1 2 3 4])
```

Enter apply. You supply a function and a collection of arguments, and apply will call that function with the arguments, returning the result. Armed with apply we can get the job done like this:

```
(apply the-function args)    ; (the-function args0 args1 args2 ...)
```

The apply function is particularly useful for converting from one kind of value to another. Thus, if you have a vector like this:

```
(def v ["The number " 2 " best selling " "book."])
```

you can use the combination of apply and str to turn it into a string:

```
;; More or less the same as:
;; (str "The number " 2 " best selling " "book.")

(apply str v)
```

or apply and list to turn it into a list:

```
;; More or less the same as:
;; (list "The number " 2 " best selling " "book.")

(apply list v)
```

and then back into a vector:

```
(apply vector (apply list v))
```

Another incredibly useful function is partial. It's called partial because it partially fills in the arguments for an existing function, producing a new function of fewer arguments in the process. For example, Clojure includes a function called inc that adds one to the number you pass in, so that (inc 1) gives you 2 and (inc 41) is 42. It's easy enough to cook up your own version of inc:

```
(defn my-inc [n] (+ 1 n))
```

But consider that my-inc is simply filling in the first argument of + with 1. Which is exactly the kind of thing that partial does:

```
(def my-inc (partial + 1))
```

Returning to our book example, we can use partial to rework and simplify our cheapness-discriminating functions:

```
(defn cheaper-than [max-price book]
  (when (<= (:price book) max-price)
    book))
```

```
(def real-cheap? (partial cheaper-than 1.00))
(def kind-of-cheap? (partial cheaper-than 1.99))
(def marginally-cheap? (partial cheaper-than 5.99))
```

Each call to partial there is giving us back a new function that—when called—calls cheaper-than with one of the prices as the first argument.

Another handy function-producing function that comes packaged with Clojure is complement. With complement every day is opposite day. complement wraps the function that you supply with a call to not, producing a new function that is, well, the complement of the original. For example, earlier we wrote adventure?, which could tell adventure books from those of other genres:

```
(defn adventure? [book]
  (when (= (:genre book) :adventure)
    book))
```

But what if we needed a function that looked for nonadventure books? Clearly we could write it by hand:

```
(defn not-adventure? [book] (not (adventure? book)))
```

But we did say we were trying to get out of the hand-coding business, so instead we turn to complement:

```
(def not-adventure? (complement adventure?))
```

As I say, complement produces a function that returns the truthy negation of the function that you pass to complement.

One more example of a function-generating function is every-pred. It combines predicate functions into a single function that *ands* them all together. With every-pred we can dispense with our home-grown both-f:

```
(def cheap-horror? (every-pred cheap? horror?))
```

Even better, every-pred will take any number of arguments, so that this:

```
(def cheap-horror-possession?
  (every-pred
    cheap?
    horror?
    (fn [book] (= (:title book) "Possession"))))
```

will do exactly what you want it to do.

Function Literals

Another way that Clojure comes to your aid in creating new functions is to supply an alternate, minimalistic syntax for defining them. So for those moments when even the sleek lines of fn seem like too much syntactical overhead, you can use a function literal: just a # followed by the function body, wrapped in the usual parentheses. Here, for example, are the guts of adventure? recast as a function literal:

```
#(when (= (:genre %1) :adventure) %1)
```

Note there are no named arguments in function literals; instead they use the very shell script-ish notation of %1 to stand for the first argument, %2 for the second argument, and so on. So if we needed a function that would double a number, we might use partial or we might do this:

```
#(* 2 %1)
```

Or if we need a function to add three numbers together, we might cook this up:

```
#(+ %1 %2 %3)
```

There are a few things to keep in mind about function literals, or *lambdas*, as they are sometimes known. First, function literals and fn produce exactly the same kind of thing (a function value); the only difference is the syntax.

Second, remember that Clojure infers the number of arguments that your literally defined function takes from the highest-numbered argument in the function body. Thus, if we modified our *double the number* function into this:

```
#(* 2 %11)
```

we would end up with a (very inconvenient) function that takes 11 arguments and ignores the first 10.

Finally, function literals have a special feature aimed directly at the very common case of creating a one-argument function. If the function you're building takes a single argument, you can use plain old %—without a number—for the one and only argument. So a minimal version of our number doubler would be as follows:

```
#(* % 2)
```

The trade-off between defining a full-blown named function with defn and using the streamlined fn or a completely stripped-down function literal is one of those familiar software-engineering choices. If you're going to be reusing the function, then by all means use defn and give it a name. Giving your function a name is also worthwhile if the name will help you (and those who come later) understand some intricate bit of code. You also probably will want to use defn on lengthy functions to visually break up the code.

On the other hand, fn and function literals are wonderful when you're cooking up short, single-use functions and when you need to take advantage of a closure to pick up some values.

The choice between fn and function literals centers on complexity and number of arguments. Lean toward function literals for really short, simple functions. If, for example, you need a function to double a number, then by all means write #(* % 2). Conversely, lean toward fn if you have a longer function, and especially one that takes more than a very few arguments. Examples aside, no one really writes function literals that have a %11.

In the Wild

And now we have the answer to the opening question of this chapter: the thing that makes Clojure a functional programming language is that you do basic things by writing functions and you do more sophisticated things by treating the functions as values—values that you can pass around and call and combine.

Possibly the best demonstration of the *functions are values* idea can be found inside the machinery of defn itself. defn is just a thin layer over def and fn. So when you define a new function with defn, perhaps this:

```
(defn say-welcome [what]
  (println "Welcome to" what "!"))
```

what gets evaluated is something like this:

```
(def say-welcome
  (fn [what] (println "Welcome to" what "!")))
```

As the name suggests, defn is def plus fn.

If you are not used to the idea, functional values can seem a bit special and magical, the kind of technique you would use only in extreme circumstances. Not so; in Clojure they are just part of the everyday programming landscape.

Take, for example, the mundane update function. As the name suggests, you use update to modify values, specifically the values inside of a map.

You Can't Modify That Map

To be precise, update produces a new map that's a lot like the input map, only different. But I'm getting as tired of writing that as you are of reading it.

So if we wanted to record that we've sold another copy of a book, we might write this:

```
;; Start with 1,000 copies sold.
(def book {:title "Emma" :copies 1000})
;; Now we have 1,001.
(def new-book (update book :copies inc))
```

As you can see, update takes three parameters: the map, the key whose value you want to update, and *a function* to do the updating. Your function will get called with the old value of the key (in this case 1000) and the map you get back will be just like the old map, except that the key will have the result of evaluating the function.

If you happen to have nested maps, you can reach for the slightly less mundane update-in function, which works like update but will also let you drill down through several layers of maps using a pathlike vector of keys:

```
(def by-author
  {:name "Jane Austen"
   :book {:title "Emma" :copies 1000}})
(def new-by-author (update-in by-author [:book :copies] inc))
```

But to see how much you can do with functional values, look no further than Ring,[1] the popular Clojure library that helps you build web applications.

To build a web application with Ring you first need to utter the proper incantation to load Ring (we'll talk about require in Chapter 9, *Namespaces*, on page 95):

```
(ns ring-example.core
  (:require [ring.adapter.jetty :as jetty]))
```

Then you create a function that takes in an HTTP request—in the form of a map—and returns a response, also in the form of a map, like this:

```
(defn handler [request]
  {:status 200
   :headers {"Content-Type" "text/html"}
   :body "Hello from your web application!"})
```

Having written your function, you now need to tell Ring that *this* is the function Ring should look to when a web request comes in. You can do that by passing the handler function to Ring's run-jetty function, which kicks off a simple web server called Jetty:

```
(defn -main []
  (jetty/run-jetty handler {:port 8080}))
```

---

1. https://github.com/ring-clojure/ring

And now your handler function will get called for requests on port 8080.

Aside from plain handlers, Ring applications also commonly use *middleware*. Middleware are functions that take a handler function as a parameter and return a new handler function. Ring programmers use middleware to layer additional features onto their handlers. For example, we might define a middleware function that logs the response:

```
(defn log-value
  "Log the message and the value. Returns the value."
  [msg value]
  (println msg value)
  value)

(defn wrap-logging
  "Return a function that logs the response."
  [msg handler]
  (fn [request]
    (log-value msg (handler request))))
```

and a second handler to specify the content type:

```
(defn wrap-content-type
  "Return a function that sets the response content type."
  [handler content-type]
  (fn [request]
    (assoc-in
      (handler request)
      [:headers "Content-Type"]
      content-type)))
```

As I say, middleware functions take in a handler—a function—and return another handler. The new handler typically runs the old handler while adding its own goodness along the way. Our first middleware function, wrap-logging, runs the handler function passed to it, prints the response, and then returns the response. The second middleware function does something more interesting: it adds a header (for the content type) to the response.

Assoc-in?

You may have noticed that the content-type handler in the example uses a function called assoc-in. This function is a lot like assoc in that it adds a new key/value association to a map. The difference is that you pass assoc-in a vector of keys and it will go spelunking down through multiple levels of maps for you. To put it another way, in the same way that update-in is the multistory version of update, assoc-in is the multistory version of assoc.

Traditionally Ring applications call the final, fully wrapped handler the app, short for application. So this is how we set up our final app and kick off Ring:

```
(defn handler [request]
  {:status 200
   :body "Hello from your web application!"})

(def app
  (wrap-logging
    "Final response:"
    (wrap-content-type handler "text/html")))
```

You can get a feeling for the power of the *functions as values* view of the world by noting that in the preceding example we're logging the final response—that is, the response after wrap-content-type has had its say. But with a little rearranging we can log the response before the content type gets added:

```
(def app
  (wrap-content-type
    (wrap-logging  "Initial response:" handler)
    "text/html"))
```

or we can log both:

```
(def app
  (wrap-logging
    "Final response:"
    (wrap-content-type
      (wrap-logging  "Initial response:" handler)
      "text/html")))
```

This last bit of code is a great example of the power of functional programming. It assembles four separate functions, three of them dynamically generated, into a working whole that is greater than the sum of its parts.

Staying Out of Trouble

Going from the simple-minded idea of functions as something you write and call manually to the *functions as values* idea has some interesting implications. Chief among these is that you don't always know the exact context in which your function will be called. Since functions are values, they can get passed around and evaluated any number of times:

```
(defn execute-that-function-three-times [your-function]
  (your-function)
  (your-function)
  (your-function))
```

Or they might get called sometime later. For example, we might use Thread/sleep to wait 372 milliseconds before calling your function:

```
(defn execute-that-function-later [your-function]
  (Thread/sleep 372)       ; Pause for 372 ms.
  (your-function))
```

Or it might never get called:

```
(defn execute-that-function-never [your-function]
  (+ 2 2))
```

Or it might get called in some odd combination:

```
(defn some-odd-combination [your-function]
  (execute-that-function-three-times
    #(execute-that-function-later your-function)))
```

Given all this, the functional programmer's Prime Directive is simple: try to write functions that *don't care* about the context in which they are called. In practice this means you should avoid writing functions that rely on or generate side effects. In functional programming, the best functions are the ones that look only at their arguments and produce only their return value. They don't read, create, or delete files; they don't roll the current time or date into their answer; and they certainly don't consult the user for input. They just look at their arguments and come up with a result. We even have an appropriately positive term for functions that follow these rules. We call them *pure functions*.

The good news is that pure functions are not hard to write. In fact, take out the printfs that we've sprinkled here and there, and all the functions we've written in this chapter are indeed pure. From adventure? to cheap-horror?, we've managed—without even trying—to write functions that look only at their arguments to come up with a return value. The goal of writing pure functions also explains the immutability of Clojure's data structures: by disallowing in-place modification of vectors and maps and all the rest, Clojure outlaws a whole class of side effects.

Note that the directive is to *try* to write pure functions. Much of the value that we programmers generate comes out in side effects—we read or write or delete the file, we update the database, or we increment the hit count on a web page. The only thing wrong with side effects is that functions that depend on them aren't the easy-to-assemble building blocks that pure functions are. So we try to write pure functions when we can. Because life is a lot easier without side effects.

Wrapping Up

In this chapter we had our first look at the deeper ideas of functional programming. We saw that in Clojure functions are values—values that you can create, bind to names, and pass around. We also saw that closures allow you to create custom-tailored functions that remember the bindings that existed when they were created. We also looked at some of the helpers that Clojure provides to aid you in the task of creating just the function you need for the task at hand. Finally, we took a quick look at the idea of a pure function: a function that neither relies on nor generates side effects.

Now that you understand what makes Clojure a functional language, it's time to turn to one of the stickiest issues of any programming language: naming things.

CHAPTER 7

Let

There's an old bit of wisdom that contends that naming things is one of the two hardest problems in programming. Difficult or not, putting names to values is something programmers do constantly. But in programs not all names are created equal. Sometimes we want to name a value that is going to stick around for a long time and we want that name to be widely visible. But sometimes we want a temporary name, a name that we can use *right here, right now* and then dispose of without another thought. The good news is that we have the first kind of names, the long-lasting ones, covered: that's what def—and if you think about it, defn—are for.

So in this chapter we'll look at let, which takes care of those local, temporary naming chores. We'll see how, along with enabling you to mix intention-revealing names into your code, let is also surprising helpful in writing higher-order functions. We'll also explore how if-let and when-let enable you to combine a let with an if and a when. And, as usual, we'll look at some uses of let in real-world programs and at some of the ways you can let yourself in for trouble.

A Local, Temporary Place for Your Stuff

We'll begin our exploration of local naming in Clojure by imagining that our book store runs periodic specials. Every now and then we offer our customers a percentage discount on their book purchases. Unfortunately, our deal does come with some fine print: there's a minimum charge for each order that overrides the discount.

Armed with our hard-won knowledge of functions and if, it's not difficult to turn this discount policy into Clojure code:

let/examples.clj
```
(defn compute-discount-amount [amount discount-percent min-charge]
  (if (> (* amount (- 1.0 discount-percent)) min-charge)
    (* amount (- 1.0 discount-percent))
    min-charge))
```

As a bit of everyday software engineering, compute-discount-amount is a mixed bag. On the plus side, it does work. Unfortunately, compute-discount-amount is hardly a model of clarity. Come back to this code after a few months' absence, and there's a fair chance you'll be muttering, *Wait, what times who is greater than huh?*

Clearly a bit of intention-revealing naming is called for. The code would be a lot easier to follow if we could bind a symbol—perhaps called discounted-amount—to the appropriate value and have that binding disappear once we're done computing discounts. But how?

You might be tempted to do something like this:

```
;; Don't do this!

(defn compute-discount-amount [amount discount-percent min-charge]
  (def discounted-amount (* amount (- 1.0 discount-percent)))   ; NOOOOO!
  (if (> discounted-amount min-charge)
    discounted-amount
    min-charge))
```

There are two reasons that you should avoid using def like this, inside of a function. The first reason is that, as we have seen, symbols bound with def have reasonably global visibility. Calling this version of compute-discount-amount will have the ugly side effect of changing the value bound to discounted-amount, and that change will be visible *outside of the function*:

```
;; A nasty side effect is brewing here.

(def discounted-amount "Some random string.")

(compute-discount-amount 10.0 0.20 1.0)

discounted-amount   ; Is now 8.00
```

The second, more philosophical reason is that using def this way is actually misusing it: def is designed to bind more or less global symbols to their more or less stable values. Instead of def you should use let for your local-naming needs:

```
;; Do use let!

(defn compute-discount-amount [amount discount-percent min-charge]
  (let [discounted-amount (* amount (- 1.0 discount-percent))]
    (if (> discounted-amount min-charge)
      discounted-amount
      min-charge)))
```

The mechanics of let couldn't be simpler: you call let like a function, passing in a name and a value—wrapped in square brackets—followed by an expression. In essence you say, *Execute this expression with this symbol bound to this value.* In our example, the symbol was discounted-amount and the value was the order amount less the percentage discount. As you can probably figure out from the example, the value returned by the let is the value computed by the expression—the *body*—of the let. Critically, the bindings manufactured by let go away once the let is done, so that you can get on with the rest of the code without littering your mental landscape with stray names.

One nice feature of let is that you can bind multiple names inside a single let. We could, for example, make the code a bit clearer by doing the percentage-off calculation in two steps:

```
(defn compute-discount-amount [amount discount-percent min-charge]
  (let [discount (* amount discount-percent)
        discounted-amount (- amount discount)]
    (if (> discounted-amount min-charge)
      discounted-amount
      min-charge)))
```

The rule is that let will bind each name to its corresponding value, starting with the first one. Each name becomes available immediately after it's bound, which is why we can use discount to compute discounted-amount.

You can also have more than one expression inside the body of the let. If, for example, you wanted to print our intermediate values for debugging purposes, you could do this:

```
(defn compute-discount-amount [amount discount-percent min-charge]
  (let [discount (* amount discount-percent)
        discounted-amount (- amount discount)]
    (println "Discount:" discount)
    (println "Discounted amount" discounted-amount)
    (if (> discounted-amount min-charge)
      discounted-amount
      min-charge)))
```

Keep in mind that while all the expressions in the body of a let get evaluated, only the last expression has anything to say about the value returned by the let.

Let Over Fn

While the ideas behind let aren't terribly challenging—it binds names to values in a purely local and temporary way—let does have some hidden superpowers, which only become visible when you combine it with fn. To get a glimpse of these hidden powers, imagine our book discounts are customer-dependent. Somewhere we have a map of the user's name to the discount that user gets:

```
(def user-discounts
  {"Nicholas" 0.10 "Jonathan" 0.07 "Felicia" 0.05})
```

We could certainly add some parameters to compute-discount-amount to deal with this:

```
(defn compute-discount-amount [amount user-name user-discounts min-charge]
  (let [discount-percent (user-discounts user-name)
        discount (* amount discount-percent)
        discounted-amount (- amount discount)]
    (if (> discounted-amount min-charge)
      discounted-amount
      min-charge)))
```

The trouble with this approach is that we now have to carry the "user names and discounts" table around every time we want to compute a price. If all that extra lifting turns out to be a problem, a better strategy might be to create a higher-level function, one that produces variants of the compute-discount-amount function tailored to a particular customer:

```
(defn mk-discount-price-f [user-name user-discounts min-charge]
  (let [discount-percent (user-discounts user-name)]
    (fn [amount]
      (let [discount (* amount discount-percent)
            discounted-amount (- amount discount)]
        (if (> discounted-amount min-charge)
          discounted-amount
          min-charge)))))
```

```
;; Get a price function for Felicia.
```

```
(def compute-felicia-price (mk-discount-price-f "Felicia" user-discounts 10.0))
```

```
;; ...and sometime later compute a price
```

```
(compute-felicia-price 20.0)
```

There are quite a few moving parts in mk-discount-price-f, but it's just a combination of features we've already seen. The first thing mk-discount-price-f does, in that initial let, is look up the discount percentage for the user. With the percentage rate in hand, mk-discount-price-f then constructs an anonymous function with an fn whose body is nearly identical to compute-discount-amount.

The interesting thing about mk-discount-price-f is how discount-percent gets bound in the initial let, *outside* of the fn and then used *inside* the fn. That means that while discount-percent is only visible inside the body of the let, it can live on long after the call to mk-discount-price-f has completed, buried inside of the anonymous function.

This *compute it in a let, use it in an fn* is such a great way to build anonymous functions that are both efficient and clear. It's efficient because you can use the outside let to compute everything you need to construct the anonymous function. And it's clear because inside of the anonymous function you can use descriptive names for those precomputed values.

Variations on the Theme

In addition to the plain vanilla version of let that we've looked at so far, Clojure comes packaged with a couple of handy variations. The most commonly used of these is probably if-let. As you might guess from the name, if-let is an if and a let rolled into one. To see if-let in action, imagine that we decide to represent anonymous books with our now-familiar book map, sans the :author key:

```
(def anonymous-book
  {:title "Sir Gawain and the Green Knight"})

(def with-author
  {:title "Once and Future King" :author "White"})
```

Now imagine we needed to write a function that will return the uppercase version of the author's name, or nil if there is no author. The twist is that we need to avoid computing the uppercase version of nil, which will blow up with an exception. Given that, we might do something like this:

```
(defn uppercase-author [book]
  (let [author (:author book)]
    (if author
      (.toUpperCase author))))
```

That will work, but we can say it a bit more succinctly with if-let:

```
(defn uppercase-author [book]
  (if-let [author (:author book)]
    (.toUpperCase author)))
```

In essence, if-let takes a single binding and uses the value bound—in the example, the author's name—as the condition of an if. Like a plain if, if-let will take a second expression, for the else case:

```
(defn uppercase-author [book]
  (if-let [author (:author book)]
    (.toUpperCase author)
    "ANONYMOUS"))
```

And if you think it would make more sense to call it let-if, well, me too.

Unsurprisingly, there is also a when-let which does about what you would expect:

```
(defn uppercase-author [book]
  (when-let [author (:author book)]
    (.toUpperCase author)))
```

There really is nothing terribly deep about if-let and when-let: They are just the kinds of things that grow out of the observation that people frequently combine let with if and when.

In the Wild

Real-life Clojure functions are full of let expressions. In fact, let is one of the most commonly used Clojure features, up there with defn and def. If, for example, you look at the Ring source code you will find the parse-params function. Here's a slightly simplified version of it:

```
(defn parse-params [params encoding]
  (let [params (codec/form-decode params encoding)]
    (if (map? params) params {})))
```

Without diving into the belts and pulleys of Ring, we can deduce that parse-params decodes some raw parameter data into a value that is either a map or something else, presumably nil. Once it has the result of that decoding bound to params—courtesy of let—it proceeds to return the decoded value if it is indeed a map, or an empty map if it's not.

If you dig around in Ring some more you'll discover the assoc-query-params function, which uses parse-params. Here is a slightly simplified version of that function, which has a vanilla let embedded in an if-let:

```
(defn assoc-query-params
  "Parse and assoc parameters from the query string
  with the request."
  [request encoding]
  (merge-with merge request
    (if-let [query-string (:query-string request)]
      (let [params (parse-params query-string encoding)]
        {:query-params params, :params params})
      {:query-params {}, :params {}})))
```

Pull the query string out of the request and call it query-string and, if you actually got something, proceed to parse the parameters and call the result in params and then ... well, you get the picture.

For a truly imposing example of a let, we need to look no further than this, from Incanter[1]:]

```
(let [opts (if options (apply assoc {} options) {})
      data (or (:data opts) $data)
      _x (data-as-list x data)
      nbins (or (:nbins opts) 10)
      theme (or (:theme opts) :default)
      density? (true? (:density opts))
      title (or (:title opts) "")
      x-lab (or (:x-label opts) (str 'x))
      y-lab (or (:y-label opts)
                  (if density? "Density" "Frequency"))
      series-lab (or (:series-label opts) (str 'x))
      legend? (true? (:legend opts))
      dataset (HistogramDataset.)]
  ;; Do something heroic with x-lab and density?
  ;; and title and...
  )
```

The preceding code, which is used in drawing histograms, binds no less then a dozen names. Glossing over the details—which thankfully need not concern us here—we can see that opts, which is defined right out of the gate, is used nine times later on in the let. Look a little more closely, and you can see that the value of opts comes out of an if expression, while the value of y-lab is computed with an if embedded in an or. Behold the power of an expression-based language.

The other thing to behold is how much computing gets done inside the square brackets of this let. There are ifs and ors and a number other function calls going off in there. The lesson here is that if you have an intricate set of step-by-step values to compute, consider doing it inside the square brackets of let, giving each intermediate result an informative name. Your future self will thank you.

Staying Out of Trouble

As simple as it seems, there are a few things to keep in mind about let. The first is that the names defined in a let are exactly that: defined inside the let. Technically, let relies on *lexical scope*. In plain English this means the bindings created by let only exist inside the code that makes up the let body.

You can't, for example, do this:

---

1. http://incanter.org

```
;; We can use title inside of the let.
(let [title "Let's Pretend This Never Happened"]
  (println "The title is" title)
  (print-the-title))

;; But now we're outside of the let.
(defn print-the-title []
  (println "The title is" title)) ; Boom!
```

Since title is only defined inside of the let, this shouldn't come as a surprise. After all, we started this trip by asking for local bindings, and so local bindings are what we got.

Second, keep in mind that if you nest let expressions, then a binding in a let can mask a binding in an outer let. For example, this code:

```
(let [title "Pride and Prejudice"]
  (let [title "Sense and Sensibility"]
    (println title)))                  ; Sense & Sensibility.
```

will print Sense and Sensibility. You can also override a binding inside of the *same* let, so that this:

```
(let [title "Pride and Prejudice"         ; Classic novel.
      title (str title " and Zombies")]   ; Now with the undead.
  (println title))                        ; Brains!
```

will leave us with a romantic horror mashup.

Wrapping Up

In this chapter we had a look at the let expression and its friends if-let and when-let. We saw how let and company enable you to bind a name to a value as you compute it, a binding that lasts only as long as you need it. We've also seen how you can use let to organize and illuminate long sequences of computing by giving a name to each intermediate value. As usual, we also looked at some of the programming pits that you can fall into when using let—and happily discovered that those pits were both few in number and fairly easy to avoid.

Now that you know all about let, it's time to dig deeper into Clojure's other naming mechanism, def.

CHAPTER 8

Def, Symbols, and Vars

So far in our Clojure adventures we've been using def to associate names with values without thinking about what exactly we were doing. There is more to def than meets the eye. So in this chapter we're going to take a long look at the machinery behind def. We'll start with a quick review of the syntax and intent of def before we move to an exploration of the remarkably transparent mechanisms lurking just behind the scenes. And along the way we'll discover two new Clojure data types, the symbol and the var. Finally we'll come back to the difference between the bindings created by def and let and look at some interesting real-world uses of def. Let's get started.

A Global, Stable Place for Your Stuff

As we discovered all the way back in Chapter 1, def is about as simple as programming-language features come. You just hand it a symbol and a value:

def/examples.clj
```
(def title "Emma")
```

And it binds the symbol to the value. We've also seen that in contrast to the very local and temporary let, you use def for longer-lasting, more stable name-to-value bindings. Let's start with the *stable* part: the rule is that a binding created with def will hang around until either you change it or the program terminates. This makes def perfect for constants:

```
;; Everyone's favorite universal constant.
(def PI 3.14)
;; Length of a standard book ID.
(def ISBN-LENGTH 13)
;; Company names are more or less constant.
(def COMPANY-NAME "Blotts Books")
```

The stable lifespan of def bindings also makes it a great tool for pulling the parts of your program together into a functioning whole. Thus we have defn, which is, as the name suggests, a functional mash-up of def and fn, so that this:

```
(defn book-description [book]
  (str (:title book)
       " Written by "
       (:author book)))
```

is just a more convenient way of writing the following:

```
(def book-description
  (fn [book]
    (str (:title book)
         " Written by "
         (:author book))))
```

The other advantage that def offers is that the bindings it creates are widely visible. Once defined, like this:

```
;; Length of a standard book ID.
(def ISBN-LENGTH 13)
;; Before 2007 ISBNs were 10 characters long.
(def OLD-ISBN-LENGTH 10)
```

you can use the bindings that come out of def in other defs:

```
(def isbn-lengths [OLD-ISBN-LENGTH ISBN-LENGTH])
```

and inside of functions:

```
(defn valid-isbn [isbn]
  (or (= (count isbn) OLD-ISBN-LENGTH)
      (= (count isbn) ISBN-LENGTH)))
```

The rule is that once you've bound a symbol to a value with def it's just there, part of the environment.

Symbols Are Things

But what exactly is the *it* that is part of the environment? In other words, what does def do, precisely? The answer is implicit in the terminology: We say that def binds a symbol to a value. The thing to note here is that the word *symbol* is not just Clojure jargon for what most other languages call an identifier. The reason it's not just jargon is that symbols are first-class *takes up bytes in memory* values in Clojure, similar to strings and keywords. So this expression:

```
(def author "Austen")
```

involves *two* values: the string "Austen" and the symbol author.

Symbols have a lot in common with keywords: both are just strings of characters that are meaningful to humans. And both symbols and keywords stand for some value. The difference is that while keywords always stand for themselves—evaluate :title and you always get :title back—symbols are typically bound to some other value. So if you evaluate the symbol author you will get back the value to which it is bound, "Austen".

Since symbols are actual things in Clojure, you can, with a little effort, reach in and get at the symbol itself as opposed to the value that the symbol is bound to. All you need is our old friend the single quote to prevent the symbol from being evaluated:

```
'author     ; The symbol author, not the string "Austen"
'title      ; A symbol that starts with a 't'.
```

The idea is that symbols are not magical things that are built into the language. In Clojure, a symbol is just another kind of value. You can, for instance, turn them into strings:

```
(str 'author)  ; The string "author".
```

and compare them:

```
(= 'author 'some-other-symbol)  ; Nope.
(= 'title 'title)               ; Yup.
```

Being a value also means that a symbol can exist on its own, without being bound to another value. You can, in fact, make stand-alone symbols as fast as you can type, so that 'some-other-symbol and 'still-another-symbol are perfectly good expressions, even if neither symbol has ever appeared in a def.

Bindings Are Things Too

Surprisingly, the bindings between symbols and values, the things created by def, are also ordinary values. When you evaluate a def, Clojure creates a *var*, a thing that represents the binding between a symbol and a value. As illustrated in the figure on page 88, you can think of vars as having two slots: there's a place for the symbol (maybe author) and a place for the value (perhaps "Austen").

In a lovely bit of introspection, you can also get at a var with the proper incantation, this time a # followed by a ':

```
(def author "Austen")  ; Make a var.

#'author               ; Get at the var for author -> "Austen".
```

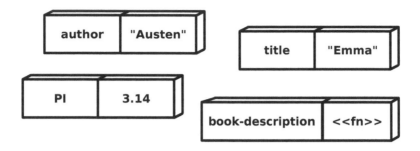

Like any other Clojure value, you can use vars in the business end of a def:

```
(def the-var #'author) ; Grab the var.
```

And, if you know the API, you can get at both the symbol and the value buried inside of the var:

```
(.get the-var)          ; Get the value of the var: "Austen"
(.-sym the-var)         ; Get the symbol of the var: author
```

Don't worry about the strange .get and .-sym syntax—we'll get to that in Chapter 16, *Interoperating with Java*, on page 189. Focus instead on the idea that when you evaluate a def you are dealing with three separate values. First there's the symbol you're binding, in this case author. Then there's the value you're binding to that symbol, "Austen" in the example. Finally we come to the punchline, the var that binds the symbol to the value, #'author.

Varying Your Vars

If vars are all about providing the global, stable environment for your code, you might wonder why vars are mutable. After all, Clojure loves immutability. But we can def and re-def our vars with wild abandon. The answer is as simple as it is pragmatic: mutable vars make for more productive Clojure programmers. Most Clojure programming is done in some form of REPL or other. So while developing, we might start out by creating a couple of vars:

```
user=> (def PI 3.14)
#'user/PI

user=> (defn compute-area [diameter]
  #_=>   (* PI diameter diameter))
#'user/compute-area
```

and then realize that we need more precision:

```
user=> (def PI 3.14159)
#'user/PI
```

and we also got the calculation wrong:

```
user=> (defn compute-area [diameter]
  #_=>    (* PI radius (/ diameter 2.0)))
#'user/compute-area
```

While your code is under development, mutable vars are a gift from heaven.

Things are different in production. The vars in a production program are just as mutable as those in development, but *you should avoid changing them*. In production code you should def (and defn) things and let them be.

Changing State?

 So what's a programmer to do if you have some state that you need to model and that state changes over time? The longer answer starts with the advice that you use atoms or refs or agents. The shorter answer is to read Chapter 18, *State*, on page 215.

Well, mostly you should leave your vars alone. There are times when it's handy to be able to temporarily change the value bound in your vars. Imagine, for example, that you write a simple logging function that uses a var to turn the actual output off and on:

```
;; First cut at debugging, needs some work.

(def debug-enabled false)

(defn debug [msg]
  (if debug-enabled
    (println msg)))
```

But how do you turn the logging on without violating the Clojure prime directive of *no defs in a function*?

It's for situations like this that Clojure gives you binding. Syntactically a binding expression looks a lot like let: you supply binding with a vector containing pairs of symbols and values, along with one or more expressions that make up the body of the binding. The binding expression will temporarily set the vars corresponding to the symbols with the supplied values as it evaluates the expressions:

```
(binding [debug-enabled true]
  (debug "Calling that darned function")
  (some-troublesome-function-that-needs-logging)
  (debug "Back from that darned function"))
```

In the example, debug-enabled gets set to true while the calls to debug and some-troublesome-function are evaluated, so that we will actually see output from the debug function. Note that any function called by some-troublesome-function will also see the temporary value of debug-enabled, and so on down the call stack.

There is one other wrinkle to binding: Any var that we use in binding needs to be declared as *dynamic*, like this:

```
;; Make debug-enabled a dynamic var.
(def ^:dynamic debug-enabled false)
```

The ^:dynamic adds a bit of metadata—which we'll talk about in Chapter 19, *Read and Eval*, on page 229—to the debug-enabled var. For now just accept it as the incantation you need to do to enable you to use binding. Finally, there is a Clojure convention for naming dynamic vars. The convention is that dynamic vars should begin and end with *. So our final exercise in debugging is as follows:

```
(def ^:dynamic *debug-enabled* false)

(defn debug [msg]
  (if *debug-enabled*
    (println msg)))

(binding [*debug-enabled* true]
  (debug "Calling that darned function")
  (some-troublesome-function-that-needs-logging)
  (debug "Back from that darned function"))
```

By surrounding your dynamic vars with asterisks—charmingly referred to as *earmuffs*—you can tell at a glance which vars are usable inside of binding and which are not. Note that since being dynamic entails a bit more overhead, you should only hang the ^:dynamic tag on vars that really need it.

Staying Out of Trouble

Perhaps the biggest danger vars pose to the new Clojure programmer grows out of the fact that vars look a lot like the familiar variables that we find in traditional programming languages. And the name *var* doesn't help.

Don't try to use vars as variables. In particular, don't rely on changing the value of a var to model the changing state of the outside world. Clojure has other, more appropriate tools for modeling the changing state of the world, tools that we'll look at in Chapter 18, *State*, on page 215.

Do use vars to weave the parts of your program together with intention-revealing names. For the most part you want to def your values, defn your functions, and then *leave them alone*. Yes, you can bind a symbol to a value with def and then go right back in and bind that same symbol to a different value with a second def. And yes, binding also exists. But you should *not* be doing any of that terribly often.

One last thing to keep in mind is that let does not create vars. Thus, if you do this:

```
;; Don't do this!

(let [let-bound 42] #'let-bound)
```

you will see something like this:

```
CompilerException java.lang.RuntimeException:
   Unable to resolve var: let-bound...
```

That's because there are no vars behind let bindings. Instead the bindings produced by let are more like the variables are in other programming languages, implemented by some behind-the-scenes magic performed by the Clojure compiler.

In the Wild

Since garden-variety vars are the mortar that binds Clojure code together, they are everywhere in real-world code. In fact, def figures into some of the first code that runs when Clojure boots up.[1] Here are slightly simplified versions of a couple of defs that get run very early on:

```
(def second (fn second [x] (first (next x))))

(def ffirst (fn ffirst [x] (first (first x))))
```

These are just two handy functions: second, which pulls the second item off of a collection, and ffirst, which takes the first item from a collection—which itself should be a collection—and pulls the first item off of it. You might wonder why this code goes to the trouble of using def and fn instead of the sleeker defn. The answer is simple: these two functions get defined *before* defn.

Dynamic vars are less common, but still out there. For example, if you're dealing with large collections in the REPL you may not want to see them printed in their full glory. Fortunately, Clojure provides a dynamic var called *print-length*, which limits how much of a collection gets printed. As you might imagine, somewhere in the depths of Clojure itself,[2] *print-length* is set up as a dynamic var. Here it is in all its well-documented glory:

---

1.   https://github.com/clojure/clojure/blob/master/src/clj/clojure/core.clj
2.   https://github.com/clojure/clojure/blob/master/src/clj/clojure/core_print.clj

```
(def ^:dynamic
  ^{:doc "*print-length* controls how many items of each collection the
    printer will print. If it is bound to logical false, there is no
    limit. Otherwise, it must be bound to an integer indicating the maximum
    number of items of each collection to print. If a collection contains
    more items, the printer will print items up to the limit followed by
    '...' to represent the remaining items. The root binding is nil
    indicating no limit."
    :added "1.0"}
  *print-length* nil)
```

A bit later, just before actually executing your program, Clojure sets up a binding for *print-length*, conceptually like this:

```
(binding [*print-length* nil]
  (run-your-code))
```

That brings us to set!, which changes the value of a dynamic var from *inside* the binding. So if you have this vector:

```
user=> (def books ["Emma" "2001" "Jaws" "Oliver Twist"])
```

and you set! *print-length* to 2:

```
user=> (set! *print-length* 2)
```

you will only see the first couple of items of your vector:

```
user=> books
["Emma" "2001" ...]
```

There are a couple of other dynamic vars that can improve your REPL experience. For example, *1—and yes, it only has the left earmuff—is always bound to the last result you got from the REPL:

```
user=> (+ 2 2)
4
user=> *1
4
```

Similarly, *2 is bound to the second-to-last result, and *3 to the one before that:

```
user=> "Austen"
"Austen"
user=> "King"
"King"
user=> "Orwell"
"Orwell"
user=> *3
"Austen"
```

Finally there is *e, which the REPL binds to the last exception:

```
user=> (/ 1 0)

ArithmeticException Divide by zero   clojure.lang.Numbers.divide
(Numbers.java:158)

user=> *e
#error {
 :cause "Divide by zero"
 :via
 [{:type java.lang.ArithmeticException
   :message "Divide by zero"
   :at [clojure.lang.Numbers divide "Numbers.java" 158]}]
 :trace
 [[clojure.lang.Numbers divide "Numbers.java" 158]
 << And so on for quite some time... >>
```

Now you always have a reminder of your last programmatic screw-up!

Wrapping Up

In this chapter we took a hard look at the mechanisms behind def. They're remarkably transparent: def creates a var (a Clojure value) which is an association between another Clojure value (a symbol) and a third value. We also looked at dynamic vars—vars that let you swap in a new value while you evaluate an expression or six.

Armed with an understanding of def and vars, we're now ready to look at namespaces, the mechanism Clojure uses to organize vars into related buckets.

CHAPTER 9

Namespaces

One of the best things about programming is that you are never done. Solve one problem, and chances are that three other issues tag along with your solution. You can find a great example of this in naming things in programs. It's hard to imagine anything more important to a clear and concise program than well-chosen names. But create enough names, and now you have a new problem: how do you tell the difference between the book var in your book-store application, the book function that records revenue for the accounting department, and the function that registers a police arrest? In short, how do you manage the names?

In this chapter we're going to look at Clojure's answer to that question, the *namespace*. We'll see how you can wall off groups of related vars in their own namespaces and how you can share vars between namespaces. Along the way we'll also see how Clojure programs ensure that the code they need is actually loaded, and we'll uncover some related tricks for ensuring that your code isn't cluttered with overly long names.

A Place for Your Vars

In the last chapter we saw how def creates vars—vars that represent the binding between a symbol and a value. What we skipped over in that chapter is how vars are organized. But really it's very simple. As illustrated in the figure on page 96, vars live in *namespaces*.

Conceptually, a Clojure namespace is just a big lookup table of vars, indexed by their symbols. And since you can have as many namespaces in your program as you want, each namespace itself has a unique name. At any given moment there is one special namespace, called the current namespace. So if you do this:

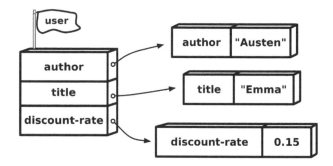

namespace/examples.clj
```
(def discount-rate 0.15)
```

it's the current namespace that gets updated with a var associating discount-rate with 0.15. If you mention discount-rate a little later in your code, Clojure will consult the current namespace to come up with 0.15.

When it boots up, Clojure creates a fresh namespace for you, called user, and makes it the current namespace.

Thus every def and defn that we have evaluated so far—with the example of our file-based project back in *Hello, Clojure*—has gone straight into the user namespace.

While user is the default namespace, it's certainly not your only namespace choice. As I say, you can create as many namespaces as you need, and the easiest way to create a new namespace is with ns:

```
(ns pricing)
```

Just feed ns the name of your new namespace, no quoting required. Conveniently, ns not only creates the new namespace, but also makes it the current namespace. Thus this:

```
(ns pricing)
```

```
(def discount-rate 0.15)
```

```
(defn discount-price [book]
  (* (- 1.0 discount-rate) (:price book)))
```

creates the pricing namespace and adds the discount-rate and discount-price vars to it.

If you supply ns with the name of an existing namespace, it will skip the creation and simply switch the current namespace to the existing namespace. If, for example, we switch from pricing to user:

```
(ns user)
```

and then back to pricing:

```
;; Back to the pricing namespace.
(ns pricing)
```

we discover that discount-price is still alive and well:

```
(println (discount-price {:title "Emma" :price 9.99}))
```

By default, the vars inside of one namespace are completely separate from the vars in another. Thus I can have as many functions or plain values called discount-price as I want, as long as I keep them in separate namespaces. That raises the question of how to get at the vars defined in one namespace from a different namespace. For example, what happens if we're in the user namespace, as here:

```
(ns user)
;; How do I get at discount-price?
```

and we want to call discount-price?

The simplest solution to the *I need something from another namespace* issue is to use a *fully qualified symbol*. A fully qualified symbol is just a long version of a symbol, one that includes the namespace. To write a fully qualified symbol you start with the namespace, follow it with a slash, and follow that with the symbol name. So discount-price becomes pricing/discount-price:

```
(ns user)
;; I can get at discount-price in pricing like this!
(println (pricing/discount-price {:title "Emma" :price 9.99}))
```

Again, namespaces are simple: they're just a place for your stuff, with their own names. And if you need something from a namespace, all you have to do is qualify the symbol with the namespace name.

Loading Namespaces

While namespaces are conceptually simple, especially if you're working in the REPL, things do get a bit more complicated when you want to use namespaces that are stored in .clj files—either files you have written or those authored by others. The rub is that you need to ensure that Clojure knows to read the .clj file and compile it into a namespace that you can use. In short, you need to make sure the namespace you want to use is *loaded* before you try to use it.

For example, your Clojure installation comes equipped with a ready-made namespace called clojure.data. The clojure.data namespace—and the period *is* part of the name—contains a handy function called diff, which will compare two data structures, perhaps vectors, and tell you which values are only in the first, which are only in the second, and which are in both.

So if you had some vectors of book titles:

```
(user=> (def literature ["Emma" "Oliver Twist" "Possession"])
#'user/literature
user=> (def horror ["It" "Carry" "Possession"])
#'user/horror
```

and you wanted to compare them, you might try to use clojure.data/diff. Sadly, you'll be disappointed:

```
user=> (clojure.data/diff literature horror)
ClassNotFoundException clojure.data
  java.net.URLClassLoader.findClass (URLClassLoader.java:381)
```

The problem is that while clojure.data comes packaged with your Clojure installation, it isn't loaded by default. To use clojure.data—and this is true of most of the namespaces you'll use in your Clojure career—you need to tell Clojure to read and compile the code behind the namespace.

Fortunately, that's not difficult. All you need is require:

```
user=> (require 'clojure.data)
```

```
user=> (clojure.data/diff literature horror)
[["Emma" "Oliver Twist"] ["It" "Carrie"] [nil nil "Possession"]]
```

As you can see from the example, require takes the name of the namespace, which you will need to quote, and loads the code behind that namespace. And once you've done the require, you can start using the contents of the namespace.

A Namespace of Your Own

Now that you've seen how to create new namespaces in the REPL and how to get namespaces loaded with require, we're ready to take the final step: defining a namespace of our own in a real *.clj file in a directory* project.

Let's start by creating a new Clojure application. Recall from *Hello, Clojure* that we can use Leiningen to create a new Clojure project like this:

```
$ lein new app blottsbooks
```

Run those commands, and you will end up with a fully functional, if skeletal, Clojure project. For our purposes, the key bit of the project is a single source file that you'll find at src/blottsbooks/core.clj.

Inside of that file you'll find the following:

hello/blottsbooks-1/src/blottsbooks/core.clj
```
(ns blottsbooks.core
  (:gen-class))

(defn -main
  "I don't do a whole lot ... yet."
  [& args]
  (println "Hello, World!"))
```

So far this is the same ground we covered back in *Hello, Clojure*, but now the ns at the top of the file should make a bit more sense: we're setting up a new namespace called blottsbooks.core.

There are a couple of things to watch as you build file-based namespaces. The first and most important is the correspondence between the namespace name —blottsbooks.core in the example—and the name of the file—blottsbooks/core.clj. This correspondence is neither an accident nor optional. In order for tools like require to work, Clojure assumes that it can do a simple transformation of a namespace name and come up with the name of the file harboring the code for the namespace. This transformation is about as simple as it comes: take the namespace name, convert any periods to directory-separating slashes, slap a .clj on the end, and voilà: blottsbooks.core is found in blottsbooks/core.clj.

Class Paths

Along with the namespace-to-file-name transformation, Clojure also relies on the Java class path—essentially a list of places that the JVM looks for code—to help it locate namespaces. This is how Clojure knows to look in the src directory, and how it manages to locate the built-in Clojure library code. More on this in *Interoperating with Java*.

Thus if we wanted to add a second namespace to our blottsbooks project (a namespace to hold our pricing code), we might create a file called src/blottsbooks/pricing.clj. Given that file name, the namespace name *must* be blottsbooks.pricing:

namespace/blottsbooks-1/src/blottsbooks/pricing.clj
```
(ns blottsbooks.pricing)

(def discount-rate 0.15)

(defn  discount-price [book]
  (- (:price book)
     (* discount-rate (:price book))))
```

If you happen to have any dashes in your namespace name—perhaps it's called blotts-books.current-pricing—then the dashes get converted to underscores in the file name: blotts_books/current_pricing.clj.

The other thing you should keep in mind as you create files full of namespaces is that it is possible to fold require expressions into the ns expression. So if we wanted to use the discount-price function from blottsbooks.pricing in blottsbooks.core, we could do it like this:

```
namespace/blottsbooks-1/src/blottsbooks/core.clj
(ns blottsbooks.core
  (:require blottsbooks.pricing)
  (:gen-class))

(defn -main []
  (println
    (blottsbooks.pricing/discount-price
      {:title "Emma" :price 9.99})))
```

Generally Clojure programmers prefer to use the stand-alone require when they're working in the REPL—it's just convenient to be able to require in namespaces as you go—and the ns version when writing source files. You should too, but you should also be aware that the syntax of the two forms of require is maddeningly different. In the stand-alone version it's require, a symbol. In the ns version it's :require, a keyword. In the stand-alone version you *must* quote the argument. In the ns version you *must not* quote the argument.

As and Refer

The downside of using fully qualified names like blottsbooks.pricing/discount-price is that they can get *long*, and long names tend to clutter up your code and make it less readable. Fortunately, Clojure provides a couple of shortcuts to minimize the clutter.

One way you can make your code less noisy is to create an alias for the namespace, like this:

```
(require '[blottsbooks.pricing :as pricing])
```

or like this:

```
(ns blottsbooks.core
  (:require [blottsbooks.pricing :as pricing])
  (:gen-class))
```

Note that we're now feeding require a three-element vector instead of just the name of the namespace. As shown in the figure on page 101, the extended version of require not only pulls in the blottsbooks.pricing namespace but also gives it an alias of plain old pricing.

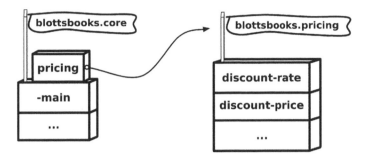

Given this, we can now refer to blottsbooks.pricing/discount-price as pricing/discount-price:

```
(defn -main []
  (println
    (pricing/discount-price {:title "Emma" :price 9.99})))
```

The alias that you supply with :as is completely arbitrary. We could have said [blottsbooks.pricing :as p] and then called p/discount-price. Also keep in mind that the alias created by :as is local to the namespace where you evaluated the require. If you want to use the pricing alias in a second namespace, you're going to need a second require.../:as. Finally, aliases don't mask ordinary bindings, so if you did have that pricing alias in your namespace you could also have a pricing function without a problem.

The require.../:as combination should be your first choice when those fully qualified names are getting in the way. In extreme situations you can take things one step further, with :refer:

```
(require '[blottsbooks.pricing :refer [discount-price]])
```

As shown in the following figure, when you use :refer you are essentially pulling the vars from the other namespace into the current namespace.

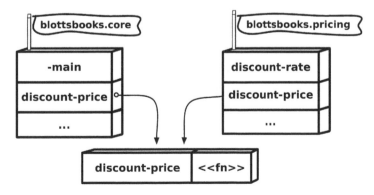

That means you don't have to worry about using fully qualified names or aliases:

```
;; Now that I've done the :refer...
(discount-price {:title "Emma" :price 9.99})
```

While :refer might seem like a great way to get to the most concise code possible, there is a danger lurking in all that convenience: what if we already have a discount-price function defined? In that case :refer will overwrite it. As perilous as this is for application functions, consider that you can also accidentally overwrite standard, Clojure-supplied functions with :refer. Who's up for debugging some code where first or list has been redefined? Since namespaces exist precisely to prevent these kinds of clashes, you should use :refer very sparsely, if at all.

REPL Prompts

 Now that we've looked at namespaces, we can finally resolve the Great REPL Prompt Mystery. REPLs generally include the name of the current namespace in their prompts. If you start a REPL with Leiningen outside of a project directory, your initial namespace will be user, and that's what you will see in your prompt. On the other hand, if you start a REPL from inside of a Clojure project directory, Leiningen will default to the core namespace of that project.

Namespaces, Symbols, and Keywords

Like symbols and vars, namespaces are just ordinary Clojure values, accessible to the mortal Clojure programmer. You can, for example, get at the current namespace: it's always bound to the symbol *ns*, so that

```
(println "Current ns:" *ns*)
```

will print something like

```
Current ns: #object[clojure.lang.Namespace 0x76c706bf user]
```

You can also look up any existing namespace by name:

```
(find-ns 'user)  ; Get the namespace called 'user.
```

With a namespace in hand, you can discover all the things defined in that namespace, so that this:

```
(ns-map (find-ns 'user))    ; Includes all the predefined vars.
```

will give you a very large map of symbols to vars, essentially everything the user namespace knows about:

```
{primitives-classnames #'clojure.core/primitives-classnames,
 +' #'clojure.core/+',
 Enum java.lang.Enum,
 decimal? #'clojure.core/decimal?,
 << and on and on >>
}
```

Conveniently, ns-map will find the namespace for you if you pass in a symbol, so we can shorten our last example to this:

```
(ns-map 'user)
```

and still get a map of everything the namespace knows about.

Namespaces and symbols have an interesting relationship. As we've seen, you can write fully qualified symbols by including a namespace name, followed by a slash, followed by the symbol proper: pricing/discount-price. The namespace is actually part of the symbol, a part that you can get at with the namespace function:

```
;; Gives us "pricing".
```

```
(namespace 'pricing/discount-print)
```

The thing to keep in mind about the namespace part of a symbol is that it's just a name, not a reference to a namespace value. Thus we can make up symbols with nonexistent namespaces, so that 'narnia/caspian is a fine symbol even if the narnia namespace doesn't actually exist. Of course, if you remove the quote, as in narnia/caspian, then you are trying to look up caspian in the narnia namespace, which had better be there.

Keywords also have room for a namespace, which you can add by either explicitly calling out the namespace:

```
:blottsbooks.pricing/author
```

or by doubling up the colon in the front:

```
::author
```

If you double up the colon, the keyword will pick up the current namespace. Given that there is no automatic lookup of keywords, adding a namespace to a keyword is mainly about preventing keyword collisions. Thus if you are worried that your :book may be confused with someone else's :book, you can always slap an extra colon on it: ::book. In practice most keywords go sans namespace.

In the Wild

When it comes to Clojure namespaces, there is one giant walking the land: clojure.core. The clojure.core namespace is where all of those fundamental, predefined functions—things like println and str and count—live. So why is it that we can just write println and count and not clojure.core/println and clojure.core/count? We rarely need the clojure.core/ because just after it creates a new namespace, ns does the equivalent of this:

```
(require '[clojure.core :refer :all])
```

The :all option is an even more dramatic version of the :refer that we saw earlier. It pulls in *all* the bindings from the other namespace. That's great for booting up a language environment, but perhaps not something you should use in everyday code.

If you are curious about what goodies come wrapped in clojure.core, you could read the documentation (in fact, you *should* read the documentation), but given what we've covered in this chapter, you can also use ns-map to reveal all the wonders hiding in clojure.core:

```
(ns-map 'clojure.core)
```

Not only that, but you can also deduce that the clojure.core namespace lives in a file called clojure/core.clj. In fact, if you look at the Clojure source code, that is exactly what you will find.[1]

This source file is full of all sorts of wonders, including the definition of not, here shown in a lightly edited form:

```
(ns clojure.core)

;; Lots of code omitted...

(defn not
  "Returns true if x is logical false, false otherwise."
  [x] (if x false true))
```

It also holds the definition of not=:

```
(defn not=
  "Same as (not (= obj1 obj2))"
  ([x] false)
  ([x y] (not (= x y)))
  ([x y & more]
   (not (apply = x y more))))
```

---

1. https://github.com/clojure/clojure/blob/master/src/clj/clojure/core.clj

A great way to explore your new programming language is to do exactly that: explore your new programming language, from the inside.

Of course, there is more to Clojure than just the bits that come built into the language. The Clojure world is a living, breathing technical ecosystem full of people writing and releasing code. Happily, getting to other people's code from a Leiningen project only requires one additional step: you need to add a dependency in the Leiningen-generated project.clj file.

For example, if we wanted to use the Korma SQL library in our book-store application, we would just add it and its current version number—which we can get from the Korma project page—to the :dependencies value:

```
namespace/blottsbooks-2/project.clj
(defproject blottsbooks "0.1.0-SNAPSHOT"
  :description "FIXME: write description"
  :url "http://example.com/FIXME"
  :license {:name "Eclipse Public License"
            :url "http://www.eclipse.org/legal/epl-v10.html"}
  :dependencies [[org.clojure/clojure "1.8.0"]
                 [korma "0.4.0"]]
  :main ^:skip-aot blottsbooks.core
  :target-path "target/%s"
  :profiles {:uberjar {:aot :all}})
```

and restart our REPL:

```
$ lein repl
nREPL server started on port 54569 on host 127.0.0.1 - nrepl://127.0.0.1:54569
...
```

then require in the Korma namespace:

```
blottsbooks.core=> (require '[korma.db :as db])
nil
```

We're in business.

Staying Out of Trouble

There is nothing terribly complicated about the namespace. Each namespace is just a big name/value lookup table which itself has a name. Keep in mind that there's no hierarchy of namespaces. Each namespace has a name and somewhere behind the scenes Clojure maintains a mapping between the namespace name, perhaps clojure.core or maybe clojure.core.data, and the actual namespace. But as far as Clojure is concerned there is no more of a relationship between clojure.core.data and clojure.core than there is between clojure.core and blottsbooks.pricing. In particular, Clojure does not look at clojure.core.data as somehow *under* clojure.core. You can call your namespace whatever you want, and names like clojure.core and clojure.core.data do help us humans make sense of the code. But as far as Clojure is concerned the names are arbitrary.

Loading namespaces is equally straightforward, especially in production, where you set up your namespace, perhaps require in some other namespaces, and leave it there. Life can get a little more complicated in development, where you frequently want to require in a namespace, modify it, and require it in again—and then do it all again.

For example, imagine that you're working in the REPL, trying out the blottsbooks.pricing namespace.

```
blottsbooks.core=> (require '[blottsbooks.pricing :as pricing])
nil
blottsbooks.core=> (pricing/discount-price {:title "Emma" :price 20.0})
17.0
```

and you decide to rename the discount-price function to the more descriptive compute-discount-price. You start up your favorite text editor and modify src/blottsbooks/pricing.clj to look like this:

```
namespace/blottsbooks-2/src/blottsbooks/pricing.clj
(ns blottsbooks.pricing)

(def discount-rate 0.15)

(defn  compute-discount-price [book]
  (- (:price book)
     (* discount-rate (:price book))))
```

Having done that, you return to the REPL and re-require the namespace:

```
blottsbooks.core=> (require '[blottsbooks.pricing :as pricing])
nil
```

Sadly, it doesn't work:

```
blottsbooks.core=> (pricing/compute-discount-price
                      {:title "Emma" :price 20.0})

CompilerException java.lang.RuntimeException:
  No such var: pricing/compute-discount-price, ...
```

The problem is that require knows that the blottsbooks.pricing namespace is already loaded and will quietly refuse to load it a second time. This is what you want in production: require in a namespace any number of times, and it only gets loaded once. But this *load once* policy gets in the way during development. Fortunately, the solution is easy: just add the :reload keyword to your require:

```
blottsbooks.core=> (require :reload '[blottsbooks.pricing :as pricing])
nil
blottsbooks.core=> (pricing/compute-discount-price
                      {:title "Emma" :price 20.0})
17.0
```

Now require will reload your code every time, existing namespace or not.

Keep in mind that the :reload option does *not* clear out the existing contents of the namespace when it reloads it. That means that when you renamed discount-price to compute-discount-price in the source and then reloaded the namespace, you did indeed define a new function called compute-discount-price. But the old discount-price is still wandering around zombielike in your REPL. Mostly this isn't a problem, but if it is, you can always deploy ns-unmap to remove it:

```
blottsbooks.core=> (ns-unmap 'blottsbooks.pricing 'discount-price)
```

One other unfortunate twist with :reload is that sometimes you have code you don't want to execute every time the namespace gets reloaded. Perhaps you're calling a function that takes a long time to run or has some side effect:

```
;; I really only want this to happen once.

(def some-value (function-with-side-effects))
```

Again, Clojure comes to the rescue, this time with defonce, which you use in place of def:

```
;; Just set some-value the first time.

(defonce some-value (function-with-side-effects))
```

As the name suggests, defonce binds the symbol to the value exactly once—the first time. Thus, in the example the function-with-side-effects will only get evaluated once, the first time you load the namespace. After that, you can :reload until your keyboard wears out and some-value will not get redefined.

If you change your mind you can always use ns-unmap to persuade defonce that it's time to actually do something:

```
(ns-unmap *ns* 'some-value)
```

And the circle is complete.

Wrapping Up

Congratulations: you've reached a milestone in your Clojure journey. Having read this far you know how about the basic Clojure data types. You know how to build flexible units of code in the form of functions. And you know how to assemble those functions into coherent packages called namespaces.

This means you have the fundamentals of Clojure covered. Certainly there is more to learn about Clojure and that will be true even when you finish the last page of this book. But you now have the basic outlines penciled in and from here on out it's all about filling in the details.

And now we'll turn to a lovely detail. In the next chapter we'll take a look at sequences. In the same way that namespaces pull your code together, sequences unify the collection types.

Part II

Intermediate

CHAPTER 10

Sequences

There's a pleasant mystery about Clojure that most newly arrived programmers notice sooner or later. On one hand the language has this rich variety of collection types, everything from the map to the set to the vector and the list, each one good at some operations and less so at others. And Clojure programmers use the range of collection types with reasonably wild abandon.

Now for the mystery: There is very little *Oh, this is a vector but this is a map* special pleading in real-world Clojure code. Certainly you can find code here and there that is concerned with specific collection types, but you can also find vast stretches of Clojure code that seem to simply ignore the differences between the collection types.

So in this chapter we'll have a hard look at sequences, the feature of Clojure that makes this all possible. We'll see how Clojure has a sort of programmatic gravitational field that tends to pull collections into sequences. We'll also discover how Clojure supplies you with a huge toolkit of functions that lets you do interesting things with sequences. We'll round out the chapter by looking at some examples of sequences in action and at some ways you can get into sequential trouble.

One Thing After Another

Let's start our exploration of sequences by asking a simple question: how does the *count* function work? Specifically, how does this one function manage to count the elements in a vector, the items in a list, the characters in a string, and the entries in a map? After all, we know that behind the scenes lists and vectors and maps and strings are all very different data structures, and if you want to count the elements of each one, somewhere there needs to be code to deal with the structural differences.

One possible design for this would be to write in special-case code for each collection type, maybe by using a multimethod. So if we were building our own count, we might write this:

sequences/examples.clj

```clojure
;; Is this how count is implemented?

(defn flavor [x]
  (cond
    (list? x) :list
    (vector? x) :vector
    (set? x) :set
    (map? x) :map
    (string? x) :string
    :else :unknown))

(defmulti my-count flavor)

(defmethod my-count :list [x] (list-specific-count x))

(defmethod my-count :vector [x] (vector-specific-count x))

;; And so on...
```

Alternatively, we can imagine that my-count has access to a number of generic wrappers, one per collection type. There would be a wrapper for lists, and one for vectors, and so on. Internally each kind of wrapper would know how to deal with its own collection type, but from the outside the different wrapper types would present the same, generic interface. The count function could then start by encasing the collection in the correct flavor of wrapper and then work with the uniform interface of the wrapper from there.

And now for the big reveal: *Clojure opts for the wrapper method.* Clojure calls its generic collection wrappers *sequences*. Under the hood there are as many flavors of sequences as there are collection types, but to the outside world all sequences provide a very uniform interface: no matter if it's a vector or a map or a list or a set behind a sequence, one sequence looks exactly like another.

Sequence Adapter

 If you have an object-oriented programming background, then the wrapper design of sequences might look familiar: hidden behind those sequences is the adapter pattern.

There's even a function for wrapping your collection in a sequence: that function is called seq. Here's a sequence made from a vector:

```clojure
(def title-seq (seq ["Emma" "Oliver Twist" "Robinson Crusoe"]))
```

Run this code, and you will get back the sequence view of your vector. So, if you print title-seq you will see this:

```
("Emma" "Oliver Twist" "Robinson Crusoe")
```

Don't be fooled by its round-parentheses disguise. title-seq is not a list; it's a sequence, or *seq* for short.

You can also get a seq from a list:

```
(seq '("Emma" "Oliver Twist" "Robinson Crusoe"))
```

A little more interesting is that you can call seq on a map: do this, and you will end up with a sequence of key/value pairs. Thus this:

```
(seq {:title "Emma", :author "Austen", :published 1815})
```

will give you

```
([:title "Emma"] [:author "Austen"] [:published 1815])
```

Well, more or less. Since Clojure makes no guarantees on the order of the keys in a map, it's possible that the elements of the map sequence might come out in a different order.

You can even call seq on a sequence, like this:

```
;; Calling seq on a sequence is a noop.
(seq (seq ["Red Queen" "The Nightingale" "Uprooted"]))
```

and get exactly the same sequence back.

A slightly more surprising thing about seq is that it will return a nil when handed an empty collection:

```
(seq [])    ; Gives you nil.
(seq '())   ; Also nil.
(seq {})    ; Nil again.
```

This *empty sequence becomes a nil* behavior is handy because it means we can use (seq collection) as a truthy value to detect empty collections.

A Universal Interface

Getting at the contents of a sequence is easy—and familiar. You just call first to get the lead-off element:

```
;; Returns "Emma".
(first (seq '("Emma" "Oliver Twist" "Robinson Crusoe")))
```

and rest to get everything *except* the first element:

```
;; Returns the sequence ("Oliver Twist" "Robinson Crusoe")
(rest  (seq '("Emma" "Oliver Twist" "Robinson Crusoe")))
```

Alternatively, you use next to get at the *all but the first* sequence. The difference between next and rest is that while rest of an empty sequence is an empty sequence, next of an empty sequence is nil. While most of the time rest works fine, occasionally nil comes in handy.

You can also add a new element to the front of your sequence with cons:

```
(cons "Emma" (seq '("Oliver Twist" "Robinson Crusoe")))
```

And that's it. Once you have a sequence, the only things you can do with it are get the first element with first, get the other ones with next or rest, and slap a new element on the front with cons.

Armed with all this, implementing my-count is reasonably straightforward:

```
(defn my-count [col]
  (let [the-seq (seq col)]
    (loop [n 0 s the-seq]
      (if (seq s)
        (recur (inc n) (rest s))
        n))))
```

The first thing my-count does is turn the collection into a sequence (in the let). The rest is just a loop that runs through the sequence—using rest—counting as it goes. Notice there is no special-case code in my-count for vectors or maps or sets. Once we have the sequence we don't need to worry about which kind of collection we have.

The only remotely tricky thing going on in my-count is the way we determine when we've run out of items to count. We call seq on our sequence. If seq returns nil we know that we're out of items, since seq of an empty sequence is nil.

Watch Those nils!

 If you're thinking that my-count would be clearer if we simply checked whether (first s) was nil, consider trying to count the items in [nil nil nil].

Aside from the thrill of understanding how count works, there is a very practical reason for diving into all of this sequence talk. While functions like count and first can manage to keep their involvement with sequences quiet, the same is not true of functions like rest, next, and cons. These three functions always (aside from the occasional nil) return sequences:

```
(rest [1 2 3])                         ; A sequence!
(rest {:fname "Jane" :lname "Austen"}) ; Another sequence.
(next {:fname "Jane" :lname "Austen"}) ; Yet another sequence.
```

```
(cons 0 [1 2 3])                    ; Still another.
(cons 0 #{1 2 3})                   ; And another.
```

And now we finally have the explanation for why (rest some-vector) gives you back a collection that prints with round parentheses: the rest function always returns a sequence.

A Rich Toolkit ...

If all we were talking about was first and rest, this whole sequence kerfuffle wouldn't amount to much. The real power of sequences lies in the mountain of useful library functions that—like our my-count function—take any kind of collection, convert it to a sequence, and then do something interesting with the sequence. For example, if you have a seqable collection but it's in the wrong order, you can sort it with sort:

```
(def titles ["Jaws" "Emma" "2001" "Dracula"])

(sort titles) ; Sequence: ("2001" "Dracula" "Emma" "Jaws")
```

Like count, sort converts the collection you pass in into a sequence, sorts it, and returns the resulting sequence.

Seqa What?

 Yes, *seqable* is a word, at least if you are a Clojurist. A seqable is something that the seq function can turn into a sequence.

The reverse function works the same way, except that it reverses instead of sorts:

```
;; A Sequence: ("Dracula" "2001" "Emma" "Jaws")

(reverse titles)
```

And since sequences are also (trivially) seqable you can feed the output of sort into reverse to get your titles sorted in the other direction:

```
;; A Sequence: ("Jaws" "Emma" "Dracula" "2001")

(reverse (sort titles)) ;
```

There is also partition, which chops up a big sequence into a sequence of smaller sequences, enabling you to take a flat vector:

```
(def titles-and-authors ["Jaws" "Benchley" "2001" "Clarke"])

(partition 2 titles-and-authors)
```

and turn it into something more structured:

```
(("Jaws" "Benchley") ("2001" "Clarke"))
```

There is also interleave, which weaves two sequences together into one:

```
;; A vector of titles and a list of authors.
(def titles  ["Jaws" "2001"])
(def authors '("Benchley" "Clarke"))

;; Combine the authors and titles into a single sequence
;; ("Jaws" "Benchley" "2001" "Clarke")

(interleave titles authors)
```

Not to mention interpose, which sprinkles a separator value between the elements of a sequence:

```
;; Gives us ("Lions" "and" "Tigers" "and" "Bears")
;; Oh my!

(def scary-animals ["Lions" "Tigers" "Bears"])

(interpose "and" scary-animals)
```

Functions like sort, reverse, partition, interleave, and interpose all share the same basic processing skeleton. They start by turning their collection arguments into sequences with seq. They then do their thing using only first, rest, and cons, or using functions that rely on the magic foursome. Finally they return the result as—you guessed it—a sequence.

… Made Richer with Functional Values

As convenient as functions like partition and interpose are, the real power of sequences only comes into play when you mix in the *functions are values* idea. A great example of this is the filter function. You can probably guess from the name what filter does: you pass filter a predicate and a collection, and it gives you back a new sequence populated with only those items from the original sequence that measured up to the predicate. The predicate is, of course, expressed as a function. So if we needed all the negative numbers in a list, we could combine filter with the neg?:

```
;; Returns the sequence (-22 -99 -77)

(filter neg? '(1 -22 3 -99 4 5 6 -77))
```

More realistically, if we had this vector of maps:

```
(def books
  [{:title "Deep Six" :price 13.99 :genre :sci-fi :rating 6}
   {:title "Dracula" :price 1.99 :genre :horror :rating 7}
   {:title "Emma" :price 7.99 :genre :comedy :rating 9}
   {:title "2001" :price 10.50 :genre :sci-fi :rating 5}])
```

Map • 117

we could use our old buddy the cheap? function:

```
(defn cheap? [book]
  (when (<= (:price book) 9.99)
    book))
```

to find all the inexpensive books:

```
(filter cheap? books)
```

which are as follows:

```
({:genre :horror, :title "Dracula", :price 1.99 :rating 7}
 {:genre :comedy, :title "Emma", :price 7.99 :rating 9})
```

Similar to filter is some. Like filter, some takes a predicate and a seqable collection. And like filter, some will go looking for items for which the predicate will return a truthy value. The difference is that some quits when it finds the first passing item, returning the value from the predicate. So while filter will always return a (possibly empty) sequence, some will return either the first truthy value from the predicate function, or nil if it can't find anything. Since our predicate function cheap? returns either the book or nil, if you write this:

```
(some cheap? books)
```

you will get the first cheap book, {:genre :horror, :title "Dracula", :price 1.99}. Even better, since the example will return either a book or nil, its return value follows the rules of truthy logic. And that means you can use it in an if:

```
(if (some cheap? books)
  (println "We have cheap books for sale!"))
```

You can think of some as posing the question, *Is there some item that passes this test?*

Map

Another thing we might want to do with a collection is transform it by evaluating a function on each element. We might, for example, have a collection of numbers and want a collection of all the numbers doubled. Here Clojure provides you with a choice.

Behind door number one is map. The map function takes a function and a collection and gives you back a sequence cooked up by applying the function to each member of the original collection. So if we started with some numbers:

```
(def some-numbers [1, 53, 811])
```

and we wanted to double them, we could write this:

```
(def doubled (map #(* 2 %) some-numbers))
```

Or if we had our collection of book maps and we just wanted the titles, we could do this:

```
(map (fn [book] (:title book)) books)
```

which would give us this:

```
("Deep Six" "Dracula" "Emma" "2001")
```

Actually, we can take a shortcut here. Remember that when it comes to looking themselves up in maps, keywords *are* functions. That means that in the last example we don't need the fn; we can just use :title as the function that we feed into map:

```
;; Turn the collection of books into a collection of titles.
;; The easy way!
(map :title books)
```

But if we wanted a collection of the *lengths* of our book titles—(8 7 4 4)—we would seem to need an fn again:

```
(map (fn [book] (count (:title book))) books)
```

But a cleaner way would be to build our mapping function with yet another function-producing function, comp. The comp function takes any number of functions and returns a function that applies each of the input functions in turn. For example, (comp str inc) will get you a function that increments a number and turns the result into a string. That means we can get our book-title-producing code down to this:

```
(map (comp count :title) books)
```

Behind door number two is the map function's less popular cousin, for. On the surface, for looks like the loops that you find in more traditional languages. Here, for example, is our title-length code, recast with for:

```
(for [b books]
  (count (:title b)))
```

Like an old-school loop, for successively sets b to each value in the books collection and executes the expressions in the body. But that's where the resemblance ends: like map, for is in the business of building new sequences from the old. Like the good functional citizen it is, for produces a value—in this case a sequence of all the title lengths.

Reduce

Sometimes you don't need to transform each item of a collection the way that map or for does. Sometimes what you need is to combine all the elements of a collection into a single value. For this we have reduce. Like map, reduce takes a function and a sequence and calls the function for each item in the sequence. Unlike map, reduce passes two arguments to the function—along with the element from the collection, your function gets called with the current result. Each time reduce calls your function, it updates the current result with the return value from that call. When reduce runs out of elements, it returns the last result.

Although there are a lot of variations on how you can use reduce, the easiest to grasp is where you pass in three things: a two-argument function, an initial value, and the collection. Do this, and reduce will kick things off by calling the function with the initial value and the first item in the collection and then roll from there. To make this a little more real, let's imagine we wanted to sum up all the numbers in this vector:

```
(def numbers [10 20 30 40 50])
```

We've already seen that you could do this with apply, but you can also get it done with reduce:

```
(defn add2 [a b]
  (+ a b))
(reduce add2 0 numbers)
```

Run the preceding code, and you will get the sum.

You get that sum because reduce called the add2 function, first with your starting value (0) and the first element of the numbers (10). It got the result (again 10), and then called the function again with the new result (10) and the second element (20), and so on down the line, eventually returning the last result.

We can simplify this last example quite a bit. Take the add2 function: all it does is add its arguments together. Well, we already have a function that does that. It goes by the name of +:

```
(reduce + 0 numbers)
```

We don't even need the initial value. If you omit the initial value from the call to reduce, reduce will use the first element of the collection as the initial value, which—since we're just adding up numbers—works fine:

```
(reduce + numbers)
```

There is something elegant and wonderful about the brevity of code like this.

Don't get the idea that reduce is only for adding numbers. Think of reduce as the basic tool for combining—or *reducing*—the items of a sequence into a single value. For example, you can use reduce to find the highest-priced book in your collection:

```
(defn hi-price [hi book]
  (if (> (:price book) hi)
    (:price book)
    hi))
```

```
(reduce hi-price 0 books)
```

Composing a Solution

You can get a huge amount of programming mileage out of sequences and the panoply of functions that Clojure provides to process them. For example, imagine that you were working on a sales application for your book business and, starting with the books vector we saw earlier, you needed to format a string proclaiming the three top-rated books, something like this:

```
"Emma // Dracula // Deep Six"
```

Step one is to find the top three books, by rating. We could start by sorting the books by their rating:

```
(sort-by :rating books)
```

That will give us the books from lowest to highest rating, but the other way around is more useful:

```
(reverse (sort-by :rating books))
```

Then we can then pull out the three highest-rated books, with take, a function that produces a sequence consisting of the first N items of another sequence. In this case it's the first three items:

```
(take 3 (reverse (sort-by :rating books)))
```

But we don't really need the whole book map, just the title. Looks like a job for map:

```
(map :title (take 3 (reverse (sort-by :rating books))))
```

We now have a sequence that looks like ("Emma" "1984" "Jaws"). From here it's just a matter of assembling the string. We can put the slashes into our sequence with interpose:

```
(interpose
  " // "
  (map :title (take 3 (reverse (sort-by :rating books)))))
```

Which gives us a five-string sequence:

```
("Emma" " // " "1984" " // "  "Jaws")
```

And then we just need to assemble the whole thing into a single string and wrap the code in a convenient function:

```
(defn format-top-titles [books]
  (apply
    str
    (interpose
      " // "
      (map :title (take 3 (reverse (sort-by :rating books)))))))
```

You can get a lot of computing out of a few sequence functions.

Other Sources of Sequences

Given all the leverage you can get out of sequences, it's not surprising that you can turn lots of things besides maps, vectors, and lists into sequences. The line-seq function, for example, will turn the contents of a text file into a sequence. So if we had all our authors' names in a file called authors.txt, we could write a function to determine if an author is listed:

```
(require '[clojure.java.io :as io])

(defn listed-author? [author]
  (with-open [r (io/reader "authors.txt")]
    (some (partial = author) (line-seq r))))
```

Let's put aside the require and with-open (it opens and closes a file) expressions for the moment and focus on the last line. In that last line we use line-seq to turn the contents of the authors.txt file into a sequence of strings, one string per line, and then use some to go looking for our author.

Or perhaps instead of a file you have a string and you want to pull out all of the bits of the string that match a particular regular expression. Look no further than Clojure's built-in regular-expression literals—which are written as a string prefixed by a #. The simplest thing you can do with a regular expression is ask if it matches some string:

```
;; A regular expression that matches Pride and Prejudice followed by anything.
(def re #"Pride and Prejudice.*")

;; A string that may or may not match.
(def title "Pride and Prejudice and Zombies")

;; And we have a classic!
(if (re-matches  re title)
    (println "We have a classic!"))
```

But you can also use re-seq to generate a sequence of strings that match a given regular expression. So armed with the regular expression #"\w+", which matches a single word, you can do this:

```
(re-seq #"\w+" title)
```

You'll end up with the sequence ("Pride" "and" "Prejudice" "and" "Zombies").

In the Wild

If you're getting the feeling that sequences are pretty central to Clojure pro-graming, well, yes. You can find sequences littered through the length and breath of real-world Clojure code. To see some real-world sequence action, you might have a look at the source code for the wonderful Overtone,[1] which describes itself as a *collaborative programmable music* system. Overtone spends a lot of its code creating, shaping, tuning, and distorting (hopefully) musical sounds, and makes heavy use of sequences and sequence functions in the process. For example, here is a bit of code that is part of generating a sound *envelope*, which controls how the loudness of a sound evolves over time:

```
(map #(+ %1 bias) [0 0 level (* level sustain) 0])
```

Keep in mind that bias, level, and sustain are all bound to floating-point numbers as this expression gets evaluated. Stare at the expression for a minute, and you will see that it's just a call to map, one that uses a function literal to add bias to each of the five elements of the vector.

Alternatively, the authors of Overtone could've written this expression with a for:

```
(for [v [0 0 level (* level sustain) 0]] (+ v bias))
```

But they didn't. This is typical of real-world Clojure code, which leans on map much more frequently than on for.

You can also find some sequence-based string-building code along the lines of our book-title example in ClojureScript.[2] ClojureScript takes on the daunting task of translating Clojure programs into the equivalent JavaScript code. Part of that translation involves transforming Clojure vectors and lists into their JavaScript equivalents, complete with brackets and commas. Dig into the ClojureScript code, and you will find this gem:

```
(defn seq->js-array [v]
  (str "[" (apply str (interpose ", " (map pr-str v))) "]"))
```

---

1. http://overtone.github.io
2. https://github.com/clojure/clojurescript

Note that seq->js-array is not a terribly general function—the call to pr-str (which turns its arguments into quoted strings) means that seq->js-array can only handle one-level sequences of strings. Fortunately seq->js-array can afford to be less than general because it's only intended to help in configuring the JavaScript environment. Still, the family resemblance to our earlier example—complete with calls to map and interpose—should be clear.

One thing to note from both of these real-world examples, as well as our earlier *format the highest-rated books* sample, is how deeply nested the sequence operations tend to get. Here's the book example again:

```
(defn format-top-titles [books]
  (apply
    str
    (interpose
      " // "
      (map :title (take 3 (reverse (sort-by :rating books)))))))
```

It's a lovely example of functional code, but it does take some effort to read. You need to work from the inside out. First we sort by :ratings. Then we reverse the sorted sequence and so on until we get to using (apply str ...) to turn the resulting sequence into a single string.

Happily, Clojure provides some convenient syntactical sugar for these occasions. In this case the sugar takes the form of a very pointy arrow: ->>. Essentially ->> lets you write a nested expression like the one we just saw in a more human *do this, then that, then the other thing* order. Here's how we would recast format-top-titles with ->>:

```
(defn format-top-titles [books]
  (->>
    books
    (sort-by :rating)
    reverse
    (take 3)
    (map :title)
    (interpose " // ")
    (apply str)))
```

This new version of format-top-titles starts with books and sorts the books by their ratings. Then it takes the resulting sequence and reverses it. Next it grabs the first three elements from the reversed sequence—these are the top-rated books—and pulls out their titles and formats a string using those titles. Note that ->> is clever in that it knows how to deal with plain symbols like reverse as well as incomplete function calls like (take 3). Even better, there is no performance penalty for using ->>: behind the scenes, Clojure just turns a ->> expression into the equivalent set of nested function calls.

There is also -> (note the single >), which is very similar to ->>. The difference is in where the current result gets placed at each step of the computation. Use ->>, and the result ends up at the end of the argument list. Use ->, and the result gets slipped in at the front. It really just depends on what the functions you're using expect.

Staying Out of Trouble

The good news is that Clojure comes equipped with a large assortment of functions to do interesting things with sequences—so many that we can only scratch the surface in this chapter. There's everything from butlast (give me all but the last element) to zipmap (build a map from two sequences). The bad news is that until you're familiar with what's available you'll tend to reinvent the wheel. In particular, if you find yourself processing a sequence one item at a time, perhaps with loop and recur, like this:

```
(defn total-sales [books]
  "Total up book sales. Books maps must have :sales key."
  (loop [books books total 0]
    (if (empty? books)
      total
      (recur (next books)
             (+ total (:sales (first books)))))))
```

consider that there is probably an easier way:

```
(defn total-sales [books] (apply + (map :sales books)))
```

The other thing to keep in mind is that when you turn a specialized collection into a sequence you end up with a generic listlike thing that no longer has any of its specialized talents. Most notably, if you turn a map into a sequence it loses that rapid *key to value* superpower that makes maps so useful:

```
(def maze-runner {:title "The Maze Runner" :author "Dashner"})

; Gives you back "Dashner"

(:author maze-runner)

; But this give you a nil - a seq is not a map!

(:author (seq maze-runner))
```

And it's not just explicit calls to seq you need to watch for, but also all those library functions that quietly return seqs, like this:

```
(:author (rest maze-runner)) ; Also nil: rest returns a seq.
```

Happily, there are functions that *do not* return sequences, most notably conj. Recall that, like cons, conj is in the business of adding new items to collections:

```
;; A *vector* ending with "Jaws".
(conj ["Emma" "1984" "The Maze Runner"] "Jaws")
;; A *list* starting with "Jaws".
(conj '("Emma" "1984" "The Maze Runner") "Jaws")
```

The difference is that conj pays attention to the type of collection you pass in and, critically, conj will give you back the same flavor of collection that you pass it. That's why conj can do the *new element goes at the front of lists but the back of vectors* thing. It has special-case code for each collection type. By contrast, the cons function just calls seq on your collection and proceeds to slap the new item on the front of the resulting sequence:

```
;; A *seq* starting with "Jaws".
(cons "Jaws" ["Emma" "1984" "The Maze Runner"])
;; A *seq* starting with "Jaws".
(cons "Jaws" '("Emma" "1984" "The Maze Runner"))
```

None of this means sequences are bad or that you should always fight the natural drift toward them. On the contrary, having a universal abstraction that allows you to work with vectors and sets and lists without constantly worrying about which you have is incredibly useful. But you do need to be mindful of when you have the actual thing and when you have the sequence.

Wrapping Up

In this chapter we looked at sequences, the Clojure abstraction that erases the differences between the various Clojure collection types and allows us treat them all like *one darned thing after another*. We also thought a bit about how sequences are implemented and we looked at the rich toolkit of functions that lets you do useful things with your sequences. Finally, we looked at some situations when it's best not to forget that a vector is a vector and a map is a map.

In the next chapter we'll explore lazy sequences, which combine the ideas of functional programming with the sequence abstraction to come up with something powerful and extraordinary.

CHAPTER 11

Lazy Sequences

Larry Wall, the creator of Perl, is famous for saying that the three virtues of a good programmer are laziness, impatience, and hubris. People tend to only remember the part about laziness, perhaps because impatience and hubris are so easy to come by. But Larry Wall is right: laziness is a great thing. Since there's always more to do than you can ever possibly get to, wise programmers save their strength for the tasks that are absolutely necessary.

What is true for programmers is frequently also true for programs. There's a lot of programmatic mileage to be gained by not running off and computing every value in sight the moment it comes into view. It turns out that laziness —the programmatic variety—is more than just a handy way of saving cycles. You can, in fact, use laziness as an organizing principle in your programs. If all of this seems unlikely, keep reading.

Sequences Without End

As we saw in the last chapter, the useful thing about sequences is that they are abstract. Instead of being a linked list or an array or some other definite kind of collection, a seq captures the idea of a sequential collection. A sequence is a thing that will give you the first value when you call first, and another sequence—representing the remaining contents—when you call rest or next. That is pretty much it.

Now consider that sequences are defined in terms of function calls. You can get the lead item in your sequence by calling the first function and a sequence representing the remaining items by calling another function, either next or (more likely) rest. We've seen how we can take advantage of the function-driven nature of sequences to abstract away the differences between the various collection types: once you turn it into a sequence, you don't care if you started with a list or a map or a vector.

But our assumption has been that behind every sequence is some concrete data structure like a list or a vector. But nowhere in the sequence API is this a requirement: The rules just say that first needs to return the first thing and rest and next need to return another sequence. This flexibility brings up an interesting possibility: perhaps we could dispense with the collection and make up the values returned by first and rest and next on the fly.

For example, imagine we were testing our book-store software and we needed to create some test books filled with nonsense text. We decide to take our cue from Stephen King:

lazy/examples.clj
```
(def jack "All work and no play makes Jack a dull boy.")

(def text [jack jack jack jack jack jack jack jack jack jack])
```

But repeatedly typing jack is both tedious and quite possibly not enough. What if we wanted 11 repetitions or 111 or 10,011? The typing is also unnecessary. After all, the sequence we're looking for is just the same value repeated over and over.

Wouldn't it be nice if we could say, *Conjure up a sequence that is a boring repetition of this value*? It would indeed, and that's why we have the repeat function. Using repeat is simultaneously simple and mind-blowing. The simple part is that to use repeat you just supply it with a value:

```
;; Be careful with repeated-text in the REPL.
;; There's a surprise lurking...

(def repeated-text (repeat jack))
```

You will get a sequence populated with the value you supplied:

```
;; Returns the "All work..." string.

(first repeated-text)

;; So does this.

(nth repeated-text 10)

;; And this.

(nth repeated-text 10202)
```

That brings us to the mind-blowing part: the sequence returned by repeat does not end. No matter how many items you ask for, they are always there. Fortunately, the sequences returned by repeat are also *lazy*: they wait until they are asked before they generate anything. They can get away with this because sequences are defined in terms of what functions like rest and next return.

Now for a bit of terminology. A *lazy sequence* is one that waits to be asked before it generates its elements. An *unbounded sequence* is a lazy sequence that, in theory, can go for ever. Not all lazy sequences are unbounded—a three-element sequence can wait to generate its elements—but all unbounded sequences are lazy.

One function that is particularly handy for taming unbounded sequences is take, which you'll recall returns the first N items of a sequence:

```
;; Twenty dull boys.

(take 20 repeated-text)
```

Infinity is so much easier to deal with when you can cut it down to size.

More Interesting Laziness

While the sequences returned from repeat are impressive at scale, they are also relentlessly boring—just the same value over and over. We can get more interesting sequences with cycle. The cycle function takes a collection and returns a lazy sequence of the items in the collection repeated over and over. So this:

```
(take 7 (cycle [1 2 3]))
```

will give you (1 2 3 1 2 3 1).

We can generate still more interesting sequences with iterate. To use iterate you pass it a function and a starting value:

```
(def numbers (iterate inc 1))
```

The iterate function returns a sequence whose first element is the value you passed in, in our example the 1, so that this:

```
(first numbers)
```

returns 1. The plot thickens with the second item, which is the value returned by applying the function to the first value. In the example this would be (inc 1), so the second item is 2. And the third value is the function applied to the second value, so 3. And off we go:

```
(nth numbers 0)     ; Returns 1
(nth numbers 1)     ; Returns 2
(nth numbers 99)    ; Returns 100.

(take 5 numbers)    ; Returns (1 2 3 4 5)
```

In principle, numbers contains all the positive integers starting with 1.

Keep in mind that what we got back from iterate is not some value or object that is somehow changing as it goes from 1 to 2 and so on. Instead what we get is a solidly immutable sequence whose first element is 1 and whose second element is 2 and then 3 and so on.

Lazy Friends

Interestingly, take is itself lazy. It does indeed return the first N items of the sequence you pass to it, but it doesn't actually grab anything off of the sequence until you ask for it. Thus this:

```
(def many-nums (take 1000000000 (iterate inc 1)))
```

doesn't create a billion-item collection immediately. Instead take knows that it should limit itself to the first billion items, but like the lazy sod that it is, take waits to be asked before it does anything. So this:

```
(println (take 20 (take 1000000000 (iterate inc 1))))
```

will print the first 20 integers and is only microscopically slower at doing so than the version sans the inner take.

take isn't alone in being surprisingly lazy. A lot of the sequence functions that we've been using are lazy. For example, our old friend map is lazy. We can, for example, use map to create a lazy sequence of all the even numbers and then just grab the first 20:

```
(def evens (map #(* 2 %) (iterate inc 1)))
```

```
(take 20 evens)
```

Also lazy is interleave, which you will recall weaves sequences together. Since it's lazy, we can safely interleave infinite sequences. We might, for instance, want to number our even numbers:

```
;; Returns (1 2 2 4 3 6 4 8 5 10)
```

```
(take 10 (interleave numbers evens))
```

An expression like (take 10 (interleave numbers evens) is more like an assembly line ready to start spewing out numbers than an actual list of numbers. Production only kicks off when you start asking for the contents of the resulting sequence.

Laziness in Practice

To really get our arms around lazy sequences, let's try a more interesting example. Suppose we needed some more or less randomly generated book maps for testing. We could sit down and manually cook up some nonsense books like this:

```
(def test-books
  [{:author "Bob Jordan", :title "Wheel of Time, Book 1"}
   {:author "Jane Austen", :title "Wheel of Time, Book 2"}
   {:author "Chuck Dickens", :title "Wheel of Time, Book 3"}
   {:author "Leo Tolstoy", :title "Wheel of Time, Book 4"}
   {:author "Bob Poe", :title "Wheel of Time, Book 5"}
   {:author "Jane Jordan", :title "Wheel of Time, Book 6"}
   {:author "Chuck Austen", :title "Wheel of Time, Book 7"}])
```

This will work, but armed with lazy sequences we can generate as many nonsense titles as we could ever want. To see how, let's start by building some titles. We could combine a base title with some numbers to get a very finite sequence of titles:

```
(def numbers [1 2 3])
```

```
(def trilogy (map #(str "Wheel of Time, Book " % ) numbers))
```

to end up with this:

```
("Wheel of Time, Book 1"
 "Wheel of Time, Book 2"
 "Wheel of Time, Book 3")
```

But since we have easy access to as many numbers as we can handle, and we know that map is lazy, it's a short step to an unlimited sequence of sequels:

```
(def numbers (iterate inc 1))
```

```
(def titles (map #(str "Wheel of Time, Book " % ) numbers))
```

We might also need authors for our generated books. Let's take a different tack here and generate a number of unique authors from a limited set of first names and last names. It's easy enough to build a modest vector of canned first names:

```
(def first-names ["Bob" "Jane" "Chuck" "Leo"])
```

But what we really need (you'll see why in a second) is the names repeated over and over:

```
(cycle first-names)
```

We also need some last names:

```
(def last-names ["Jordan" "Austen" "Dickens" "Tolstoy" "Poe"])
```

And we need a repeating sequence of those names:

```
(cycle last-names)
```

We also need a function to combine a first name with a last name to give us a full name:

```
(defn combine-names [fname lname]
  (str fname " " lname))
```

We can now use map to combine our names together to get a lazily infinite list of first- and last-name combinations:

```
(def authors
  (map combine-names
    (cycle first-names)
    (cycle last-names)))
```

Finally we can pull our authors and titles together into a lazy sequence of book maps:

```
(defn make-book [title author]
  {:author author :title title})
```

```
(def test-books (map make-book titles authors))
```

We end up with test-books bound to a lazy sequence that starts out like the manually generated one at the beginning of this section but then goes on forever, providing us with as many *Wheel of Time* sequels as we can stand.

It's wonderful to think that every time we look at a book, perhaps by doing (first test-books), we trigger a cascade of computing that generates a number, then a title, then a fresh first name and last name, and then a full name, and finally a book map. And yet on the outside test-books looks like a garden-variety sequence.

This underlines something important about lazy sequences: they are the ultimate *pay only for what you use* programming technique. By setting up the test-books sequence we have provided our system with a way to generate a huge amount of data. But—and the *but* here is key—we only pay the CPU and memory price for the data that we actually use. It's only when we grab something from the sequence that the data gets generated.

Behind the Scenes

Now that we have a feeling for how lazy sequences work from the outside, let's look at how they are built. The key tool for building a lazy sequence from scratch is the aptly named lazy-seq. The lazy-seq function is similar to seq. Like with seq, you give lazy-seq an expression and it will turn it into a sequence. So this:

```
(lazy-seq [1 2 3])
```

will give you the three-element sequence (1 2 3). The difference is that lazy-seq, being lazy, will hold off on evaluating the expression until you actually start pulling things off the sequence that it returns. For example, if you wrapped your vector in a chatty function:

```
(defn chatty-vector []
  (println "Here we go!")
  [1 2 3])
```

and then made a lazy sequence out of it:

```
;; No output when we do this.
```

```
(def s (lazy-seq (chatty-vector)))
```

you would *not* immediately see the output from the println. It's only seen when you start expanding the sequence, perhaps by pulling off the first element:

```
;; This will cause "Here we go!" to print.
```

```
(first s)
```

Under the hood, lazy-seq uses some macro magic (we'll talk about macros in Chapter 20, *Macros*, on page 241) to wrap its argument in an anonymous function, a function that only gets called when the time is right. And it's this *delay until the last possible second* behavior that is the key to laziness.

To see how it works in practice, we can implement our own version of repeat. Recall that the repeat function takes a value and produces an infinite sequence of that value repeated over and over. How would we write our own repeat? Like this:

```
;; Note that the real `repeat` has a couple of arities
;; that we won't bother to implement here.
(defn my-repeat [x]
  (cons x (lazy-seq (my-repeat x))))
```

The my-repeat function starts reasonably enough—it returns a sequence, manufactured with cons. Recall that cons takes a value and a sequence and returns a new sequence consisting of the value followed by the contents of the old sequence. In my-repeat we use cons to build a sequence consisting of the value passed in followed by the sequence created by—wait for it—a call to my-repeat. And that sequence starts with the value passed in, followed by another call to repeat, and so on. The magic that prevents this from flying off into recursive Neverland is the delaying action of lazy-seq. The only time those additional calls to my-repeat get fired is when you start accessing the resulting sequence. Lazy sequences are concise, marvelous, and recursively insane.

Now that we have the hang of it, it's not hard to implement some of the more involved functions. Here, for example, is a perfectly serviceable version of iterate:

```
(defn my-iterate [f x]
  (cons x (lazy-seq (my-iterate f (f x)))))
```

You start the sequence with the value passed in, followed by a new lazy sequence that starts with the function applied to the value, followed by the same again, ad infinitum.

Implementing a simple version of map is also not hard, and illustrates how to bring your lazy sequence to an end:

```
(defn my-map [f col]
  (when-not (empty? col)
    (cons (f (first col))
          (lazy-seq (my-map f (rest col))))))
```

Like my-repeat and my-iterate, my-map will keep building as much of the sequence as it needs. The difference is that my-map is limited by the input collection. When the my-map detects that there are no more elements in the input collection, it returns nil. This is the signal to lazy-seq that the end has arrived. Lazy sequences are indeed a bit mind-bending, so it's not surprising that their implementations are, as well.

Staying Out of Trouble

While lazy—and particularly unbounded— sequences are a powerful programming tool, dealing with them in the REPL has its issues. You certainly don't want to try to print an entire infinite sequence, either explicitly, like this:

```
user=> (def numbers (iterate inc 1))
#'user/numbers

user=> (println numbers)    ; Say goodnight!
```

or implicitly:

```
user=> numbers              ; And that is it!
```

Never try to stare into the face of the infinite. This is where the *print-length* dynamic var and set!, both of which we saw back in Chapter 8, *Def, Symbols, and Vars*, on page 85, come in handy:

```
user=> (set! *print-length* 10)
10

user=> numbers
(1 2 3 4 5 6 7 8 9 10 ...)
```

More subtly, you also need to be careful about side effects when dealing with lazy sequences, since your code might run at unexpected times. For example, imagine that we had the text for each chapter of a book stored in files with names like chap1.txt and chap10.txt. We could use the built-in Clojure function slurp (yes, that's really the name) to read the contents of a chapter file into a string:

```
;; Get the contents of the file as a string.
(slurp "chap1.txt")
```

Add in some map and take cleverness and we can create a sequence of the text of the first 10 chapters:

```
(def chapters (take 10 (map slurp (map #(str "chap" % ".txt") numbers))))
```

Except that while we have just set up a pipeline for reading the files we haven't actually read anything yet. Think about it: take and map both produce lazy sequences, so we need to actually *do* something with the elements of chapters before any slurping occurs. This can be a problem, because while Clojure's collections are immutable, the contents of files are not.

Slurp and Spit

The slurp function is the Clojure programmer's universal *I need to read something* friend. Most notably, slurp will do exactly what you want if you hand it a URL: (slurp "http://russolsen.com/index.html").

If your interest lies more in writing than reading, there is spit, which will take a path and a string to write the string to that file, as in: (spit "/tmp/chapter1.txt" "It was a dark...").

As I say, these functions are your friends. The names ... well, I guess you had to be there.

It's for just these occasions that Clojure provides the doall function:

```
;; Read the chapters NOW!
(doall chapters)
```

The doall function runs down your lazy sequence, accessing each element, and returns the sequence, effectively wringing the laziness out. If you want it done *right now*, doall is your friend.

Along the same lines is doseq, which realizes each item in a lazy sequence one at a time but doesn't try to hold onto the whole thing. Syntactically, doseq looks a lot like for:

```
;; Read the chapters NOW!
(doseq [c chapters]
  (println "The chapter text is" c))
```

The difference is that while for returns a lazy sequence—not much help when we're trying to de-lazy our sequence—doseq is emphatically eager.

In the Wild

We can see one of the more useful applications of lazy sequences in nREPL,[1] a library that enables you to create a client/server rendition of a REPL, where the client sends Clojure expressions off to a server, which evaluates them and sends back the results. Here's the sequence:

```
(repeatedly #(transport/recv transport timeout))
```

The repeatedly function is the function-driven equivalent of repeat. Instead of returning the same value over and over, repeatedly calls the function you pass in over and over, returning a lazy sequence of the resulting values. The repeatedly function is useful in those situations where you are dealing with side effects —presumably you will get something different back from the repeated calls to the function. That's certainly true in the preceding code, where transport/recv reads one message after another from some sort of message stream.

The key thing here is that this code is converting a series of side effect–driven events—the messages showing up to be read—into a lazy sequence of values that can be then be processed further using the ordinary tools of Clojure programming.

Lazy sequences—and the functions that produce them—are common enough in Clojure that it is probably more productive to point out some functions that are *not* lazy, functions that will try to immediately realize any sequence you hand them. Obviously there is count; try to count the elements of a sequence, and you're going to realize the whole thing, or try to do this:

```
;; Say goodnight.
(count (iterate inc 0))
```

Similarly, it's a bad idea to try to sort or reduce over an infinite sequence.

Wrapping Up

In this chapter we explored lazy sequences, those Zen collections full of elements that are not there until you look. We saw how Clojure is full of functions

---

1.   https://github.com/clojure/tools.nrepl

like repeat and iterate that create lazy sequences, and functions like map and take that are capable of processing them. We also looked at how you can use these functions to build up useful sequences, and at how it's all implemented. Along the way we saw how laziness can sometimes come as a bit of a surprise and how to use doall and doseq to ensure that your sequence is populated *right now*.

Now that you know a lot about putting data *into* collections, it's time to look at reversing the process. So in the next chapter we're going to turn to a feature that will enable us to pluck just the value we need from a collection, even if that collection is nested inside of another collection. Or two. Or three.

CHAPTER 12

Destructuring

One of the secrets of Clojure's power is that it gives you basic tools—things like functions and vectors and maps—that let you do the simple things simply. But Clojure also provides facilities to compose those tools into more capable conglomerates that can take on the bigger jobs. On the code side, we have higher-order functions and vars and namespaces. On the data side, we have a set of simple data structures that you layer. If your problem requires it, there's nothing stopping you from putting that vector inside of a map inside of a set inside of another map.

The downside of all this convenient data packaging is that peeling off the wrapping can be tedious. If you do have that vector inside of a map inside of a set, you could spend a lot of time—and programming energy—cutting through the wrapping to get at the actual data.

So in this chapter we'll look at *destructuring*, a tool that you can use to cut through the data structure packaging. We'll see how destructuring works and how it's seamlessly integrated into key parts of Clojure. We'll also look at how you can use destructuring to make your code cleaner and clearer, and at how to avoid letting destructuring defeat its own purpose by obscuring your code.

Let's get started.

Pry Open Your Data

To see how we can use destructuring to peel back the layers of our data structures, we'll start by disassembling something simple and work from there. Take this not-very-intimidating vector:

destructuring/examples.clj
```
(def artists [:monet :austen])
```

and imagine you wanted to separate out the two keywords. There are a lot of ways to do that separation, but given that we're only dealing with a two-element vector, we might go for the first function and its convenient sibling, second. So running this:

```
(let [painter (first artists)
      novelist (second artists)]
  (println "The painter is:" painter
           "and the novelist is" novelist))
```

will give you the right values in painter and novelist.

Destructuring provides an alternative to this kind of hand disassembly. Here's the destructuring version of the same let:

```
(let [[painter novelist] artists]
  (println "The painter is:" painter
           "and the novelist is:" novelist))
```

Notice how the left side of the let binding equation, instead of being a simple symbol, is now a vector of symbols: [painter novelist]. That left-side vector acts as a sort of template for the artists vector. Essentially we're saying, *Match up—and bind—the symbols in the first vector with the corresponding values in the second vector.* Thus the symbol painter gets bound to :monet and novelist gets bound to :austen. The nice thing about destructuring is how well it scales. If we had more values in our vector, perhaps like this:

```
(def artists [:monet :austen :beethoven :dickinson])
```

we could just add more names to the names vector:

```
(let [[painter novelist composer poet] artists]
  (println "The painter is" painter)
  (println "The novelist is" novelist)
  (println "The composer is" composer)
  (println "The poet is" poet))
```

and get our symbols bound.

Getting Less than Everything

Conveniently, we don't have to have a one-to-one correspondence between the names and the data. For example, if we are only interested in the first three elements of our four-item vector, we could say this:

```
(let [[painter novelist composer] artists]
  (println "The painter is" painter)
  (println "The novelist is" novelist)
  (println "The composer is" composer))
```

and simply ignore the leftover data, in this case :dickinson.

But what if we wanted to ignore some of the *leading* items of the vector? No problem—we can put a dummy name in as a placeholder:

```
(let [[dummy dummy composer poet] artists]
  (println "The composer is" composer)
  (println "The poet is" poet))
```

There's nothing special about the symbol dummy; we're just using it to soak up the values for :monet and :austen. There's also nothing earth-shattering about using the same name twice in a let. The name simply ends up bound to the last value, which is fine since we don't care about either value. In fact, Clojure programmers have a convention for this sort of *I don't really care about this* name. We use a symbol consisting of a single underscore. Thus, a better rendition of that last example would be as follows:

```
(let [[_ _ composer poet] artists]
  (println "The composer is" composer)
  (println "The poet is" poet))
```

We're also not limited to a single level of destructuring. If we started with this two-level vector:

```
(def pairs [[:monet :austen] [:beethoven :dickinson]])
```

we could get hold of the first member of each pair with this:

```
(let [[[painter] [composer]] pairs]
  (println "The painter is" painter)
  (println "The composer is" composer))
```

Notice the two-level structure of the leftmost template vector mirrors the two-level structure of the pairs vector. Run the preceding code and you'll see this:

```
The painter is :monet
The composer is :beethoven
```

Alternatively, you can mix things up and pull out the first item of the first pair and the second item of the second pair, so that if your were looking for :monet and :dickinson you could say:

```
(let [[[painter] [_ poet]] pairs]
  (println "The painter is" painter)
  (println "The poet is" poet))
```

The idea behind destructuring is that instead of painfully navigating your way through a data structure, API call by API call, you provide a rough sketch of the data structure—a sketch that includes a programmatic arrow marking the data you're looking for.

Destructuring in Sequence

Although so far we have limited ourselves to destructuring vectors, all of the tricks we've seen so far will work with any of Clojure's sequential data types. Thus if we switch our names from a vector to a list:

```
(def artist-list '(:monet :austen :beethoven :dickinson))
```

the destructuring stays exactly the same:

```
(let [[painter novelist composer] artist-list]
  (println "The painter is" painter)
  (println "The novelist is" novelist)
  (println "The composer is" composer))
```

Note especially that even when we're destructuring a list, we continue to use square brackets around our template. The left side of the binding equation remains [painter novelist composer]. In this context you can think of those square brackets as standing in for the delimiters around *any* sequential data type.

And I do mean *any* sequential data type. Aside from lists and vectors, you can destructure any Clojure value that can be turned into a sequence. Strings, for example, destructure into their individual characters:

```
(let [[c1 c2 c3 c4] "Jane"]
  (println "How do you spell Jane?")
  (println c1)
  (println c2)
  (println c3)
  (println c4))
```

Run the preceding code and you will see this:

```
How do you spell Jane?
J
a
n
e
```

The rule is, if you can turn it into a sequence, you can destructure it.

Destructuring Function Arguments

Not only does destructuring work with all the sequential types (and, as we'll see in a minute, with maps), but it's also not limited to let. Most notably, you can use destructuring to drill into the arguments passed to a function. Using destructuring with your function arguments is nearly identical to using it in a let, except that you don't supply the value—that comes from the call to the function. Here, for example, is a function that's looking for a two-element vector:

```
(defn artist-description [[novelist poet]]
  (str "The novelist is " novelist " and the poet is " poet))
```

As I say, the value to be destructured is supplied when you *call* the function, so that this:

```
(artist-description [:austen :dickinson])
```

will return "The novelist is :austen and the poet is :dickinson".

You can even mix and match normal and destructured arguments. Here, for example, is a function that has a garden-variety argument along with a destructured one:

```
(defn artist-description [shout [novelist poet]]
  (let [msg (str "Novelist is " novelist
                 "and the poet is " poet)]
    (if shout (.toUpperCase msg) msg)))
```

This latest version of artist-description returns an uppercase version of the message if the nondestructured parameter shout is truthy.

Digging into Maps

There's even more good news with destructuring: it also works with maps. The idea behind destructuring a map is the same as with the sequential types. You provide a template for the data structure—a template that includes the symbols that you want to bind to various values in the map. To see how map destructuring works, consider that when you build a map, you supply a bunch of keys and values:

```
(def artist-map {:painter :monet  :novelist :austen})
```

Here we're saying *Associate :monet with :painter and :austen with :novelist.* That is, *this* key with *that* value. In the template that you provide in a map destructuring, you do something very similar. You provide a series of *symbols* and keys. Like this:

```
(let [{painter :painter writer :novelist} artist-map]
  (println "The painter is" painter)
  (println "The novelist is" writer))
```

This *symbol* with this *key*:

```
The painter is :monet
The novelist is :austen
```

In this last example we're binding the value associated with the key :painter to painter, and the value associated with :novelist to writer.

The important thing to note about map destructuring is that in the left side of the destructuring equation the keys come second; the symbol painter is *followed by* the key :painter. Also keep in mind that since map destructuring is all about the keys, the order of the symbol/key pairs is not important. Thus we could have written our last example as follows:

```
(let [{writer :novelist painter :painter} artist-map]
  (println "The painter is" painter)
  (println "The novelist is" writer))
```

without changing the result.

Diving into Nested Maps

In the same way that you can use destructuring to dig into several layers of sequential data structures such as lists or vectors, you can also excavate several layers of maps. For example, given this two-level description of Jane Austen:

```
(def austen {:name "Jane Austen"
             :parents {:father "George" :mother "Cassandra"}
             :dates {:born 1775 :died  1817}})
```

we can extract the names of her parents with this:

```
(let [{{dad :father mom :mother} :parents} austen]
  (println "Jane Austen's dad's name was" dad)
  (println "Jane Austen's mom's name was" mom))
```

A good way to look at this kind of two-level map destructuring is from the outside in. At the very outside, we have the basic let structure:

```
(let [<<something-to-bind-to>> austen]
  ;; Do something with the data...
  )
```

Digging into the next level, we see that we have a map destructuring, one that is going to grab the :parents key:

```
(let [{<<something-to-bind-parents-to>> :parents} austen]
  ;; Do something with the data...
  )
```

And what are you going to do in the something-to-bind-parents-to spot? Yet another destructuring, of course, which takes us back to this:

```
(let [{{dad :father mom :mother} :parents} austen]
  ;; Do something with the data...
  )
```

Once you have the idea, you can pull as little or as much as you want out of the maps. We could, for example, grab Jane's name along with her mother's name and her year of birth:

```
(let [{name :name
       {mom :mother} :parents
       {dob :born} :dates} austen]
  (println name "was born in" dob)
  (println name "mother's name was" mom))
```

Just keep in mind that the order of things in the left side of the destructuring is reversed from what you would expect if you were creating a map. When it comes to destructuring, it's value *then* key all the way down.

The Final Frontier: Mixing and Matching

So far we have seen how to destructure sequential things like vectors and lists. We've also seen how to destructure our way into maps. What we haven't done yet is destructure a mixture of the two, perhaps a map in a vector or a vector in a map. Fortunately, it's just more of the same: to destructure a mix of sequences and maps, you mix the destructuring syntax in exactly the way that you would guess.

Take this vectors-inside-of-a-map conglomeration:

```
(def author {:name "Jane Austen"
             :books [{:title "Sense and Sensibility" :published 1811}
                     {:title "Emma" :published 1815}]})
```

We can get hold of Jane's name and the information about *Emma* with a simple

```
(let [{name :name [_ book] :books} author]
  (println "The author is" name)
  (println "One of the author's books is" book))
```

Alternatively, if we had a couple of maps inside of a vector, perhaps like this:

```
(def authors  [{:name "Jane Austen" :born 1775}
               {:name "Charles Dickens" :born 1812}])
```

we could easily dig down into the dates of birth:

```
(let [[{dob-1 :born} {dob-2 :born}] authors]
  (println "One author was born in" dob-1)
  (println "The other author was born in" dob-2))
```

Going Further

Destructuring is one of those convenience features that always seems to leave you wanting more. For instance, consider that when destructuring a map with keyword keys, people tend to use symbols that look just like the keys. If, for example, we were working with maps that looked like this:

```
{:name "Romeo" :age 16 :gender :male}
```

we might be inclined to bind the value of :name to name, :age to age, and :gender to gender:

```
(defn character-desc [{name :name age :age gender :gender}]
  (str "Name: " name " age: " age " gender: " gender))
```

This does work, but there's a lot of repetition in the code as we repeat our way through name :name age :age gender :gender. If only we could just say, *Oh, and pull out :name, :age, and :gender as name, age, and gender.* Turns out we can:

```
(defn character-desc [{:keys [name age gender]}]
  (str "Name: " name " age: " age " gender: " gender))
```

Essentially :keys says that you are going with the convention of using the keyword names as your local names. Instead of endlessly repeating the symbol and the keyword (name :name) you just list the values you want to extract in a vector following the :keys.

Even better, you can mix and match :keys with ordinary *by hand* destructuring; thus we could have said

```
(defn character-desc [{:keys [name gender] age-in-years :age}]
  (str "Name: " name " age: " age-in-years " gender: " gender))
```

Don't be fooled by the syntax. :keys is a special value, used by destructuring to mark off the *same symbol as key* vector. Destructuring knows this is a special value because when we're doing normal destructuring we don't have keywords (with their leading colon) on the left side of the destructuring equation.

Another seeming drawback of destructuring, at least when used with functions, is that it eats the value you're destructuring. Nowhere, for example, in the preceding code's character-desc function do we have access to the complete name/gender/age map. You can certainly have your map and your destructuring too, with the proper application of let:

```
(defn add-greeting [character]
  (let [{:keys [name age]} character]
    (assoc character
           :greeting
           (str "Hello, my name is " name " and I am " age "."))))
```

The add-greeting function in our code example wants to add a new key/value pair to the character map passed in, but the new value depends on some of the existing values (:name and :age). Thus it needs both the destructured name and age but also the whole, untouched character map.

Happily, destructuring provides a convenient shortcut for this, as well, in the form of :as.

```
(defn add-greeting [{:keys [name age] :as character}]
  (assoc character
         :greeting
         (str "Hello, my name is " name " and I am " age ".")))
```

In this last version of add-greeting we're using :as to pick up the whole map without the need to write an additional let.

Staying Out of Trouble

Like most programming tools, destructuring works best when mixed with a healthy dose of common sense. The real value of destructuring is that it makes those deep dives into data structures easier to code and easier to read. There is something about the *look for the value here* approach of destructuring that clicks with the human brain. Or it clicks to a point: digging too far into a complex data structure with a single destructuring expression is one sure way to make your code confusing.

For example, if you had a vector of reader information, like this:

```
[{:name "Charlie",  :fav-book {:title "Carrie", :author ["Stephen" "King"]}}
 {:name "Jennifer", :fav-book {:title "Emma", :author ["Jane" "Austen"]}}]
```

and you wanted the full name of the author of the second reader's favorite book—say that three times fast—you might write this:

```
(defn format-a-name [[_ {{[fname lname] :author} :fav-book}]]
  (str fname " " lname))
```

Most programmers would have to stare at this gem for a few minutes in order to understand it. A better approach might be to go at this problem in a couple of stages, like this:

```
(defn format-a-name [[_ second-reader]]
  (let [author (-> second-reader :fav-book :author)]
    (str (first author) " " (second author))))
```

There's nothing like some intention-revealing names to, well, reveal your intentions.

The other thing to keep in mind about destructuring is that it's purely a creature of local bindings. While you can use destructuring with function parameters and with let, you can't use destructuring directly in a def. So this:

```
;; No!!

(def author {:name "Jane Austen" :born 1775})

(def author-name [{n :name} author])
```

will not compile. But don't despair. This will:

```
(def author-name
  (let [{n :name} author] n))
```

A little let goes a long way.

In the Wild

Examples of destructuring are easy to find if you look around in the Clojure ecosystem. For example, Korma,[1] the database library, contains this function, which helps set up connections to MySQL databases:

```
(defn mysql
"Create a database specification for a
 mysql database. Opts should include
 keys for :db, :user, and :password.
 You can also optionally set host and port.
 Delimiters are automatically set to \"`\"."
  [{:keys [host port db make-pool?]
    :or {host "localhost", port 3306, db "", make-pool? true}
    :as opts}]

    ;; Do something with host, port, db, make-pool? and opts
)
```

Again we have the typical *function with a docstring* setup, but this function is using some interesting destructuring to dig into the map that it's expecting as an argument. Things begin innocently enough. At the front we have some :keys-based destructuring to get at values such as the host and port. And at the end of the destructuring we have a familiar :as, which gives the function access to the entire map that is passed in.

But in between the :keys and the :as, we have something we haven't seen before: :or. The :or feature helps you deal with the situation where you look for some value in your destructuring and it's not there. Take another look at the preceding code and ask yourself, what if the caller doesn't pass in a value for :host? Or :port? The answer is that host and port would end up set to nil. Or they would without the :or. The :or lets you specify default values in the form of a map. So if you leave out :host in the map that you pass to the mysql function, you will get the default value of "localhost". Similarly, leave out the port and you will get 3306.

---

1. https://github.com/korma/Korma/blob/master/src/korma/db.clj

Wrapping Up

In this chapter we looked at destructuring. Clojure is full of deep, interesting ideas, things like programming with immutable data structures and lazy sequences. Destructuring isn't one of them. Destructuring makes up for its lack of deep philosophical implications by being a practical, clever alternative to picking through your data one API call at a time. Instead of all that first-ing and nth-ing your way through a data structure, destructuring lets you build a sort of treasure map of the data that you want. *Start in the first slot of this sequence, then turn right at this keyword and go 20 paces down that vector.*

Next, and continuing with the *dealing with your data* theme, we're going to turn to records, which are like maps that have been specialized to a particular purpose.

CHAPTER 13

Records and Protocols

One of the things that makes programming such a joyous challenge is that it's full of trade-offs. One day you might find yourself choosing between making the program faster at the cost of a more complicated algorithm or a bit more memory. Twenty-four hours later you're trying to strike a balance between ease of use and a more powerful interface. And by the third day you're wrestling with the tension between building code that works decently everywhere versus a more specialized implementation that works better, but only *right here*.

It's this last *generic versus specialized* question that we're going to take up in this chapter as we look at Clojure records. In the pages that follow we'll see how records are a more specialized data-storage alternative to maps. We'll start by reviewing just what a record is and how you create them. We'll move on to the question of when to use a record and when to use a map. That will bring us face to face with the question of how you do polymorphism in Clojure, and *that* will bring us to protocols. Finally we'll round out this chapter in our usual way by looking at some real-world uses of records and protocols and how to avoid some of the sharp edges of records.

The Trouble with Maps

The great thing about Clojure maps—those lovely {:key "value"} creatures—is that they are very flexible. You can use a map to associate just about any key with essentially any value. It's this *I can deal with anything* flexibility that makes maps so useful and ubiquitous in Clojure programs.

But this flexibility of maps does not come for free. Part of the cost of flexibility can be measured in CPU seconds at runtime. Maps are wonderfully speedy, but the *deal with anything* flexibility does come with a runtime penalty. Since maps need to deal with arbitrary keys, they are a bit slower than a data structure designed to deal with just these keys. Mostly the speed penalty doesn't matter, but sometimes—for example, when you're trying to process huge amounts of data—it matters a lot.

A second—and more commonly felt—drawback of maps is their cost in terms of code coherence and documentation. Since you can put anything into any map, the only way to discern the intent of maps like these:

```
record/examples.clj
(let [watson-1 (get-watson-1)
      watson-2 (get-watson-2)]
      ;; Do something with our watsons...
      )
```

is to see if you have a fictional character or a *Jeopardy!*-winning supercomputer:

```
;; A fictional character.

(defn get-watson-1 []
  {:name "John Watson"
   :appears-in "Sign of the Four"
   :author "Doyle"})

;; A Jeopardy playing computer.

(defn get-watson-2 [] {:cpu "Power7" :no-cpus 2880 :storage-gb 4000})
```

Striking a More Specific Bargain with Records

Happily, Clojure provides an alternative to maps that mitigates some of these shortcomings: the *record*. You can think of records as maps with some predefined keys. To make a record you need to first define the record type:

```
(defrecord FictionalCharacter[name appears-in author])
```

As you can see from the code, the record type has a name and a list of the predefined fields. So if you evaluate the expression in our example, you end up with a record type called FictionalCharacter that has three fields, one for the character's name, one for the name of the fictional work the character appears in, and one for the author. Behind the scenes, defrecord creates a couple of functions, whose names are based on the record type. In our example, we get ->FictionalCharacter and map->FictionalCharacter.

Instant Vars

 Since defrecord begins with def it's reasonable to assume that it is in the var-creation business. In fact, defrecord creates a number of vars. There's one for the record type, and one each for the two factory functions. The same is true of defprotocol, which we'll meet presently.

There are a couple of ways to kick off the second stage of record creation, which is to create instances of your record type—actual fictional characters in our example. First, we can use the ->FictionalCharacter function to create our first FictionalCharacter instance:

```
(def watson (->FictionalCharacter "John Watson" "Sign of the Four" "Doyle"))
```

As you can see from the example, ->FictionalCharacter takes values for each of the fields in the record, in the order that they were specified in defrecord, and gives you back a new record instance, which will print in the REPL like this:

```
#records.core.FictionalCharacter{:name "John Watson",
                                 :appears-in "Sherlock Holmes",
                                 :author "Doyle"}
```

Alternatively, we can use map->FictionalCharacter, which expects its arguments rolled up in a map, like this:

```
(def elizabeth (map->FictionalCharacter
                {:name "Elizabeth Bennet"
                 :appears-in "Pride & Prejudice"
                 :author "Austen"}))
```

Just make sure the map you pass in has keyword arguments that match the names of the fields in the record.

Records Are Maps

No matter how you create your record instances, once you have them in hand you can treat them just like maps with keyword keys:

```
(:name elizabeth)        ; => "Elizabeth Bennet"
(:appears-in watson)     ; => "Sign of the Four"
```

The resemblance between records and maps is much more than skin- (or keyword?) deep: Any function that works with a map will also work with a record:

```
(count elizabeth)        ; => 3
(keys watson)            ; => (:name :appears-in :author)
```

You can also use assoc to modify the values in your record:

```
(def specific-watson (assoc watson :appears-in "Sign of the Four"))
```

You can even assoc brand-new, not-in-the-record-type keys into your record instances:

```
(def more-about-watson (assoc watson :address "221B Baker Street"))
```

You will get back a new FictionalCharacter instance that has the three predefined fields along with the new :address entry. Note that any extra values you assoc into your records are exactly that: extra. They get carried around like any other map fields, but they don't affect the record type in any way *and* they don't get the magic speed boost of the built-in fields.

The Record Advantage

So if records are just maps with some fields wired in, are they really worth the bother? As usual, the answer is *it depends*. One concrete advantage of records is that getting at the hard-wired fields is faster than getting at the equivalent fields in a map. Thus, if you had this:

```
(def irene {:name "Irene Adler"
            :appears-in "A Scandal in Bohemia"
            :author "Doyle"})
```

you would expect that *this* would be faster:

```
(:name watson)
```

than *this*:

```
(:name irene)
```

How much faster? Certainly not enough to matter if you are only dealing with a few novels—or a few tens of thousands. But if you are dealing with seriously large mounds of data, the performance advantages of records are something to consider.

Another reason to use records is the one that I touched on at the beginning of this chapter: they can help you make your code clearer. For example, a glance at this code:

```
;; Define the record types.

(defrecord FictionalCharacter[name appears-in author])
(defrecord SuperComputer [cpu no-cpus storage-gb])

;; And create some records.

(def watson-1 (->FictionalCharacter
                 "John Watson"
                 "Sign of the Four"
                 "Doyle"))

(def watson-2 (->SuperComputer "Power7" 2880 4000))
```

leaves no doubt that watson-1 is a fictional detective's assistant, while watson-2 is an eerily intelligent quiz show–playing machine. And if you're still puzzled about what kind of thing you've gotten hold of, you can always use the class function, which will return the type of the record.

```
(class watson-1)     ; user.FictionalCharacter
(class watson-2)     ; user.SuperComputer
```

You can also use instance? to test if a value has a particular type:

```
(instance? FictionalCharacter watson-1)    ; True.
(instance? SuperComputer watson-2)         ; Nope.
```

Keep in mind that while class and instance? are great tools for poking around in the REPL, you should generally avoid using them in real code. This sort of thing:

```
;; Don't do this!

(defn process-thing [x]
  (if (= (instance? FictionalCharacter x))
    (process-fictional-character x)
    (process-computer x)))
```

is bound to lead you to spaghetti code and grief. Fortunately, Clojure has a better way of dealing with this sort of type-sensitive code: protocols.

Class?

 The class function works for all values, not just records. A good rainy-day programming project is to spend some time feeding values into class to see what comes out.

Protocols

The word *protocol* is one of those nontechnical terms—it originally meant the set of rules for coping with a visit from the ambassador from Naboo and similar situations—that has picked up a variety of technical meanings, mostly around networking and communications. The meaning of *protocol* in Clojure is closer to the diplomatic original. A Clojure protocol is a set of *how to behave* rules expressed in code.

To see how protocols work, let's imagine that along with the FictionalCharacter. we had a second record type, one used to track employees at a company:

```
(defrecord Employee [first-name last-name department])
```

Nothing is really new here: Employee is just a record type with three fields. Armed with this new definition, we can cook up an Employee instance:

```
(def alice (->Employee "Alice" "Smith" "Engineering"))
```

Now imagine that—for reasons beyond understanding—we had instances of Employee and FictionalCharacter floating around in the same program. Clearly, employees and fictional characters have some things in common. They both have names and they are both in some sense *from* somewhere. It would be great if we had a mechanism for treating these two kinds of records as the same thing whenever it's convenient.

Enter protocols. Here's a protocol definition that we might use to leverage the common aspects of employees and fictional characters:

```
(defprotocol Person
  (full-name [this])
  (greeting [this msg])
  (description [this]))
```

This code does a number of things. First, and most obviously, it creates a new protocol called Person. Less obvious is that the expression in the code example also creates three new functions, full-name, greeting, and description. The special thing about the functions generated by protocols is that they are polymorphic. Exactly what they do depends on the *type* of their first argument.

And at the moment our full-name greeting, and description functions do exactly nothing—we still need to provide implementations for each record type that implements Person. To do that we recast our FictionalCharacter and Employee definitions to implement Person:

```
(defrecord FictionalCharacter[name appears-in author]
  Person
  (full-name [this] (:name this))
  (greeting [this msg] (str msg " " (:name this)))
  (description [this]
    (str (:name this) " is a character in " (:appears-in this))))

(defrecord Employee [first-name last-name department]
  Person
  (full-name [this] (str first-name " " last-name))
  (greeting [this msg] (str msg " " (:first-name this)))
  (description [this]
    (str (:first-name this) " works in " (:department this))))
```

Notice how the name of the protocol is tacked on to the end of each record definition, followed by implementations for full-name, greeting, and description. These *method* definitions, to use the proper jargon, look a bit like defns without the defn—just the name of the method followed by the parameters, followed by the body of the method. Each method needs to have at least one parameter, the record we're operating on, which is conventionally called this. If you happen to have more than one this parameter—as we do in the greeting method in the preceding example—then this must be the *first* parameter.

So in the new FictionalCharacter definition from our example, we implement the full-name method by returning the :name field from the record: (:name this). The implementations of description and greeting are a bit more complicated, but not much: we just assemble an appropriate string based on the name of the character and the fictional work that character appears in.

Once we have FictionalCharacter and Employee implementing the Person protocol we can start churning out instances:

```
(def sofia (->Employee "Sofia" "Diego" "Finance"))

(def sam (->FictionalCharacter "Sam Weller" "The Pickwick Papers" "Dickens"))
```

And then we can take advantage of our new polymorphic functions:

```
;; Call the full-name method. Returns "Sofia Diego".

(full-name sofia)

;; Call description.
;; Returns "Sam Weller is a character..."

(description sam)

;; Returns "Hello! Sofia"

(greeting sofia "Hello!")
```

Finally, note that since the author field of FictionalCharacter takes no part in the Person protocol, it doesn't show up in any of the method definitions. But the author is still there in the record and you can still get at it, so that (:author sam) will give you exactly what you expect.

Decentralized Polymorphism

One interesting—and useful—aspect of protocols is that you can define and implement them after the fact. Imagine, for example, that you are working on a Clojure application and six months ago one of your colleagues implemented the Employee, FictionalCharacter, and SuperComputer records. And now, for reasons that need not concern us, you have just been handed the job of producing a positive marketing slogan for instances of each of these record types. So you start by defining a new protocol:

```
(defprotocol Marketable
  (make-slogan [this]))
```

And then you go back and modify the Employee, FictionalCharacter, and SuperComputer defrecords so that they support the new protocol. Well, you could do that, but you don't have to. Armed with Clojure's extend-protocol, you can implement the new protocol for existing types independently of those type definitions:

```
(extend-protocol Marketable
  Employee
    (make-slogan [e] (str (:first-name e) " is the BEST employee!"))
  FictionalCharacter
    (make-slogan [fc] (str (:name fc) " is the GREATEST character!"))
  SuperComputer
    (make-slogan [sc] (str "This computer has " (:no-cpus sc) " CPUs!")))
```

Notice how extend-protocol is a sort of inside-out defrecord. It starts with a single protocol and then enumerates the implementations of that protocol. Armed with extend-protocol you can call make-slogan on employees, fictional characters, and supercomputers. In fact, you can even extend your protocol to embrace data types that aren't records:

```
(extend-protocol Marketable
  String
    (make-slogan [s] (str \" s \" " is a string! WOW!"))
  Boolean
    (make-slogan [b] (str b  " is one of the two surviving Booleans!")))
```

This means that protocols and records are as mutually flexible as they can be. You can cook up new protocols as you need them and use extend-protocol to implement your new protocol on any existing type, without touching the original definition of that type.

Record Confusion

If you're coming to Clojure from an object-oriented language, then this record and protocol talk probably rings a very familiar bell. Record types and their instances do look a lot like the classes and objects that you find in object-oriented languages. And protocols clearly resemble the abstract types or interfaces that you also find in the object-oriented world. None of this is by chance. Records are Clojure's approach to building a structured, composite data type with predefined fields. Similarly, protocols are Clojure's riff on type-based polymorphism—the idea that you can have a single operation implemented in different ways by different types.

But record types and values part company with object-oriented classes and objects in important ways. Clojure record values are exactly as immutable as Clojure's vectors and maps. Records are also innocent of implementation inheritance. There are no super record types. And, as we saw in the last section, records and protocols are independent of each other in time and space.

At any given moment you can decide to implement some protocol—including one you have just constructed—on any record type.

Perhaps the biggest practical difference between Clojure's records and protocols and the objects and classes that you find in an object-oriented language is that many significant Clojure programs get along just fine without them. That leads us to the best approach to using records and protocols: start without them. Start with plain old maps and functions and see how things go. If, as you go along, your code starts to drift toward the unreadable, and records help, then put in some records. If you are having performance problems and it seems like records, with their speedy field access, would make things better, then try some records. And if you find that you need some polymorphism, and perhaps need to leave the door open for some polymorphic extensions in the future, then reach for the protocols. But start simple: you may just find that maps and functions are enough.

Protocols raise a different question, one that can be summed up with *Don't we have this polymorphic thing covered with multimethods?* Recall that multimethods (which we covered in Chapter 5, *More Capable Functions*, on page 49) let you create completely arbitrary polymorphic functions.

While there is a lot of overlap between protocols and multimethods, there is also a fair bit of daylight. Each multimethod defines a single, stand-alone operation. Protocols can include a whole bundle of related operations. Multimethods support a completely arbitrary dispatch mechanism. Protocols dispatch based on a type mechanism. If you don't need all of the generality of a multimethod you are better off using a protocol.

In the Wild

The best way to get a feeling for records and protocols is to see them in action in real code.

For that let's return to the Clostache templating library, which you will recall takes most of the pain out of the *substitute this value in the HTML* task that virtually all web applications need to perform. To make Clostache work you need a template string and a map of values:

```
(require 'clostache.parser)
(def template "The book {{title}} is by {{author}}")
(def values {:title "War and Peace" :author "Tolstoy"})
```

And you can use the Clostache render function to populate the template with your values:

```
;; Gives you "The book War and Peace is by Tolstoy"
```

```
(clostache.parser/render template values)
```

One of the more powerful features of Clostache is the ability to conditionally include or omit parts of the output with *sections*. Here's a template with a section:

```
(def data {:author "Tolstoy" :show-author true})
```

```
(def section-templ "{{#show-author}} by {{author}} {{/show-author}}")
```

Here the {{#show-author}} and {{/show-author}} define a section. The text in the section will only be rendered if the section value—show-author in this case—is truthy.

If you dig into the Clostache source code you will discover that sections are represented by record values:

```
(defrecord Section [name body start end inverted])
```

The key fields in Section are name, which is the name of the controlling value—show-author in the example—and body, which is the text of the section.

Look a little further, and you will see Section values in action:

```
(defn- render-section
  [section data partials]
    (let [section-data ((keyword (:name section)) data)]
      (if (:inverted section)
        (if (or (and (seqable? section-data)
                     (empty? section-data))
                (not section-data))
          (:body section))
      ; Lots of code omitted
      )))
```

Notice how render-section treats the section value—which is an instance of Section—like a garden-variety map with :name, :body, and :inverted keys. This is record use at its most basic. Clostache harbors no protocols, no polymorphism, not even a second record type. It's just the Section record type there to make the code a little clearer.

You can find a great example of a protocol in Stuart Sierra's Component library.[1] Component takes on the task of helping you build real-world applications—applications that frequently need to do things when they start up

---

1.   https://github.com/stuartsierra/component

(perhaps connect to a database or initialize some data) and other things when they shut down (maybe close that database connection).

The Component library is built around a protocol called Lifecycle. Here it is in all its starkly simple glory:

```
(defprotocol Lifecycle
  (start [component]
    "Begins operation of this component. Synchronous, does not return
until the component is started. Returns an updated version of this
component.")
  (stop [component]
    "Ceases operation of this component. Synchronous, does not return
until the component is stopped. Returns an updated version of this
component."))
```

With just two methods, start and stop, Lifecycle may seem trivial, but it provides the glue that you can use to build basic components, composite components made up of other little components, and so on.

Occasionally you may need to create a one-off implementation of a protocol. Perhaps you are using—or testing—a function that takes a protocol implementation and you just don't have an appropriate record at hand. For example, perhaps you're trying to test your Component system and you need an implementation of Lifecycle. For these occasions Clojure provides us with reify, which takes a protocol name and some method implementations and creates a one-off implementation of that protocol:

```
(def test-component (reify Lifecycle
                      (start [this]
                        (println "Start!")
                        this)
                      (stop [this]
                        (println "Stop!")
                        this)))
```

Run the preceding code, and you will end up with value in test-component that implements Lifecycle. Even better—especially for testing purposes—is that reify doesn't require you to implement the *whole* protocol:

```
;; A partial implementation of Lifecycle. We can call start, but
;; we will get an exception if we call stop.

(def dont-stop
  (reify Lifecycle
    (start [this]
      (println "Start!")
      this)))
```

As defined in the preceding code, dont-stop will be an instance of Lifecycle, but one that will throw an exception if you try to call the stop method.

Staying Out of Trouble

Possibly the easiest mistake you can make with a record is to attempt to get a value into a field and to miss. While this code may look plausible, it's nonsense:

```
(map->FictionalCharacter {:full-name "Elizabeth Bennet"
                          :book "Pride & Prejudice"
                          :written-by "Austen"})
```

The trouble is that fields in FictionalCharacter are called name, appears-in, and author, *not* full-name, book, and written-by. The expression in the preceding code will give you a six-field record, with the three built-in fields set to nil, complemented by three additional fields—remember, records are also maps— set to the values we see in the code.

You can come to the same unfortunate end with botched uses of assoc:

```
(assoc elizabeth :book "Pride & Prejudice")
```

Another thing to keep in mind is that protocols take up more room in your namespace than is immediately apparent. As we've seen, evaluating (defprotocol Person...) binds the symbol Person to the protocol definition. That's implied in the def part of defprotocol. The thing that can bite you is that when you define a protocol you are also defining functions, one for each method in your protocol. This means you need to be careful with the names you pick for your method. If, for example, instead of using full-name in our Person protocol we had gone with name like this:

```
(defprotocol CollidingPerson
  (name [this])
  (greeting [this msg])
  (description [this]))
```

we would have seen the following warning from Clojure:

```
Warning: protocol #'user/CollidingPerson is overwriting function name
```

The problem is that defprotocol is trying to define a function called name but name is already a built-in function that comes with Clojure. This is not necessarily fatal, as long as you know which name you're using at any given moment. In the same vein, you should watch out for dueling protocols:

```
(defprotocol Person
  (full-name [this])
  (greeting [this msg])
  (description [this]))

(defprotocol Product
  (inventory-name [this])
  (description [this]))
```

Again you will see a warning as description from Product overrides the Person description:

```
Warning: protocol #'user/Product is overwriting method
description of protocol Person
```

The solution to these kinds of protocol-versus-protocol name conflicts is simple: when in doubt, put each protocol in its own namespace.

Finally, you should be aware that records have a more generic cousin in *types*. In the same way that you define a new record type with defrecord, you define new types (or perhaps a type type?) with deftype. The difference is that while records come with a fair bit of built-in behavior—think of all those maplike talents that records just *have*—types are more of a blank slate. When you define a type it's up to you to define *all* of the behavior of instances of your new type. This is more work, but it also means you have full control. Types are one of those language features that you may never use, but they are there if the need ever arises.

Wrapping Up

In this chapter we looked at records and protocols. We saw how records are specialized maps. Like a map, a record lets you associate any key with any value. But records have an attitude. They know about a particular set of keys that they want to work with. We also saw how protocols are collections of functions that you can use to build polymorphic operations on your records.

You've now accumulated a lot of Clojure know-how. You can write code that generates functions on the fly and that puts data into collections and pulls it back out. Perhaps it's time to talk about how you can make sure it's all working.

CHAPTER 14

Tests

If there is one thing programmers have learned over the past few decades, it's that seeing is believing. No matter how carefully you think out your design, and no matter how brilliantly you implement your code, if you haven't actually seen your system working, you don't know that it does. The *seeing is believing* philosophy is why we need to actively test our code. And since there are at most 24 hours in a day, hours that we would like to spend doing things besides testing, we try to automate that testing.

So in this chapter we're going to look at some of the tools that Clojure provides to help you convince yourself that your code is, in fact, working. We'll start by looking at how you can write traditional unit tests. From there we'll move on to *generative property-based testing*, which allows you to specify—and then test—the properties of your program.

And since the world is full of buggy programs, let's get going!

Spotting Bugs with clojure.test

Let's begin our adventures in testing by building a brand-new book store inventory project:

$ lein new inventory

Now imagine we're going to have a book inventory that looks like this:

```
[{:title "2001"   :author "Clarke" :copies 21}
 {:title "Emma"   :author "Austen" :copies 10}
 {:title "Misery" :author "King"   :copies 101}])
```

And we write some functions to do useful things with it:

```
test/inventory/src/inventory/core.clj
(ns inventory.core)

(defn find-by-title
  "Search for a book by title,
  where title is a string and books is a collection
  of book maps, each of which must have a :title entry"
  [title books]
  (some #(when (= (:title %) title) %) books))

(defn number-of-copies-of
  "Return the number of copies in inventory of the
  given title, where title is a string and books is a collection
  of book maps each of which must have a :title entry"
  [title books]
  (:copies (find-by-title title books)))
```

And now we need to convince ourselves that this code does what it claims to do. Happily, Clojure comes equipped with a simple and capable library for writing traditional unit tests: clojure.test.

In a Clojure project the test typically lives in the test subdirectory. The convention is to put the tests for a namespace in a parallel -test module. So to test the inventory.core namespace, we create inventory.core-test. Inside the test namespace we'll need to pull in clojure.test, and since writing a test is all about using the facilities that clojure.test provides, we can be forgiven for using :refer :all as we do it:

```
test/inventory/test/inventory/core_test.clj
(ns inventory.core-test
  (:require [clojure.test :refer :all])
  (:require [inventory.core :as i]))
```

Obviously we also need to require in the namespace that we're testing, in this case inventory.core.

Now that we have all the infrastructure, building tests is easy. You use deftest. For example, if we wanted to convince ourselves that we could find a book by its title, we might write this:

```
(def books
  [{:title "2001"   :author "Clarke" :copies 21}
   {:title "Emma"   :author "Austen" :copies 10}
   {:title "Misery" :author "King"   :copies 101}])

(deftest test-finding-books
  (is (not (nil? (i/find-by-title "Emma" books)))))
```

As you can see, deftest takes a symbol—the name of the test—followed by the code for the test. In our example we use the clojure.test-supplied is to assert we can find one of the books in our inventory by title. Using is couldn't be easier: If the expression you supply is truthy, the test passes. If not, it fails.

Under the hood deftest binds a zero-argument function to the test name, a function that runs the test. Thus one—but certainly not the only—way to run your test is to call the function:

```
test/inventory/dev/run_test.clj
(require '[inventory.core-test :as ct])

(ct/test-finding-books)
```

If the test succeeds the function will quietly return nil. If the test fails you will get a reasonably informative exception—something like this:

```
FAIL in (test-something-that-fails) (form-init8361253184899189179.clj:2)
expected: (not (nil? (i/find-by-title "Some other book" inventory)))
  actual: (not (not true))
```

You're also not limited to one expression per test. So if it makes sense to test more than one condition in your test, you can write this:

```
test/inventory/test/inventory/core_test.clj
(deftest test-finding-books-better
  (is (not (nil? (i/find-by-title "Emma" books))))
  (is (nil? (i/find-by-title "XYZZY" books))))
```

You can even organize your tests into subtests—or contexts—with testing:

```
(deftest test-basic-inventory
  (testing "Finding books"
    (is (not (nil? (i/find-by-title "Emma" books))))
    (is (nil? (i/find-by-title "XYZZY" books))))
  (testing "Copies in inventory"
    (is (= 10 (i/number-of-copies-of "Emma" books)))))
```

The combination of deftest and testing means that you can organize your tests in just about any way that makes sense.

Testing Namespaces and Projects

So far we have run our tests one at a time, but this gets old fast. Happily, clojure.test provides the run-tests function, which makes it easy to run all of the tests in a namespace:

```
test/inventory/dev/run_tests.clj
;; Three ways to run the tests in a namespace.

(test/run-tests)
(test/run-tests *ns*)
(test/run-tests 'inventory.core-test)
```

Call run-tests without any arguments, and it will run all the tests in the current namespace. Pass it either a namespace value or a namespace name (as a symbol), and it will run all the tests in that namespace.

Better still, Leiningen provides a task to run all the tests in all the namespaces in your project from the command line:

```
$ lein test

Ran 1 tests containing 1 assertions.
1 failures, 0 errors.
{:test 1, :pass 1, :fail 0, :error 0, :type :summary}
```

It even supplies a nice summary of the test results.

Property-Based Testing

While clojure.test is a fine implementation of traditional unit testing, it does suffer from the common drawback of all unit-testing frameworks. To test a given property of your code, you think of some examples that exercise that property and you start typing. The problem with this approach is that the tests are one step removed from the thing you're really interested in: the property. For example, take another look at the first test we wrote in this chapter:

```
(deftest test-finding-books
  (is (not (nil? (i/find-by-title "Emma" books)))))
```

A casual observer might be forgiven for thinking that this test has something to do with the novel *Emma*. It doesn't. The test is trying to say that we should get a non-nil result when we search for a book that is in the inventory.

Now imagine that instead of testing the code one example at a time, we could state the property that we want to test along with a description of the of input data for which that property should hold. *When searching for the title of a book selected randomly from the inventory, find-by-title should return non-nil.* Being able to make assertions like *I should get a non-nil result when I do this* is the idea behind generative property-based testing. The popular test.check Clojure library can help you build these sorts of tests.[1]

To see how to use test.check we need to start with the data, and for that the test.check library provides a variety of *generators*, values you can use to generate more or less random test data custom-tailored to your needs. There is, for example, a generator called string-alphanumeric you can use to generate essentially random titles for our books. To actually generate some values you use another

---

1. https://github.com/clojure/test.check

function provided by test.check: sample. Pass a generator to sample, and it'll give you the next 10 values that come out of the generator. So if you do this:

```
test/sample_generators.clj
(require '[clojure.test.check.generators :as gen])

(gen/sample gen/string-alphanumeric)
```

you will get the first 10 values generated by string-alphanumeric:

```
("" "Q" "h" "q" "7" "ap" "6" "fdKMQ" "KcuWd" "h20")
```

As you might expect, there are also generators for numbers, Booleans, keywords, and all the other basic Clojure values with names like int, pos-int, Boolean, and keyword—all of which produce exactly the values you would expect.

Armed with these generators, we can make a start on the test data for our books:

```
test/inventory/test/inventory/core_gen_test.clj
(def title-gen gen/string-alphanumeric)

(def author-gen gen/string-alphanumeric)

(def copies-gen gen/pos-int)
```

One issue with using string-alphanumeric to generate titles is that it sometimes produces zero-length strings. Similarly, pos-int will produce zeros, which may not make sense for the number of copies of a book in inventory. Fortunately, test.check also has a solution in the form of such-that, a function that wraps an existing generator in one that will only return values OK'd by a predicate. Thus we can build a generator for (nonempty) titles, another for authors, and another for the (nonzero) number of copies:

```
(def title-gen (gen/such-that not-empty gen/string-alphanumeric))

(def author-gen (gen/such-that not-empty gen/string-alphanumeric))

(def copies-gen (gen/such-that (complement zero?) gen/pos-int))
```

But what we're really looking for is not separate titles and authors and copies, but rather a series of maps that contain those things. That brings us to hash-map. With the test.check rendition of hash-map you pass in alternating keys and generators, and you get an endless supply of maps with the keys associated to values from the generators. Armed with hash-map we can build a generator that will provide us with an endless supply of random book maps:

```
(def book-gen
  (gen/hash-map :title title-gen :author author-gen :copies copies-gen))
```

We can use those to generate an endless supply of inventories:

```
(def inventory-gen (gen/not-empty (gen/vector book-gen)))
```

But an endless supply of inventories isn't quite what we need. We also need a book from each inventory, a book that we can search for and find. For this we can use element (which will pluck a random element out of a collection) and the generator version of let (which lets us build a composite generator, one based on the *values* of existing generators):

```
(def inventory-and-book-gen
  (gen/let [inventory inventory-gen
            book (gen/elements inventory)]
    {:inventory inventory  :book book}))
```

Do this, and in inventory-and-book-gen we get a generator that will produce a series of maps, where each map contains a book inventory along with an individual book, plucked from the inventory, something like this:

test/sample_generators.clj
```
{:inventory [{:title "S0" :author "po" :copies 2}
             {:title "B2d" :author "fN" :copies 2}]
 :book {:title "S0" :author "po" :copies 2}}
```

And now we have the data for our test.

Generator Magic?

Don't fret if the test.check generators seem like magic. It is a bit magical, but it's all implemented with sophisticated-but-nevertheless-ordinary Clojure. For example, each generator is actually a record instance with a function buried inside. And as you might imagine from our adventures generating random books back in *Lazy Sequences*, there are some lazy sequences in play, as well.

Checking Properties

The final piece of the property-based testing puzzle is expressing the property. Happily, test.check provides a lovely syntax for doing just that. To start with a simple example, here we're stating that each positive integer is smaller than the next positive integer:

test/sample_generators.clj
```
(prop/for-all [i gen/pos-int]
  (< i (inc i)))
```

But we're not quite done: since we're defining a test and not a theorem, we need to supply a limit on the number of integers we'll try. Here we pare the infinite run of positive integers down to the first 50 produced by the pos-int generator:

```
(tc/quick-check 50
  (prop/for-all [i gen/pos-int]
    (< i (inc i))))
```

There, the quick-check function will check the property that we specified for 50 randomly generated cases. The quick-check function returns a map describing the results, something like this:

```
{:result true, :num-tests 50, :seed 1509151628189}
```

Now (finally!) we can write the test for our inventory code:

test/inventory/test/inventory/core_gen_test.clj
```
(tc/quick-check 50
  (prop/for-all [i-and-b inventory-and-book-gen]
    (= (i/find-by-title (-> i-and-b :book :title) (:inventory i-and-b))
       (:book i-and-b))))
```

Conceptually we say, *For all the inventory/book combinations we care to generate, looking for a book in the inventory with a given title should produce a book with that title.*

There is also a smooth integration with clojure.test in the form of defspec, found in yet another namespace, clojure.test.check.clojure-test. So do this:

```
(ctest/defspec find-by-title-finds-books 50
  (prop/for-all [i-and-b inventory-and-book-gen]
    (= (i/find-by-title (-> i-and-b :book :title) (:inventory i-and-b))
       (:book i-and-b))))
```

You end up with a clojure.test test that runs the property test.

As you might imagine, there's a lot more to test.check, but this is the basic idea: define your data (in the form of generators), combine it with statements about properties, and roll the whole thing into a test.

Staying Out of Trouble

So which is better, traditional unit tests or generative tests? The answer is simple: *yes*. Both traditional tests and their generative cousins have strengths and weaknesses. And both have a place in making sure your code is doing what it is supposed to be doing.

Traditional unit tests do have one huge advantage: they are shatteringly obvious. Does it work when I do *this*? Yes. Does it work when I do *that*? Yes. OK, then we're good. So, if we were trying to test this simple function:

test/trouble_one.clj
```
(defn f [a b] (/ a b))
```

we might write this test:

```
(deftest test-f
  (is (= 1/2 (f 1 2)))
  (is (= 1/2 (f 3 6)))
  (is (= 1 (f 10 10))))
```

And we know that for these specific instances, it works. The drawback of this kind of hand-crafted unit testing is that it is tightly constrained by our patience and imagination. I'm certainly not going to write tests for more than a few dozen integers before I call it a day.

Generative testing, on the other hand, opens up vast stretches of test cases. We could, for example, write this:

```
(ctest/defspec more-complex-spec 10000
  (prop/for-all [a gen/pos-int
                 b gen/pos-int]
    (is (= (* b (f a b)) a))))
```

And we'd pretty rapidly discover that f does not work when b is zero. The danger with generative testing is that all those generated test cases will lull us into believing that we've covered *all* the possibilities. Do the math, and you will discover that even millions of test cases make up approximately zero percent of the possible pairs of integers. Change the function a bit:

```
(defn more-complex-f [a b] (/ a (+ b 863947)))
```

```
(ctest/defspec test-more-complex 10000
  (prop/for-all [a gen/pos-int
                 b gen/pos-int]
    (= (* (more-complex-f a b) (- b 863947)) a)))
```

Now the chances are excellent that the generative test will miss the division by zero. As I say, the best solution is usually a small number of traditional unit tests combined with the greater reach of generative testing:

test/trouble_two.clj
```
;; Prevent the division by zero.

(defn  more-complex-f [a b]
  (let [denominator (- b 863947)]
    (if (zero? denominator)
      :no-result
      (/ a denominator))))

;; But we still want to be sure we detect it correctly.

(deftest test-critical-value
  (is (= :no-result (more-complex-f 1 863947))))

;; And the function works in other cases.

(def non-critical-gen (gen/such-that (partial not= 863947) gen/pos-int))
```

```
(ctest/defspec test-other-values 10000
  (prop/for-all [a gen/pos-int
                 b non-critical-gen]
    (= (* (more-complex-f a b) (- b 863947)) a)))
```

Finally, keep in mind that even one test is much better than no tests at all. Let's return one more time to our original inventory test:

```
(require '[inventory.core :as i])
```

```
(deftest test-finding-books
  (is (not (nil? (i/find-by-title "Emma" books)))))
```

This test may not seem impressive, but get it to run, and you have demonstrated the following:

- There is a namespace called inventory.core.
- There are no gross syntax errors in inventory.core.
- The inventory.core namespace contains a function called find-by-title.
- You can call find-by-title with two parameters.
- Calling find-by-title with reasonable parameters doesn't throw an exception.
- The find-by-title function does not always return nil.

This is not sworn testimony that find-by-title does exactly what you want, but it is also not nothing. A little bit of testing goes a long way.

In the Wild

To find an example of clojure.test in real-world code you need to look no further than the tests for Clojure itself.[2] Here, for example, is a Zenlike statement of what + should do:

```
(deftest test-add
  (are [x y] (= x y)
       (+) 0
       (+ 1) 1
       (+ 1 2) 3
       (+ 1 2 3) 6

       (+ -1) -1
       (+ -1 -2) -3
       (+ -1 +2 -3) -2

       (+ 1 -1) 0
       (+ -1 1) 0
       ;; Much of the test omitted.
       ))
```

---

2. https://github.com/clojure/clojure/blob/master/test/clojure/test_clojure/numbers.clj

Note that as part of its meditations this test uses are instead of is. Essentially are lets you build parameterized tests. The key logic is the (= x y) at the top, while the bulk of the test specifies values for x and y.

And here we have a test of the cons function.[3] Did you know that you could cons characters onto a string to get a sequence of characters?

```
(deftest test-cons
  ;; Some of the test omitted...

  (are [x y] (= x y)
    (cons 1 nil) '(1)
    (cons nil nil) '(nil)

    (cons \a nil) '(\a)
    (cons \a "") '(\a)
    (cons \a "bc") '(\a \b \c)

    (cons 1 ()) '(1)
    (cons 1 '(2 3)) '(1 2 3)

    (cons 1 []) [1]
    (cons 1 [2 3]) [1 2 3]

    ;; More of the test omitted...
    ))
```

And in the same file we can see test.check in action:

```
(defspec longrange-equals-range 100
  (prop/for-all [start gen/int
                 end gen/int
                 step gen/s-pos-int]
                (= (clojure.lang.Range/create start end step)
                   (clojure.lang.LongRange/create start end step))))
```

This test is out to show that instances of clojure.lang.Range and clojure.lang.LongRange, which represent ranges of numbers—and unsurprisingly are produced by the range function—are equivalent.

Wrapping Up

In this chapter we covered some of the ways you can ensure that your Clojure code actually works. We took a quick look at writing traditional case-based unit tests with clojure.test and then moved on to generative tests with test.check.

We also saw that the question of how you write your tests is much less important than the decision *to write tests*. Because when it comes to building working software, neither optimism nor hubris is a strategy.

---

3. https://github.com/clojure/clojure/blob/master/test/clojure/test_clojure/sequences.clj

CHAPTER 15

Spec

One thing you may have noticed about Clojure programs—and Clojure programmers—is that they rarely talk about data types. Oh, sure, we have strings and symbols and maps and vectors along with various record types, but what's important in Clojure is less the data type than the data *shape*. Thus we tend not to think of our data as an AggregateBookCollection, which contains instances of BookEntities, each one having instances of Author and Title. Instead we look at it as a vector of maps, where each map has :title, :author, and :copies keys.

Since Clojure is more concerned with the shape of data than its type, Clojure programmers spend a fair amount of time verifying that the value they've just been handed has the right shape. *Is this really a vector of maps where each map has a :title key?* is a common sort of question to ask of a value passed to your function. So in this chapter we're going to look at a relatively recent addition to the Clojure ecosystem: clojure.spec, a library that enables you to validate the shape of your values.

This Is the Data You're Looking For

To get a feeling for how clojure.spec works, let's return to our book-store example and imagine that we're writing code to process our familiar book maps, values that look like this:

```
{:title "Getting Clojure" :author "Olsen" :copies 1000000}
```

Further, imagine that we're getting our book data from a not-terribly-reliable source, and we've decided that the first thing we need to do is validate that this value that claims to be a book is in fact a book-shaped value. Clearly we could write a function:

```
spec/inventory/src/inventory/core.clj
(defn book? [x]
  (and
    (map? x)
    (string? (:author x))
    (string? (:title x))
    (pos-int? (:copies x))))
```

While this does work, the *code it by hand* approach to validating data doesn't scale well. In any sizable system we are likely to have a significant number of complicated data shapes, and writing functions like this for each one would quickly become tedious.

Building this kind of data validation is why we have clojure.spec.[1] At its most basic, a clojure.spec is a sort of regular expression facility for Clojure data. In exactly the same way you can use a regular expression to express a pattern—perhaps an *A* followed by any number of *B*s—that either will or won't match some string, you can use clojure.spec to express a pattern—perhaps a collection consisting of only numbers—that either will or won't match some Clojure data.

To see it in action you will need to load the clojure.spec.alpha namespace:

```
(ns inventory.core
  (:require [clojure.spec.alpha :as s]))
```

The key function supplied by spec is valid?:

```
(s/valid? number? 44)      ; Returns true.
(s/valid? number? :hello) ; Returns false.
```

As you can see, valid? takes a predicate function and a value and will tell you if the value passes the test posed by the function. If this seems less than impressive, well, yes. But it's just the beginning.

Clojure Dot Spec Dot Alpha?

As I write these words clojure.spec is in the process of being finished off, which explains the alpha in the namespace name. Depending on when you're reading this, that alpha may or may not still be there.

Note also that while clojure.spec is well integrated with Clojure, it is delivered as a separate library. Thus if you are using Leiningen you will need an additional dependency entry in your project file.

For example, by using clojure.spec/and, you can combine a couple of predicates into something that will test if the value is a number and greater than 10:

---

1.   https://clojure.org/about/spec

```
(def n-gt-10 (s/and number? #(> % 10)))

(s/valid? n-gt-10 1)    ; Nope.
(s/valid? n-gt-10 10)   ; Still nope.
(s/valid? n-gt-10 11)   ; True.
```

Conveniently, and doesn't limit you to just two predicates:

```
(def n-gt-10-lt-100
  (s/and number? #(> % 10) #(< % 100)))
```

One thing to be aware of is that the terminology is a bit confusing: We generally refer to the pattern-matching values as *specs*. But people do sometimes refer to the whole clojure.spec library itself as *spec*. For clarity, I'll stick to calling the library clojure.spec and the values specs.

Along with and, clojure.spec also provides or, which lets you create a spec that will match either *this* or *that*. So if we needed a spec that would match either a number *or* a string, we might write the following:

```
(def n-or-s (s/or :a-number number? :a-string string?))

(s/valid? n-or-s "Hello!") ; Yes!
(s/valid? n-or-s 99)       ; Yes!
(s/valid? n-or-s 'foo)     ; No, it's a symbol.
```

Notice the slight twist in using or. It requires its arguments in pairs, a keyword followed by a predicate. The keyword is required to help in producing coherent feedback when a spec fails to match.

More significantly, both and and or will accept specs as well as simple predicate functions as arguments. This means we can build up arbitrarily complex specs, so that this defines a spec that will accept numbers greater than 10, or any symbol:

```
(def n-gt-10-or-s (s/or :greater-10 n-gt-10 :a-symbol symbol?))
```

Spec'ing Collections

We can also create specs for the various collections. The most basic here is coll-of, which specifies a collection of something:

```
;; Something like '("Alice" "In" "Wonderland").

(def coll-of-strings (s/coll-of string?))

;; Or a collection of numbers or strings, perhaps ["Emma" 1815 "Jaws" 1974]

(def coll-of-n-or-s (s/coll-of n-or-s))
```

To produce tighter specifications on collections, we can reach for cat. Essentially cat lets you specify *this* should follow *that* in a collection. For example, if we wanted to match only four-element collections consisting of alternating strings and numbers we could say this:

```
(def s-n-s-n (s/cat :s1 string? :n1 number? :s2 string? :n2 number?))
(s/valid? s-n-s-n ["Emma" 1815 "Jaws" 1974])    ; Yes!
```

Note that like or, cat requires descriptive keywords.

We can also write specs for maps using the keys function. Here, for example, is a spec for our familiar book map:

```
(def book-s
  (s/keys :req-un [:inventory.core/title
                   :inventory.core/author
                   :inventory.core/copies]))
```

The spec in that example will match any map that has :title, :author, and :copies keys:

```
;; Yes!
(s/valid? book-s {:title "Emma" :author "Austen" :copies 10})

;; No! :author missing.
(s/valid? book-s {:title "Arabian Nights" :copies 17})

;; Yes! Additional entries are OK:
(s/valid? book-s {:title "2001" :author "Clarke" :copies 1 :published 1968})
```

Note that there is something a bit odd going on with the keys function. We supplied namespace-qualified keys in the spec: it's :inventory.core/title, not :title. But having supplied namespace-qualified keywords, the -un part of :req-un says that when it comes time to match, the spec will look for unqualified keyword keys in the map. There is a method to this namespace madness, but to understand it we need to first talk about how you can register your specs.

Registering Specs

So far in our examples we have been treating specs like the garden-variety Clojure values that they are. But consider how useful it would be to have a global registry, a place where you could announce, *When I'm talking about books I mean a map with :title, :author, and :copies keys.* That way any bit of code anywhere can check to see if a value qualifies as a book according to the high standards of our book inventory system.

This is the motivation behind clojure.spec/def, not to be confused with our old buddy clojure.core/def! The idea of clojure.spec/def is to allow you to register your spec in a JVM-wide registry of specs any code can then use. For example, this:

```
(s/def
  :inventory.core/book
  (s/keys
    :req-un
    [:inventory.core/title :inventory.core/author :inventory.core/copies]))
```

registers our simple book spec under the keyword :inventory.core/book.

Once a spec is registered, you can use the keyword *as a spec*:

```
;; Validate a book against the registered spec.
```

```
(s/valid? :inventory.core/book {:title "Dracula" :author "Stoker" :copies 10})
```

The global registry is the reason we need all those namespace-laden keywords. In a global registry we don't want the spec for our books to collide with other book specs, perhaps entered by some accounting- (as in *cook the books*) or travel- (as in *book a flight*) related library.

Happily, we don't have to constantly write out the fully qualified keyword. Recall that ::book is the same as :inventory.core/book when the current namespace is inventory.core. So if the current namespace is inventory.core, this will give us the same effect as our previous example:

```
(s/def ::book (s/keys :req-un [::title ::author ::copies]))
```

Spec'ing Maps (Again)

That brings us back to writing specs for maps. Recall that we passed over the strangeness that while the keywords in our actual book maps were sans namespaces (:title, for example), in the spec we used keywords with a namespace (:inventory.core/title, for example).

The reason for this is both clever *and* useful, two things that don't always go together. When you specify the keys to a map, clojure.spec will try to look up the (fully qualified) keys in the registry. If it doesn't find a spec registered under that key, no problem. But if it does, *it validates the value associated with that key in the map against the spec.*

Since up to now we haven't registered specs under :inventory.core/title, :inventory.core/author, or :inventory.core/copies, the spec didn't check the values associated with the :title, :author, and :copies keys in the map. That means that up to now this is a perfectly good :inventory.core/book:

```
{:title 1234 :author false :copies "many"}
```

But it's easy to tighten up the spec. All we have to do is define specs for :inventory.core/title and :inventory.core/author. Here's the whole thing:

```
(s/def ::title string?)
(s/def ::author string?)
(s/def ::copies int?)
(s/def ::book (s/keys :req-un [::title ::author ::copies]))
```

Now we have a spec for our books that requires both the title and the author to be strings.

Why? Why? Why?

One issue with more complex specs is that it's not always immediately clear *why* a particular value doesn't match. For example, you might have to look at this expression for a while to see why valid? returns false:

```
(s/valid? ::book {:author :austen :title :emma})
```

To help you figure out why your spec isn't matching, clojure.spec provides the explain function, which takes the same arguments as valid?. If the spec matches, explain will print a celebratory message, so that if you do this:

```
(s/explain n-gt-10 44)
```

you will see this:

```
Success!
```

Things are much more interesting if the spec doesn't match. Do this:

```
(s/explain n-gt-10 1)
```

and you will see something like the following:

```
val: 4 fails predicate: (> % 10)
```

Thus we can use explain to figure out why your book map failed to match the spec:

```
(s/explain ::book {:author :austen :title :emma})
```

To wit:

```
In: [:author] val: :austen fails spec: :inventory.core/author
at: [:author] predicate: string?
```

Of course! The author and title need to be *strings*, not keywords!

Note that explain *prints* its results. Match or no, its return value is always nil.

The explain function has a positive doppelgänger in the form of conform. While explain will tell you what went wrong when a spec doesn't match, conform will

tell you all about a successful match. Like valid? and explain, conform takes a
spec and a value:

```
(s/conform s-n-s-n ["Emma" 1815 "Jaws" 1974])
```

If the spec doesn't match, conform returns the keyword :clojure.spec.alpha/invalid.
If it does match, conform will give you a detailed explanation of the match, as
a Clojure value. For simple specs, this is just the matching value itself, so
that this will give you 1968:

```
(s/conform number? 1968)
```

Things get interesting when you use conform with a spec containing descriptive
keywords, so that this:

```
(s/conform s-n-s-n ["Emma" 1815 "Jaws" 1974])
```

will return

```
{:s1 "Emma", :n1 1815, :s2 "Jaws", :n2 1974}
```

Note that unlike explain, conform actually returns results instead of printing the
results.

Function Specs

So far we've been treating clojure.spec as a general-purpose library for ensuring
that our data looks the way it should. And so it is. But think about how
useful it would be during development to have a way to automatically do some
spec matching at critical points in your code. For example, wouldn't it be
great if you could write a spec for the arguments of a function and have that
spec checked each time the function is called?

We could do this by taking advantage of function pre and post conditions:

```
;; Register a handy spec: An inventory is a collection of books.

(s/def :inventory.core/inventory
  (s/coll-of ::book))

(defn find-by-title
  [title inventory]
  {:pre [(s/valid? ::title title)
         (s/valid? ::inventory inventory)]}
  (some #(when (= (:title %) title) %) inventory))
```

This isn't bad, but there is a much more concise and maintainable way to get
the same effect. The clojure.spec library has a feature that lets you describe what

should go into and come out of a function *separately from the function*. The
trick is to use clojure.spec/fdef:

```
;; Define the function.
(defn find-by-title
  [title inventory]
  (some #(when (= (:title %) title) %) inventory))

;; Register a spec for the find-by-title function.
(s/fdef find-by-title
    :args (s/cat :title ::title
                 :inventory ::inventory))
```

As you can see from the code, fdef takes a function and a spec that matches
the arguments for that function. Since there can be a significant performance
penalty involved in checking arguments, by default the checking is disabled.
To turn the argument checking on we to need require yet another namespace:

```
(require '[clojure.spec.test.alpha :as st])
```

and explicitly instrument our function:

```
(st/instrument 'inventory.core/find-by-title)
```

Once we have all that in place, we have clojure.spec checking on our function,
so that if you pass a vector of strings instead of the expected book maps, as
follows:

```
(find-by-title "Emma" ["Emma" "2001" "Jaws"])
```

you will see this:

```
ExceptionInfo Call to #'inventory/find-by-title
did not conform to spec:
In: [1 0] val: "Emma" fails spec:
:inventory/book at: [:args :inventory] predicate: map?
...
```

Since spec-based argument checking can slow things down, it's most useful
during development and testing.

Spec-Driven Tests

Checking arguments is not the only clojure.spec-based facility you can use to
improve the reliability of your code. You also take advantage of clojure.spec—and
specifically fdef—to drive test.check generative tests. Think about it: in spec'ing
the arguments of a function you are also providing much of the information
required to *generate* those arguments.

If we have this simple marketing blurb–generating function and an fdef to go with it, we can run the function with 1,000 randomly generated books:

```
(defn book-blurb [book]
  (str "The best selling book " (:title book) " by " (:author book)))

(s/fdef book-blurb :args (s/cat :book ::book))
```

All we need is the check function:

```
(require '[clojure.spec.test.alpha :as stest])

(stest/check 'inventory.core/book-blurb)
```

Now this is not much of a test because, while we are calling book-blurb with randomly generated data, our test is not checking the return value. But that's not much of a challenge. We just add a :ret clause to our fdef:

```
(s/fdef book-blurb
  :args (s/cat :book ::book)
  :ret (s/and string? (partial re-find #"The best selling")))
```

Here we are saying that the return value must be a string and contain the words "The best selling."

If you want to go even further, you can supply a function via the :fn key. The function gets handed a map containing both the function arguments and the return value. The test passes if the function returns a truthy value. Going back to our book blurb example, we could use :fn to check that the string returned contains the author's name:

```
(defn check-return [{:keys [args ret]}]
  (let [author (-> args :book :author)]
    (not (neg? (.indexOf ret author)))))

(s/fdef book-blurb
  :args (s/cat :book ::book)
  :ret (s/and string? (partial re-find #"The best selling"))
  :fn check-return)
```

Here the check-return function pulls the author out of the arguments and checks that the name of the author does indeed appear in the book blurb.

Staying Out of Trouble

Possibly the biggest danger lurking inside of clojure.spec is related to mistyping a keyword while registering a spec. For example, if you do this you might think you are (among other things) declaring that the value associated with :title in a book map needs to be a string:

```
(s/def ::author string?)

(s/def ::titlo string?)

(s/def ::copies pos-int?)

(s/def ::book
      (s/keys :req-un [::title ::author ::copies]))

;; Register a spec for the find-by-title function.

(s/fdef find-by-title
  :args (s/cat :title ::title
               :inventory ::inventory))
```

But take a closer look and you will see that we misspelled ::title when defining the spec. This means that while books are required to have titles, since there is no spec called ::title the value can be anything.

The other thing to keep firmly in mind about specs is that when we talk about a global clojure.spec registry, we're talking about *global* in the sense of *available to other code running in this JVM*. If your system consists of a number of cooperating Clojure processes, you need to ensure that you register any specs that you intend to use in *each* JVM. In this sense you can think of specs as akin to functions and values you bind with def: they need to be loaded before you can use them.

In the Wild

You can find a great example of clojure.spec in action in the ring-spec,[2] which contains specs for the Ring web application library. For example, as we saw back in Chapter 6, *Functional Things*, on page 63, a key part of a Ring application is dealing with requests, which arrive at the application in the form of maps. But what, exactly, do those request maps contain?

I'm glad you asked:

```
(s/def :ring/request
  (s/keys :req-un [:ring.request/server-port
                   :ring.request/server-name
                   :ring.request/remote-addr
                   :ring.request/uri
                   :ring.request/scheme
                   :ring.request/protocol
                   :ring.request/headers
                   :ring.request/request-method]
          :opt-un [:ring.request/query-string
                   :ring.request/body]))
```

---

2. https://github.com/ring-clojure/ring-spec

Looks like we have a map with entries for port, a server name, a remote address, and so on. And it looks like the query string and body are optional. And if you were curious about what you might find in these fields, you just have to look a bit closer:

```
(s/def :ring.request/server-port (s/int-in 1 65535))
(s/def :ring.request/server-name string?)
(s/def :ring.request/remote-addr string?)

; And so on...
```

You can see other interesting specs in clojure.specs.alpha,[3] which contains the specs for Clojure itself. Look in that repository, and you will find the following spec definition:

```
(s/def ::defn-args
  (s/cat :name simple-symbol?
         :docstring (s/? string?)
         :meta (s/? map?)
         :bs (s/alt :arity-1 ::args+body
                    :arity-n (s/cat :bodies (s/+ (s/spec ::args+body))
                                    :attr (s/? map?)))))))
```

The name ::defn-args says it all. This is the spec for the arguments that you can pass to defn. Note that this isn't a spec for the arguments to some particular function defined with defn; it's the spec for what defn itself will accept as arguments. Notice how the spec requires a symbol—the name of the function— followed by a docstring, and then the metadata (something we'll talk about in Chapter 19, *Read and Eval*, on page 229), followed by the body of the function.

There are a couple of things to note about this spec. The first is that it's not stand-alone. It relies on the previously defined ::args+body spec and the simple-symbol? function (both of which I'm omitting here) to do much of the work. Also note that the ::defn-args spec uses a feature of clojure.spec we haven't seen before, s/?. Essentially, s/? makes the next part of the spec optional. Thus, while the function name is required, both the docstring and the metadata are optional.

You can also find the function spec for defn in the same file:

```
(s/fdef clojure.core/defn
  :args ::defn-args
  :ret any?)
```

and discover that defn takes the arguments specified by ::defn-args and (at least according to this spec) returns some value—we care not which.

---

3. https://github.com/clojure/core.specs.alpha

Wrapping Up

In this chapter we took a tour of clojure.spec, a Clojure library for verifying the shape of data. We looked at the ins and outs of specifying the various basic data types and collections and at how to assemble simple specs into more intricate ones. We also saw how you can register your specs in a JVM-wide registry and how you can use clojure.spec to improve the quality of your code.

With this look at clojure.spec you've hit another milestone in your Clojure journey. Along with the basics, you now know enough about the features of Clojure that it's time to start thinking beyond the language. So in the next part we'll look at how you can use Clojure to interact with the wider world, a world where you need to call Java libraries and maintain state and do more than one thing at a time. From there we'll return to the Clojure language itself for a last look at its syntax and at how the magic of macros works.

Part III

Advanced

CHAPTER 16

Interoperating with Java

So far our exploration of Clojure has been exactly that: an exploration of Clojure. But one of the best things about Clojure—at least Clojure on the JVM—is that it's part of the Java ecosystem. And that means that Clojure programmers can take advantage of the mountain of Java code that has been written in the past couple of decades.

But to get at all that Java code you need to know two things. First, you need to have at least a general understanding of how Java works. Second, you need to know how to call Java code from your Clojure program. So these are the two topics we'll explore in this chapter. In the pages that follow we'll discover how in Java we use classes to make objects, and objects to make things happen. From there we'll move on to the Clojure features that enable you to interact with Java classes and objects. Along the way we're going to discover how the Clojure REPL is a great tool for interactively exploring Java APIs, and we'll even gain some insight into how Clojure itself is implemented.

A Peek at Java …

Java is all about objects. A Java object is little bundle of data and code that typically represents a *thing*, possibly something in the real world like a book but possibly something more abstract like a stack or a queue. The data in objects is organized as *fields*, named values attached to the object. So an object that represents a book might have fields called title and author.

Every Java object is associated with a class. It's an object's class that determines exactly which fields and which methods the object carries. Classes typically also specify a *constructor*, a special bit of code that gets called when a new object is created. It's the constructor that initializes the fields on an object and otherwise gets it ready to go out into the world. For example, our books might be represented by a Book class, complete with three fields and a constructor:

interop/book1/Book.java
```java
public class Book {

    // The fields. Every Book instance has its own title, author, and chapter.

    public String title;
    public String author;
    public int numberChapters;

    // Constructor method.

    public Book(String t, String a, int nChaps) {
        title = t;
        author = a;
        numberChapters = nChaps;
    }
}
```

Most Java code comes packaged in *methods*, which are named, functionlike bits of program defined inside of classes. Thus an object representing a book might have methods with names like publish and payRoyalties:

interop/book2/Book.java
```java
public class Book {

    //Note the fields are public.

    public String title;
    public String author;
    public int numberChapters;

    public Book(String t, String a, int nChaps) {
        title = t;
        author = a;
        numberChapters = nChaps;
    }

    public void publish() {
        // Do something to publish the book.
    }

    public void payRoyalties() {
        // Do something to pay royalties.
    }
}
```

It's generally considered bad programming practice to expose the data fields of a Java object directly to the outside world by declaring them public as we've done so far in our Book class. A more typical Java class will declare its fields private—that is, accessible only by code defined within the class—and will include methods with names like getTitle and getAuthor to expose the data hidden inside:

interop/book3/Book.java
```java
public class Book {

    // Make the fields private, accessible only inside this class.

    private String title;
    private String author;
    private int numberChapters;

    public Book(String t, String a, int nChaps) {
        title = t;
        author = a;
        numberChapters = nChaps;
    }

    // Add getter methods to make fields available to the outside world.

    public String getTitle() {
        return title;
    }

    public String getAuthor() {
        return author;
    }

    public int getNumberChapters() {
        return numberChapters;
    }
}
```

Java organizes classes into an inheritance tree, where every class except one has a parent, or *superclass*, which supplies default methods and fields. The lone parentless exception is java.lang.Object, which sits alone at the top of the hierarchy, the ultimate ancestor of all Java classes.

Thus we might have a class called Publication:

interop/book4/Publication.java
```java
// By default, Publication is a subclass of java.lang.Object.

public class Publication {
    private String title;
    private String author;

    public Publication(String t, String a) {
        title = t;
        author = a;
    }
    public String getTitle() {
        return title;
    }
    public String getAuthor() {
        return author;
    }
}
```

And make Book a subclass of Publication:

interop/book4/Book.java

```java
// Book is now a subclass of Publication, which handles the author and title.

public class Book extends Publication {
    private int numberChapters;

    public Book(String t, String a, int nChaps) {
        super(t, a);
        numberChapters = nChaps;
    }

    public int getNumberChapters() {
        return numberChapters;
    }
}
```

The idea is that the superclass represents a more generalized version of the concept while the subclass represents something more specific.

Finally, most classes in Java are organized into *packages*, which are roughly analogous to Clojure's namespaces. We might, for example, put our Book class in the com.russolsen.blottsbooks package:

interop/book5/Book.java

```java
// Book is now in the com.russolsen.blottsbooks package.

package com.russolsen.blottsbooks;

public class Book extends Publication {
  // Guts of the class omitted.
}
```

Once we encase a class in a package, the package name becomes part of the class's *fully qualified classname*, so that the fully qualified name of Book is now com.russolsen.blottsbooks.Book. In an effort to prevent name collisions, most—but not all—Java package names are constructed using a sort of reverse domain name scheme. Hence the com.russolsen part of the com.russolsen.blottsbooks.

... And Back to Clojure

To see how we can get at the wonders of Java from Clojure, let's reach for every programmer's favorite abstraction, the file. Java comes packaged with a handy class for representing files, namely java.io.File. According to the documentation for java.io.File, we can create an instance by passing in a string, the path to the file. To create a new instance of a Java class using Clojure's interoperation facilities—*interop* for short—we use the classname with a dot on the end in the lead-off spot in the expression:

interop/examples.clj
```clojure
(def authors (java.io.File. "authors.txt"))
```

The preceding code will create a new instance of java.io.File, calling the constructor along the way, and return that instance—which represents an operating-system file called authors.txt—back to our Clojure code.

Once we have an instance in hand we can start calling its methods. For example, just having an instance of java.io.File doesn't guarantee that the file actually exists in the file system. To find out if the file authors.txt is really there, we can use the exists method:

```clojure
(if (.exists authors)
  (println "Our authors file is there.")
  (println "Our authors file is missing."))
```

Similarly, we can find out if the file is readable with the canRead method:

```clojure
(if (.canRead authors)
  (println "We can read it!"))
```

And—assuming we have the proper operating-system authority—we can even change the permissions of the underlying file:

```clojure
(.setReadable authors true)
```

As you can see, to call a method on a Java instance you stick a dot on the *front* of the method name—so that canRead becomes .canRead—and use the result like a function, passing the instance as the first argument, followed by any additional arguments.

You can also access your object's public fields from Clojure. File instances don't have any public fields, but another built-in class, java.awt.Rectangle, does. As you might guess from the name, java.awt.Rectangle represents a rectangular area on your screen—AWT being the original Java GUI library. If we create a new 10-by-20 rectangle sitting at the origin:

```clojure
(def rect (java.awt.Rectangle. 0 0 10 20))
```

we could then reach into its public fields:

```clojure
(println "Width:" (.-width rect))
(println "Height:" (.-height rect))
```

Yes, the syntax is a little odd: (.-<field> <instance>). Note the dot and dash in front of the field name.

Packages

So far we've been using the fully qualified classnames for files: java.io.File and java.awt.Rectangle. Since that can be a bit of a mouthful, Clojure provides import. In much the same way that you can use require/:as to create syntactical shortcuts for the denizens of your Clojure namespaces, you can use import to do the same with Java classes. In the REPL you can use the stand-alone form of import:

```
;; In the REPL.
(import java.io.File)
```

If you are writing a .clj file you should include the import in the ns at the top:

```
(ns read-authors
  (:import java.io.File))
```

Note that there is no quoting needed in either form. However you do it, once you have imported a class you can refer to the class without its package name:

```
(def authors (File. "authors.txt"))
```

If you happen to need a number of classes from the same Java package, you can roll all the imports into a single expression. Thus if we need the InputStream class—which also lives in java.io—we could say this:

```
;; Do this in a .clj file:
(ns read-authors
  (:import (java.io File InputStream)))
```

or this:

```
;; In the REPL.
(import '(java.io File InputStream))
```

Note that if you use the multiple-class import in the stand-alone import, you *do* (sigh) need a quote.

One Java package you will not need to import is java.lang. This package contains the very core Java classes, things like java.lang.String and java.lang.Boolean. Because it's so central to life in the Java world, Clojure automatically imports java.lang into all namespaces. Thus if you evaluate String or Boolean in the REPL, like this:

```
user=> String
java.lang.String
user=> Boolean
java.lang.Boolean
```

you will see they both originate in java.lang.

Class Methods and Fields

While Java classes mostly exist to define the behavior of their instances, the classes themselves are also objects with a class—java.lang.Class—and fields and methods of their own. The fields and methods provided by classes (*static* methods and fields in Java parlance) are independent of any particular instance of the class.

For example, the File class carries around a field called separator that contains the character that goes between the bits of your path for the operating system you're working on. In a Clojure program you can get at static fields by writing class/field. Thus if you evaluated this:

```
File/separator
```

on a Linux box or a Mac, you would get a string containing a forward slash. Evaluate the same expressions on Windows, and you will get a backslash.

You access static methods in much the same way as static fields: class/method. For example, the File class has a static method that will create a temporary file for you. Here's how you would use it from Clojure:

```
;; Create a temporary file in the standard temp directory, a file
;; with a name like authors_list8240847420696232491.txt

(def temp-authors-file (File/createTempFile "authors_list" ".txt"))
```

Remember, you call static methods on Java classes with class/method.

In the Wild

So far we have limited ourselves to the built-in libraries that come packaged with Java. But Clojure's interop features work just as well with third-party libraries. For example, you might be interested in using Google's take on reading and writing JSON, the Gson library.[1]

To get a feel for using Gson from Clojure, you might start by creating a new project:

```
$ lein new exploregson
Generating a project called `exploregson`...
$ cd exploregson
```

Next we need to tell Leiningen that our project depends on a particular version of the Gson library. So we add the Gson library and its latest version (at least

---

1. https://github.com/google/gson

it's the latest version as I write this) to the project.clj dependencies. The syntax is exactly the same for Java libraries and Clojure libraries:

```
(defproject exploregson "0.1.0-SNAPSHOT"
  :description "FIXME: write description"
  :url "http://example.com/FIXME"
  :license {:name "Eclipse Public License"
            :url "http://www.eclipse.org/legal/epl-v10.html"}
  :dependencies [[org.clojure/clojure "1.8.0"]
                 [com.google.code.gson/gson "2.8.0"]]])
```

Next, start a REPL with lein repl. Looking over the Gson documentation, you see that there seems to be a central class, com.google.gson.Gson:

```
user=> (import com.google.gson.Gson)
com.google.gson.Gson

user=> (def gson-obj (Gson.))
#'user/gson-obj
```

Once you have your Gson instance, it's easy enough to turn Clojure values into JSON strings:

```
user=> (.toJson gson-obj 44)
"44"

user=> (.toJson gson-obj {:title "1984" :author "Orwell"})
"{\":title\":\"1984\",\":author\":\"Orwell\"}"
```

And now you are off and interacting with Gson. While this kind of REPL-based exploration is not a substitute for reading the library documentation, it is a great way to get a feel for what the documentation means.

Aside from the built-in Java classes and third-party libraries like Gson, there is another giant pile of Java code lying around that is of at least academic interest to every Clojure programmer: Clojure itself.

At its most basic, Clojure is just a collection of Java classes. Even better, *every* Clojure value is just a reference to some Java object. So in the same way we can call Java methods on instances of java.io.File, we can call them on garden-variety Clojure values. For example, having peeked at the Clojure source code, I know the Java class behind vectors defines a method called count. So I can call it:

```
;; Make a Clojure value which is also a Java object.

(def v [1 2 3])

;; Call a Java method on our Clojure value/Java object.

(.count v)
```

This means that we can explore Clojure itself, using Clojure.

In fact we have already done a bit of this. Recall back in Chapter 8, *Def, Symbols, and Vars*, on page 85, when we were talking about digging into vars to get at their symbol and value:

```
(def author "Dickens") ; Make a var.

(def the-var #'author) ; Grab the var.

(.get the-var)         ; Pull the value out of the var: "Dickens"
(.-sym the-var)        ; Pull the symbol out of the var: author
```

Armed with our new insights into Java interop, we now can see that the (.get the-var) expression is calling the get method on the-var while the second expression is accessing a public field called sym.

To take one more example, let's look at the value we get back from the cons function:

```
(def c (cons 99 [1 2 3]))
```

Recall that cons prepends a value to a sequence. We can use our old buddy class to discover the class of the value returned by cons:

```
(class c)       ; clojure.lang.Cons
```

and based on that we can go looking for the Cons Java code:

```
final public class Cons extends ASeq implements Serializable {

        private final Object _first;
        private final ISeq _more;

        public Cons(IPersistentMap meta, Object _first, ISeq _more) {
                super(meta);
                this._first = _first;
                this._more = _more;
        }

  // Code omitted...

        public Object first() {
                return _first;
        }

        public ISeq more() {
                if (_more == null)
                        return PersistentList.EMPTY;
                return _more;
        }

  // Lots of code omitted...
}
```

and then try them out:

```
;; And call into the Java.
(.first c)     ; 99
(.more c)      ; (1 2 3)
```

Would I use .first this way in production code? Of course not. Is this a great way to get a feeling for how Clojure works? Absolutely!

Staying Out of Trouble

One thing to keep in mind as you dive into Java interop is that while we can use .method and class/staticMethod in place of functions, they are *not* functions. They are, instead, *special forms*, more or less hardwired into Clojure. In particular, you cannot bind a method name:

```
;; Nope. Nope. Nope.

(def count-method .count)
```

All is not lost, however: you can use the built-in memfn function to turn a method name into a function. For example, while .exists is not a function, (memfn exists) is. This can be useful when you need a function value. If, for instance, you had a collection of File instances:

```
(def files [(File. "authors.txt") (File. "titles.txt")])
```

and you needed the parallel collection of Booleans indicating which files were there, you could say this:

```
(map (memfn exists) files)
```

One thing you should *not* do is blindly wrap all of your interop forms in functions, either with memfn or with plain old defn. It can be hard to resist that inner call to write something like this:

```
(defn file-exists?
  "Wrap the exists method cause I hate that dot."
  [f]
  (.exists f))

(defn readable?
  "Wrap the canRead method cause I hate camel case."
  [f]
  (.canRead f))
```

Resist you should: generally you only want to wrap calls into Java when the wrapper adds something. Otherwise just use interop like the native Clojure it is.

The final—and most important—thing you should keep firmly in mind as you work with Java objects is that many—not all, but many—Java objects *are mutable.* To pick one example, Java's answer to Clojure's vectors is a class called java.util.Vector.

It's easy enough to work with them from Clojure. You just make one:

```
(def jv-favorite-books (java.util.Vector.))
```

and then you can start adding elements to it:

```
(.addElement jv-favorite-books "Emma")
(.addElement jv-favorite-books "Andromeda Strain")
(.addElement jv-favorite-books "2001")
```

And then you stop and realize that you are changing this Java vector *in place.* First it's an empty vector, then it has one element, then two, and then three. This is the very thing that we gave up to get all the wonders of immutability in Clojure.

Don't panic. But do avoid dealing with mutable objects if you can. For example, in the trivial preceding example, the solution is a simple *don't do that.* Just use a plain old Clojure vector: ["Emma" "Andromeda Strain" "2001"]. If you do need to deal with mutable Java objects—perhaps you are getting them back from a Java API—try to turn them into something immutable if at all possible. For example, if we did have that mutable collection of books, we can easily turn it into a safely immutable Clojure vector with vec, which also accepts Java-style collections:

```
;; Back in the immutable world!
```

```
(def thankfully-immutable-books (vec jv-favorite-books))
```

The main thing is to know when you're dealing with a mutable object and work from there.

Wrapping Up

In this chapter we covered calling Java code from your Clojure program. We looked at the mechanics of creating new Java objects, at calling methods, and even at how you can use Clojure to look into the Java code behind Clojure itself.

One aspect of Java interop that we didn't look at in this chapter was using Java threads from Clojure. Because that's what the next chapter is about.

CHAPTER 17

Threads, Promises, and Futures

One of the things that makes programming such a challenge is that many of our sharpest tools are also our most dangerous weapons. Having functional values means that we can deliver a little package of code to the right place at the right time. But functional values also separate the action from the source code in a way that can make it hard to debug your program. In the same spirit, lazy sequences are wonderful, except for those infuriating times when you forget that your sequence is indeed lazy. But nothing can compare to the potential for both good and evil that comes with the thread. Having your program do several things at once is a boon: *Hey, I can do all these jobs at the same time!* But it's also a danger: *Oh, look at those two threads fighting over that data!*

So with this chapter we start a two-chapter look into the related topics of threads and mutable state. We'll kick things off in this chapter by introducing the fundamentals. We'll look at how you can create threads in a Clojure program, at some of the havoc they can wreak if you aren't careful, and at some of the simple mechanisms that Clojure provides to keep the chaos in check.

Great Power ...

Let's start with the basics: a thread is the little computing engine that breathes life into your program, turning code into action. In fact, every program that has ever run on the JVM was pushed along by a thread:

thread/examples.clj
```
(ns blottsbooks.threads)

(defn -main []
  (println "Coming to you live from the main thread!"))
```

In the Java world the thread that you get by default, the one that runs your main program, is called the *main thread*. Things only get interesting—or scary—when you start dealing with a second thread. Or a twenty-fifth thread.

To see this in action in Clojure we can resort to some simple Java interop: there is an aptly named Java class called Thread that will take a Clojure function and run it in a separate thread when you call the start method:

```
;; Make a thread.

(defn do-something-in-a-thread []
  (println "Hello from the thread.")
  (println "Good bye from the thread."))

(def the-thread (Thread. do-something-in-a-thread))

;; And run it.

(.start the-thread)
```

While this example illustrates the basic mechanics of threads, it doesn't really show the thread magic in action. You kick off the thread and the messages print. So what?

Threads and Functions

 To be more precise, the Java Thread class takes any object that implements the Runnable interface. Conveniently, Clojure functions implement Runnable.

One way to experience the magic is to create a thread that takes a long time to run. And we can do that by inserting a Thread/sleep in our function, so that it pauses for a few seconds:

```
;; Print two messages with a three second pause in the middle.

(defn do-something-else []
  (println "Hello from the thread.")
  (Thread/sleep 3000)
  (println "Good bye from the thread."))

(.start (Thread. do-something-else))
```

In the example we've created a second thread of execution. This second thread prints a message, pauses, and then prints a second message.

So if you run this code in a REPL, the call to .start will return immediately, probably either just before or just after you see the output from the first println. There will be a pause and then you will see the second message. But since the call to .start does return immediately, you are free to do other things in the REPL while you're waiting for the second message to appear. And that is the magic of threads.

In more practical terms, if you happen to have two jobs that need doing, you can decide to do them one after the other:

```
;; Do the first thing then the second.
```
```
(do-the-first-job)
(do-the-second-job)
```
```
;; Go on with the rest of the program...
```

Or do one in a separate thread while you work on the other in the current thread:

```
;; Do the first job in another thread.
```
```
(.start (Thread. do-the-first-job))
```
```
;; Immediately start on the second job.
```
```
(do-the-second-job)
```
```
;; Go on with the rest of the program (but keep reading!)...
```

Or spin off threads to do both jobs:

```
(.start (Thread. do-the-first-job))
```
```
(.start (Thread. do-the-second-job))
```
```
;; Do something else...
```

And you can go off and do a third thing while the two threads are humming away.

... And Great Responsibility

Unfortunately, along with the *do stuff at the same time* magic there is the inevitable *hair on fire* complication: without some kind of positive control mechanism, *we know nothing about how fast a thread will run.* The implications of this ignorance are deep and pervasive. To see these implications in action we're going to break the rules a bit and embed some def expressions in a couple of functions:

```
(def fav-book "Jaws")
```
```
(defn make-emma-favorite [] (def fav-book "Emma"))
```
```
(defn make-2001-favorite [] (def fav-book "2001"))
```

As we saw in back in Chapter 8, *Def, Symbols, and Vars*, on page 85, this is not a great idea: sticking a def inside of a function creates a more or less hidden side effect, making your program harder to understand. But let's do it anyway, for the sake of the example.

Now if we run these two functions in sequence, like this:

```
(make-emma-favorite)
(make-2001-favorite)
```

it's clear that *2001* will prevail in the *last function wins* contest. Alternatively, if we reverse the order, *Emma* will win the favorite-book contest.

Now imagine we spin these two functions off in threads:

```
;; Kick off the threads.
```
```
(.start (Thread. make-emma-favorite))
(.start (Thread. make-2001-favorite))
```

And wait a few seconds. ... Now what's our favorite book?

Without actually examining the value bound to fav-book, the only correct answer to this question is *We don't know*. We don't know because we have no idea how fast the threads ran, relative to each other and relative to the main thread. Threads are independent engines of computation, with the emphasis on *independent*.

We can certainly make a guess: probably each thread will do its thing very quickly. Probably the *2001* thread—which we started second—will run a bit behind the *Emma* thread and get the last word in. That's a good guess, but it's still a *guess*. It could have happened the other way around. It's even possible that it will take both threads a long time to get going, in which case we might see *Jaws* as our favorite book. In just a few lines of code we have created Schrödinger's var.

The technical term for this sort of situation is *race condition*. The effect of our code depends on which thread happens to run a bit faster or slower. Race conditions can occur anytime you have two or more threads making changes to a shared resource. In our somewhat contrived example, the threads shared a var. But real-world programs are full of references to data structures, database tables, file systems, and the like—a whole world of things that can be shared and changed and therefore fought over by multiple threads.

Good Fences Make Happy Threads

Fortunately, all is not lost. As I say, race conditions happen when you have more than one thread trying to modify the same data structure. So our first line of defense is to make sure that our threads don't *accidentally* change a shared resource. And this brings us back to Clojure's immutable data structures.

Recall that once you make a Clojure vector or list or map or set you cannot change it: you can only make modified copies. In general, immutable data structures are a huge help in crafting understandable programs. But mix in some threads, and the immutability becomes almost indispensable. Take this book inventory for example:

```
(def inventory [{:title "Emma" :sold 51 :revenue 255}
                {:title "2001" :sold 17 :revenue 170}
                ;; Lots and lots of books...
                ])
```

Imagine you started several threads to process the inventory in different ways:

```
(.start (Thread. (sum-copies-sold inventory)))
```

```
(.start (Thread. (sum-revenue inventory)))
```

Since we haven't seen the code behind sum-copies-sold and sum-revenue, we have no idea what those functions do. They might be well behaved and do exactly what their names suggest. Or these functions might be pathological messes. What we do know is our pair of functions cannot meddle with the contents of the vector that we pass to them. We know this because the vector and all of its component parts are immutable. And that single bit of knowledge is a giant first step toward writing multithreaded programs that actually work: as long as we stick to Clojure's everyday immutable data structures—and avoid doing dumb things like embedding defs in our functions—there is zero risk of accidental thread collision.

In the same spirit, we also don't need to worry about the dynamic vars we met in Chapter 8, *Def, Symbols, and Vars*, on page 85. Clojure keeps any dynamic binding of vars safely separated by thread. Here's an example:

```
(def ^:dynamic *favorite-book* "Oliver Twist")
```

```
(def thread-1
  (Thread.
    #(binding [*favorite-book* "2001"]
      (println "My favorite book is" *favorite-book*))))
```

```
(def thread-2
  (Thread.
    #(binding [*favorite-book* "Emma"]
      (println "My favorite book is" *favorite-book*))))
```

```
(.start thread-1)
(.start thread-2)
```

This will always result in thread-1 announcing it loves the science-fiction classic *2001* while thread-2 will claim loyalty to *Emma*. This is true no matter which thread runs first or if the threads are running at exactly the same time.

Thread Local

 If you're familiar with Java threading, you will have probably worked out that Clojure's dynamic vars live in thread local storage.

Promise Me a Result

The separating effect of immutability and per-thread dynamic binding means that we don't have to worry quite so much about one thread accidentally interfering with the operation of another, which is a great first step. But it's only a first step. Having separated our threads for their own safety, we now need to figure out how to get them to work together. Sometimes this isn't a problem. Some threads are born to silently do a job and silently expire:

```
;; Delete a file in the background.
(.start (Thread. #(.delete (java.io.File. "temp-titles.txt"))))
```

But more often we want some kind of result back from the thread we just fired off. *How many copies did we sell? And what was the revenue?* Or simply, *Is this thread done?*

Let's start with the last question. All we need here is a bit more Java interop, in the form of the *join*:

```
(def del-thread (Thread. #(.delete (java.io.File. "temp-titles.txt"))))
(.start del-thread)
(.join del-thread)
```

Call join, and it will pause, returning only when the thread you pass to it has finished. The main downside of join is while it will tell you a thread is done, it won't tell you anything about what the thread *did*: join always returns nil.

A more practical way to get a result out of a thread is to use a *promise*. You can think of a promise as a sort of value trap. When you create a promise, you have set the trap but it's empty:

```
(def the-result (promise))
```

Once you have a promise you can put a value in it with the deliver function:

```
(deliver the-result "Emma")
```

And BLAM! the trap snaps shut, grabbing the value. Keep in mind that you can only deliver a single value to a promise. Once the trap shuts on a value it's trapped in the promise and there is no changing it.

To get at the value in your promise you can use the deref function:

```
(println "The value in my promise is" (deref the-result))
```

Or you can use the completely equivalent syntactical shortcut of prepending an @ to the promise:

```
(println "The value in my promise is" @the-result)
```

This brings us to the punchline: if you try to dereference a promise with no value, deref (or @) will pause until there *is* a value. This means that promises are great for transferring a single value from one thread to another.

Let's go back to our book-inventory example:

```
(def inventory [{:title "Emma" :sold 51 :revenue 255}
                {:title "2001" :sold 17 :revenue 170}
                ;; Lots and lots of books...
                ])
(defn sum-copies-sold [inv]
  (apply + (map :sold inv)))
(defn sum-revenue [inv]
  (apply + (map :revenue inv)))
```

We can run the calculations in separate threads and use promises to communicate the results back to our original, default thread:

```
(let [copies-promise (promise)
      revenue-promise (promise)]
  (.start (Thread. #(deliver copies-promise (sum-copies-sold inventory))))
  (.start (Thread. #(deliver revenue-promise (sum-revenue inventory))))

  ;; Do some other stuff in this thread...

  (println "The total number of books sold is" @copies-promise)
  (println "The total revenue is " @revenue-promise))
```

We can be serene in the knowledge that if the threads haven't finished with their sums by the time we start printing, the main thread will simply wait until they are finished.

A Value with a Future

This pattern of firing off a computation in another thread and then getting the result back via a promise is so common that Clojure provides a prepackaged version of it in the form of a *future*. You can think of a future as a promise that brings along its own thread. Creating a future could not be easier. You just supply future with one or more expressions:

```
(def revenue-future
  (future (apply + (map :revenue inventory))))
```

That's it. Sometime after you create your future, Clojure will—behind the scenes—evaluate the function in a separate thread and set the value of the future to the result.

From the programmer's point of view, a future works like a promise that magically gets loaded with a value. You can use @ or deref to get the result:

```
(println "The total revenue is " @revenue-future)
```

As with a promise, dereferencing a future will block if the future is not quite done being computed.

Staying Out of Trouble

As I pointed out at the opening of this chapter, dealing with multiple threads is one of those *great power versus great responsibility* situations. Programming with multiple threads opens up the possibility that you can keep all your CPU cores busy doing productive work. But multiple threads also means dealing with the headaches—and dangers—that come with trying to do more than one thing at a time.

So far in this chapter we have walked through some of the obvious *threads fighting over resources* problems, but threads come with some other, less obvious dangers. For example, threads are expensive: creating a new thread takes a long time, and each thread takes up a reasonable chunk of memory.

Thus if you just want to get some background processing done, use a future, not a promise, since futures will deal with the issues of creating and disposing of threads. If you do need more control, you should consider using one of the thread-pool facilities supplied by Java. The best place to start is with the java.util.concurrent.Executors class, which provides a number of static methods for building thread pools. You can, for example, use it to create a fixed-size thread pool:

```
(import java.util.concurrent.Executors)

;; Create a pool of at most three threads.

(def fixed-pool (Executors/newFixedThreadPool 3))
```

Once you have your thread pool, you can throw work at it in the form of functions to be evaluated:

```
(defn a-lot-of-work []
  (println "Simulating function that takes a long time.")
  (Thread/sleep 1000))

(defn even-more-work []
  (println "Simulating function that takes a long time.")
  (Thread/sleep 1000))

(.execute fixed-pool a-lot-of-work)
(.execute fixed-pool even-more-work)
```

The thread pool will execute those functions in one of the threads in the pool. Even better, if you happen to throw more work at the pool than there are threads, the pool will queue the work and do it as the threads free up:

```
;; Throw more jobs at the fixed-pool than it can handle...

(.execute fixed-pool even-more-work)
(.execute fixed-pool even-more-work)
(.execute fixed-pool even-more-work)
(.execute fixed-pool even-more-work)
(.execute fixed-pool even-more-work)
(.execute fixed-pool even-more-work)

;; ... and it will get it all done as quickly as it can.
```

A simple fixed-sized thread pool is not your only option. The Executors class provides methods to create thread pools with a variety of behaviors, everything from a pool that will execute your functions periodically to one that will attempt to keep all your CPU cores as busy as possible. In fact, behind the scenes, Clojure uses one of the thread-pool variants to manage the threads that drive futures.

The bottom line is that while the raw Thread class is conceptually simple—and therefore great for examples—it is also a low-level and reasonably blunt tool. In real applications you are much better off using higher-level constructs like futures and thread pools than creating your own threads manually.

You should also be careful with operations like join and deref—operations that block the current thread. The problem with this:

```
(deref revenue-promise)
```

or its syntactically sugared twin:

```
@revenue-promise
```

is that if something prevents a value being delivered to revenue-promise, then those expressions will wait *forever*—or at least until someone kills the program.

In production code you should almost always supply a timeout, and a value to return if a timeout does occur:

```
;; Wait 1/2 second (500 milliseconds) for the revenue.
;; Return :oh-snap on timeout.

(deref revenue-promise 500 :oh-snap)
```

Consistently using timeouts provides a sort of circuit breaker to guard against a cascade of endlessly waiting threads.

Finally, be aware that by default the JVM will refuse to stop if there are threads still running. So if you write something like this:

```
(defn -main []
  (let [t (Thread. #((Thread/sleep 5000)))]
    (.start t))
  (println "Main thread is all done, but..."))
```

you have just built a program that will hang around for about five seconds.

Sleeping Precision

 Keep in mind that Thread/sleep only promises to pause your thread for *at least* the interval you requested. But it might pause for longer. Threads are hard.

There are a couple of ways to deal with this. The most straightforward is to make sure that your threads are all nicely dead and cleaned up before your program terminates.

Alternatively, you can mark your threads as daemons:

```
(defn -main []
  (let [t (Thread. #((Thread/sleep 5000)))]
    (.setDaemon t true)
    (.start t))
  (println "Main thread is all done!"))
```

But be aware that the JVM will terminate daemon threads without warning when the main thread terminates.

In the Wild

A great way to get a feel for working with multiple threads in Clojure is to look at the Compojure library.[1] Compojure helps you route the requests that come into your web application to a suitable response. Here, for example, is a simple placeholder web application for our book store, built with Compojure:

```
(ns storefront.handler
  (:require [compojure.core :refer :all]
            [compojure.handler :as handler]))

(defroutes main-routes
  (GET "/" [] "Welcome to Blotts Books!!")
  (GET "/book" [title author]
      (str "Sorry " title " By " author " is not available.")))

(def app (handler/site main-routes))
```

---

1. https://github.com/weavejester/compojure

The key bit of code here is the call to defroutes, which allows you to associate
a route—/book, for example—with the code to handle requests that come in
on that route. If you peek inside the Compojure source code, you can find
the bits behind defroutes:

```
(defmacro defroutes
  "Define a Ring handler function from a sequence of routes. The name may
  optionally be followed by a docstring and metadata map."
  [name & routes]
  (let [[name routes] (macro/name-with-attributes name routes)]
   `(def ~name (routes ~@routes))))
```

and GET:

```
(defmacro GET "Generate a `GET` route."
  [path args & body]
  (compile-route :get path args body))
```

and the compile-route function called by GET:

```
(defn compile-route
  "Compile a route in the form `(method path bindings & body)` into a function.
  Used to create custom route macros."
  [method path bindings body]
  `(make-route
    ~method
    ~(prepare-route path)
    (fn [request#]
      (let-request [~bindings request#] ~@body))))
```

There are Clojure features in this code that we haven't covered yet. In particular, we'll get to those odd backquotes and tildes as well as defmacro in Chapter
20, *Macros*, on page 241.

The first thing to note is that all of this code, from our trivial book-store
application down to the deep plumbing of Compojure, needs to work in a
multithreaded environment. JVM-based web servers tend to spin off all sorts
of threads in order to handle large numbers of simultaneous requests. Thus
web applications and libraries like Compojure need to be OK with running
inside of any number of threads. So while neither our application nor Compojure is spinning off any new threads, the threads are out there.

The second thing to note is how this code, from top to bottom, is completely
devoid of any *Oh, gee, I'm working in a multithreaded application!* special
pleading. It's certainly possible to write Clojure code that will fail utterly in
the presence of multiple threads. Just carelessly write to a file or modify a
shared mutable Java object or simply suck up the available CPU cycles. But

Clojure, with its emphasis on functional programming and immutable data structures, does make it a bit easier to write thread-friendly code.

You can find a great example of the use of futures in the clojure.core/pmap function. The idea behind pmap is to farm out the work that might otherwise be done with map into a number of threads, in parallel—hence the name.

From the outside, pmap is identical to map:

```
(pmap some-computationally-intensive-f a-collection)
```

While the real implementation of pmap is complicated by practical questions like *Just how many processors does this machine have?*, a basic implementation that captures the spirit of the original is a simple application of future:

```
(defn toy-pmap [f coll]
  (let [futures (doall (map #(future (f %)) coll))]
    (map deref futures)))
```

Start by mapping each value in the collection into a future, which will eventually contain the mapped value. Then map over the futures, dereferencing them back to the mapped value.

The only twist here is the interaction between the *start working on it now so that we have the result later* nature of futures and the very lazy nature of map. Recall that map will actually not compute anything until you start looking at the elements of the lazy sequence that it returns. But in toy-pmap we want to create the futures so that they can get started pre-computing the results. To get this all to happen, we wrap the call to the first map in a doall. We do this to ensure that we get an early start on the futures, at the cost of making toy-pmap eager—don't use toy-pmap on an infinite sequence.

Industrial-Strength pmap

 Another complication that the real pmap deals with revolves around being just lazy enough to work with large, possibly unbounded, sequences while at the same time being eager enough to keep the futures working just a bit ahead of the game.

One thing that you can glean from toy-pmap is that there is quite of bit of overhead involved: Think about creating all those futures along with two invocations of map. This is also true of the real pmap, which means that pmap is likely to be *slower* than map unless the function you are passing into pmap is doing some intense computing.

Wrapping up

In this chapter we took a look at some of the ins and outs of threads. We saw how multiple threads can help you push your computing job forward on multiple fronts at once, but also how a multithreaded program can come to grief if you are not careful.

But we also saw how Clojure's immutable data structures and dynamic binding, along with promises and futures, can enable you to use multiple threads safely.

But we're not quite done with multiple threads yet. In this chapter we focused on keeping your threads separated, on keeping them from sharing state. In real life, though, in everything from a simple web application hit counter to complex data-handling systems, we need to have threads deal with shared state. And so that is what we'll tackle in the next chapter.

CHAPTER 18

State

There's a fundamental irony to the Clojure approach to programming, which arises from a principle that can be summed up—at least in part—as *avoid mutable state*. Avoiding mutable state is why you can't just jam a new value into the fifth element of an existing vector or delete a key from an existing map. It's also why Clojure has let instead of local variables and why we restrain ourselves from defing things on the fly in production. The idea is the less mutable state we have—at least in production—the easier our programs are to understand.

Now for the irony: having gotten rid of all of the mutable state, we're now at a loss when it comes to modeling things that do change over time. How, for example, do we keep track of our book-store inventory as books get sold and new stock arrives? As things stand right now we would have a hard time building an application that handles a simple *You Are the 500th Person To Visit Our Site* counter, let alone a service to, say, manage inventories.

So in this chapter we'll look at how you represent mutable state in Clojure. In the pages that follow we'll see that Clojure comes with a variety of containers for your mutable state, each with a different set of talents and drawbacks.

It's Made of Atoms

Let's start with that simple hit-counter application. Here is a basic Ring web application that counts the number of visitors to the site and congratulates every 100th visitor:

```
state/examples.clj
(def counter 0)
(defn greeting-message [req]
  (if (zero? (mod counter 100))
    (str "Congrats! You are the " counter " visitor!")
    (str "Welcome to Blotts Books!")))
;; ect
```

Except that it doesn't. The trouble is that counter stays firmly bound to zero and it's not clear how we can fix that. And as we've discussed any number of times, we cannot yield to the temptation of slipping (def counter (inc counter)) in greeting-message: vars are there to hold relatively stable values and a hit counter is anything but stable.

Fortunately, Clojure does come with a container for more volatile values: the atom. Here's our hit-counter application augmented with an atom to manage the count:

```
(def counter (atom 0))

(defn greeting-message [req]
  (swap! counter inc)
  (if (= @counter 500)
    (str "Congrats! You are the " @counter " visitor!")
    (str "Welcome to Blotts Books!")))

;; ect
```

As you can see, we create the atom by calling the atom function and passing in the initial value of the atom, zero in the example. You can also see that we get the value back out of the atom by prefixing an @ to it. We could also have gotten the value by writing the slightly longer (deref counter). If all of this looks familiar, it should: getting at the values inside of an atom is exactly the same as getting the value out of a promise or a future.

The punchline with atoms is the way that they march from one mutable state to another. The key is in the swap! function:

```
(swap! counter inc)
```

The swap! function takes two arguments, the atom and a function to produce the next value of the atom. The idea is that swap! calls the function with the old value of the atom and uses the value returned from the function as the new value for the atom. So in our example, each call to swap! will increment the value in the atom, giving us our counter. Conceptually swap! lets you march from one value of your atom to the next.

Conveniently, swap! will pass any additional arguments into the function, so if we wanted to cheat a bit and count each visitor to our site as a dozen, we could write this:

```
(swap! counter + 12)
```

The great thing about atoms is that the update mechanism ensconced in swap! is completely thread safe. Here's how it works:

- The first thing swap! does is grab the value in the atom.

- It then calls your update function with the value to get the new value.

- Next—and this is the critical bit—swap! checks that the value in the atom is still what it was when the update started. If the value is still the same, then swap! replaces the value with the new value and we're done.

- If the value has changed, swap! will grab the new value and *start the process all over.*

Thus swap! keeps trying to update the atom until it manages to do so without interference from other threads. Even better, all this happens on the thread that calls swap! so that when swap! returns, you *know* your update has been applied to the value in the atom.

Swapping Maps

Atoms are not limited to storing just numbers: in fact, you can wrap an atom around any Clojure value. Thus a more practical example might look like this:

```
(ns inventory)

(def by-title (atom {}))

(defn add-book [{title :title :as book}]
  (swap! by-title #(assoc % title book)))

(defn del-book [title]
  (swap! by-title #(dissoc % title )))

(defn find-book [title]
  (get @by-title title))
```

That gives us a simple but complete stateful inventory manager:

```
(find-book "Emma")     ; Nope

(add-book {:title "1984", :copies 1948})
(add-book {:title "Emma", :copies 100})
(del-book "1984")

(find-book "Emma")     ; Yup
(find-book "1984")     ; Nope
```

There really is not much to an atom. An atom is a container for a mutable value. You can get at the value with deref or @ and you update it with swap!.

Conceptually simple and easy to use, atoms should be the first tool you reach for when you need to manage some mutable state.

Refs: Team-Oriented Atoms

One drawback in using atoms is that each atom stands alone. For example, if we needed to track the total number of books in the inventory along with each book by title using two atoms, we might try something like this:

```
(ns inventory)

(def by-title (atom {}))

(def total-copies (atom 0))

(defn add-book [{title :title :as book}]
  (swap! by-title #(assoc % title book))

  ;; Oh no! The two atoms are out of sync right here!

  (swap! total-copies + (:copies book)))
```

We're going to have an unavoidable window where the new book is in the inventory but not counted.

It is for just such occasions that Clojure supplies us with refs. Setting up a ref is much like setting up an atom:

```
(ns inventory)

(def by-title (ref {}))

(def total-copies (ref 0))
```

As is getting at the values inside of a ref: it's still either @by-title or (deref total-copies). The difference between refs and atoms is that you can update a number of refs in a single database transactionlike operation. So now we can have our new book and count it too:

```
(defn add-book [{title :title :as book}]
  (dosync
    (alter by-title #(assoc % title book))
    (alter total-copies + (:copies book))))
```

As you can see, the ref-updating function is called alter and it uses the same *update with a function* style as swap!. The key difference between atoms and refs is that all calls to alter must happen within the body of a call to dosync. The changes inside of a dosync will either all happen together or not at all. Any intermediate states—in this case the book that's in the inventory but not counted—will not be visible to code outside of the dosync.

Refs share the same basic update and conflict-resolution strategies as atoms, only on a larger scale. The work of updating a ref happens on the thread that is trying to do the updating, and in the event of dueling updates, one of the competing calls to dosync will get reevaluated, perhaps more than once.

Agents

Returning to our book-inventory example, let's imagine that we have a new requirement: we need to notify the corporate inventory system of each change in the inventory. Happily, someone else has written a function called notify-inventory-change that takes care of all the notification details. We just need to call it at the right times.

So rolling back to our original, atom-based code, our first stab at this is to just add a call to notify-inventory-change in the inventory-update function:

```
(def by-title (atom {}))

(defn add-book [{title :title :as book}]
  (swap!
    by-title
    (fn [by-title-map]
      (notify-inventory-change :add book)
      (assoc by-title-map title book))))

;; Similar logic in del-book.
```

Life is good … until we start getting complaints from corporate about redundant notifications.

The problem is that we've forgotten one of the key aspects of atom update functions: they may get called several times in the course of resolving an update conflict. And that means that atom update functions are bad places for code that generates side effects, which is exactly what we're doing with notify-inventory-change. Since refs use the same *call it until there are no conflicts* update strategy, they are unlikely to be of any help here either.

What we need is the third Clojure mutable value container, the agent. Here's our original inventory manager—sans the notification—recast to use an agent:

```
(ns inventory)

(def by-title (agent {}))

(defn add-book [{title :title :as book}]
  (send
    by-title
    (fn [by-title-map]
      (assoc by-title-map title book))))

;; Similar logic in del-book.
```

Like atoms, agents are stand-alone value containers. And as with atoms and refs, you get at the value in an agent with an @ or deref.

On the surface, updating an agent is similar to updating an atom, except that the magic update function is called send. But it's the same *change via a function* pattern we see with atoms and refs.

Agents and atoms part company in *where* and especially *when* the update happens. While the atomic swap! is synchronous—once the call to swap! is done, you know that your atom has been updated—send is asynchronous. Behind the scenes every agent has a queue of functions associated with it. When you call send, your update function gets added to the end of the queue. Sometime later a background thread will pop your function off of the queue and execute it, updating the value in the agent in the process.

The very visible implication of the agent-update strategy is that send returns immediately after it puts the update function in the queue. Thus it's not only possible but likely that send will return before the update completes:

```
;; Queue up and add book request.

(add-book {:title "War and Peace" :copies 25})

;; At this point the agent may or may not have been updated.
```

The less visible—but critical—implication of the timing of agent updates is that the update function will get called exactly once, which is just what we need with our external inventory manager. So here is the agent-based add-book with the notification mixed back in:

```
(defn add-book [{title :title :as book}]
  (send
    by-title
    (fn [by-title-map]
      (notify-inventory-change :add book)
      (assoc by-title-map title book))))
```

And we have no more redundant notifications.

Choose Wisely

Sometimes—especially for the newly arrived Clojure programmer—it can be difficult to know which container to reach for in any given situation. After all, along with vars we now have atoms and refs and agents. It is an embarrassment of programming riches. Fortunately there are some straightforward guidelines that you can follow.

The first rule: If your value is mostly stable over the life of the program, perhaps with some thread-local variations, then put it in a var.

The second rule: If you have a number of mutable values that need to be updated together—and those updates *don't* involve side effects—then use refs. Remember, it's refs that give you that databaselike ability to build transactions.

The third rule: If there are side effects that need to happen as you update your mutable state, then use an agent. You should also consider using an agent if your update function is slow. That way you can foist the slowness off on the background thread that is updating the agent.

The last rule is simple: If you have a mutable value but your update function is side effect–free and you don't need to keep several values consistent, then use an atom. And rejoice, because atoms are by far the simplest of our mutable state trio. In fact, there is even more reason to rejoice because in most cases you *can* use atoms. Most of the time we don't need to coordinate changes with a ref or strictly serialize our updates with an agent. The bottom line is that if you are thinking about mutable state, your first thought should be an atom.

Do You Really Need That Ref?

 Since atoms are the easiest of the mutable value containers to work with, it's sometimes worth reshaping your code just so you can use an atom. In the example we used a ref to track the total number of books stored in our inventory, held by a second ref. Alternatively we could have created a single ubermap to hold both the count and our inventory and stored that in an atom. The choice comes down to a trade-off: the simplification of using an atom versus having separately updatable refs.

In the Wild

The Clojure language plugin for the LightTable text editor shows off a great example of using an atom to track some fairly complex data.[1] [2] In this case it's configuration data:

---

1. https://github.com/LightTable/Clojure
2. http://lighttable.com

```
;; Lots of code omitted.
(def my-settings (atom {:name "clj"
                         :dir (fs/absolute-path fs/*cwd*)
                         :type "lein-light-nrepl"
                         :commands [:editor.eval.clj
                                    :editor.clj.doc
                                    :editor.cljs.doc
                                    :editor.clj.hints

                                    ;; Many keywords omitted...

                                    :editor.eval.cljs
                                    :cljs.compile]}))
;; Lots of code omitted.

(defn settings! [setts]
  (swap! my-settings merge setts))
```

Here we start with an atom containing a map of program settings along with
a function that lets us merge new settings into the map. Anytime we need
one of the settings, we just have to remember to dereference the atom, perhaps
(:dir @my-settings).

While atoms are frequently bound in a top-level def, you can also create them
inside of functions. A wonderful example of this is lurking in the standard
Clojure function memoize. The purpose of memoize is to speed up your program
by caching the results of function calls. The memoize function takes an existing
function, perhaps this one:

```
(defn blurb [book]
  (str "Don't miss the exciting new book, "
       (:title book)
       " by "
       (:author book)))
```

and returns a new function:

```
(def memoized-blurb (memoize blurb))
```

You can now use the new—or memoized—function exactly as you would the
original. The first time you call the memoized function it will simply delegate
to the original. But it will also cache the result, so that if you happen to call
the memoized function with the same arguments a second—or fifty-
fourth—time, it will skip the original function and return the cached result:

```
(def emma {:title "Emma" :author "Austen"})

;; Only calls the blurb function once.
(memoized-blurb emma)
(memoized-blurb emma)
(memoized-blurb emma)
```

The memoize function is doing the classic trade-off of memory—all of those cached values—for speed—not having to make redundant calls to the original function. Of course, this all assumes that the original function is pure, that the result depends only on the values passed in. So memoizing a function that returns the current time is probably a bad idea.

Without knowing anything else about the internals of the function returned by memoize, we can deduce that it somehow has access to mutable state. After all, its behavior changes over time. Call the function once with some set of arguments, and it will call the wrapped function. Do the same thing again, and it will return the cached value. Somewhere, something changed during that first function call.

In fact, each function that is returned by memoize has its own private atom, an atom that contains a map of arguments to return values. When you call the memoized function it first consults the map to see if it has seen these arguments before. If it has, it returns the cached value. If not, it calls the original function, caches the new result in the map, and returns the result.

Here's the code for memoize, slightly reformatted:

```
(defn memoize
  "Returns a memoized version of a referentially
  transparent function. The memoized version of
  the function keeps a cache of the mapping from
  arguments to results and, when calls with the
  same arguments are repeated often, has
  higher performance at the expense of higher
  memory use."
  [f]
  (let [mem (atom {})]
    (fn [& args]
      (if-let [e (find @mem args)]
        (val e)
        (let [ret (apply f args)]
          (swap! mem assoc args ret)
          ret)))))
```

Taking this step by step, we see that the anonymous function returned by memoize starts—as predicted—with an atom containing an empty map. That's the (atom {}). When the anonymous function is called, it updates the value of the atom as needed. That's the call to swap! at the core of the function.

It's important to keep track of what is and isn't changing as the anonymous function is called. It's certainly not the function. It's also not the map: that's one of those solidly immutable Clojure maps. Instead it's the mutable value inside of the atom that changes, successively getting hold of bigger and bigger—but steadfastly immutable—maps.

You can find an interesting use of refs lurking inside the open source music system Overtone that we met back in Chapter 10, *Sequences*, on page 111. Overtone includes a software metronome, a virtual rendition of one of those *click Stay click On click The click Beat* machines so hated by 10-year-old piano students.

Here's the function that manufactures new metronomes:

```
(defn metronome
 [bpm]
 (let [start (ref (now))
       bar-start (ref @start)
       bpm   (ref bpm)
       bpb   (ref 4)]
   (Metronome. start bar-start bpm bpb)))
```

Notice all the calls to ref, which makes sense because as the software metronome is clicking away we want to carefully coordinate the time (start) it started with the number of clicks (or beats) per minute (bpm), among other things.

And here's a snippet of the code that changes the beats per minute:

```
(dosync
 (ensure bpb)
 (let [cur-beat      (metro-beat metro)
       cur-bar       (metro-bar metro)
       new-tick      (beat-ms 1 new-bpm)
       new-tock      (* @bpb new-tick)
       new-start     (- (metro-beat metro cur-beat) (* new-tick cur-beat))
       new-bar-start (- (metro-bar metro cur-bar) (* new-tock cur-bar))]
   (ref-set start new-start)
   (ref-set bar-start new-bar-start)
   (ref-set bpm new-bpm)))
```

This is a ref-oriented dosync with a couple of twists we haven't seen before. First, the ref updating is done with ref-set rather than alter. You can think of ref-set as a sort of shortcut that you can use to update a ref when the new value doesn't depend on the previous value, more or less synonymous with (alter ref (fn [_] new-value)).

The other new wrinkle is the use of (ensure bpb), which makes bpb part of the current update without altering its value. It ensures that no other dosync changes the value of bpb while the current dosync is executing.

You can also find an interesting use of agent lurking inside Overtone:

```
(def samples (load-samples "~/Desktop/tech/*.wav"))

(defn start-samples
  "Starts all samples playing at init-vol. Returns a seq containing info
  regarding all running samples. Samples start playing 1s after this
  fn is called to ensure that they are all started in sync"
  []
  (at (+ 1000 (now))
      (doall
       (reduce (fn [res samp]
                 (let [id (loop-synth samp 0)]
                   (conj res  {:ampl 0
                               :id id
                               :samp samp})))
               []
               samples))))


(def playing-samples* (agent (start-samples)))
```

Like our inventory notification example, the playing-samples* agent is there to perpetrate side effects. In this case the side effect is actual music coming out of real speakers. The *one update at a time* processing used by agents is just the thing to prevent you from playing Mozart over your hip-hop. Unless that's the effect you're looking for.

Staying Out of Trouble

Programmers new to Clojure sometimes get lost in expressions like this:

```
(def title-atom (atom "Pride and Prejudice"))
```

The thing to keep in mind is that this expression creates *two* value containers. The first is a var, which gets bound to the name title-atom. The value of that var is another container, an atom. And inside the atom we find the string "Pride and Prejudice".

If we swap! another value in, perhaps like this, the var doesn't change at all:

```
(swap! title-atom #(str % " and Zombies"))
```

It is still the same var, bound to the same name and pointing at the same atom. It's the value *inside the atom* that gains some zombies.

Another thing to keep in mind is what happens should an update function fail. The good news is that atoms and refs are easy. If something goes horribly wrong in the function you pass swap! or inside of a dosync, then the whole update fails and an exception gets thrown.

The story with agents, with their *off in another thread* update strategy, is more complex. If an agent update function fails, then that update has no effect on the value of the agent:

```
(def title-agent (agent "A Night to Remember"))

;; BOOM! You can't add 99 to a string!

(send title-agent + 99)
```

But you will not see the exception back from the send—after all, the exception happened later, on a different thread. The agent will enter a failed state and will immediately reject any further send calls by raising the *exception that caused the original failure*:

```
(send title-agent #(str % " Forever"))

;; ClassCastException java.lang.String cannot be cast to java.lang.Number
```

This is actually helpful behavior, but it can be confusing if you aren't expecting it.

Happily, you can check the state of your agent with agent-error and use restart-agent to get it back to normal:

```
;; If the agent is dead then restart it with a new value
;; and clear any pending updates.

(if (agent-error title-agent)
  (restart-agent
    title-agent
    "Poseidon Adventure"
    :clear-actions true))
```

Finally, there will probably come a time when you will wish that your agents—or at least the threads behind them—would just go away. One of the annoyances with using agents is that they rely on a behind-the-scenes thread pool managed by Clojure. And, as we saw in the last chapter, the JVM is finicky about terminating when there are live threads still around. Fortunately, Clojure provides you with the shutdown-agents function to shut down the agents in the agent thread pool, allowing your JVM to exit:

```
(defn -main []
  ;; Do some stuff with agents.

  ;; Shut down the threads that have been running the agent updates
  ;; so that the JVM will actually shut down.

  (shutdown-agents))
```

It's always a great idea to call shutdown-agents just before the end of any program that uses agents.

Wrapping Up

In this chapter we looked at Clojure's trio of state-management constructs: the atom, the ref, and the agent. We saw that the atoms, refs, and agents have a lot in common. Each one is just a mutable container for a value. Each lets you march from one value to the next by supplying a function—a function that takes the old value and produces the new one. But atoms, refs, and agents part company in the way they manage change. Atoms are simple, stand-alone containers that march from one value to the next, resolving any conflicts by reevaluating the update function. Refs are just like atoms, but can be updated in batches, inside of a dosync transaction. Agents are stand-alone, but queue up updates and execute them one at a time in a separate thread.

Next we're going to turn our attention back to Clojure itself, specifically to Clojure's syntax and how it got that way.

CHAPTER 19

Read and Eval

Programming-language syntax is a lot like politics: very few people do it for a living but virtually everyone has an opinion. And many have strong opinions. Certainly it's not hard to find strong opinions about Clojure's syntax. Many of us love what we see as its elegant terseness while some programmers can only see parentheses. Lots and lots of parentheses.

Clojure's somewhat odd syntax is not the shady outcome of a conspiracy of parentheses manufacturers. Nor is it a completely arbitrary esthetic choice. Clojure's syntax is an integral part of how the language works. So in this chapter we're going to look at the two critical functions at the heart of Clojure, read and eval, and at how they relate to all those parentheses. Along the way we'll take a moment to write our own version of eval, essentially building our very own toy Clojure implementation.

If all that sounds intimidating, take heart: like everything else in Clojure, read and eval are simple. They are also critical to getting to the next level of insight into how the language works. So let's get started.

You Got Data On My Code!

If you have read this far you probably noticed something odd about the syntax of Clojure code: it looks a lot like the syntax of Clojure data literals. If, for example, you started with this bit of nonsensical Clojure data:

read/examples.clj
```
;; Just some data: Note the quote.

'(helvetica times-roman [comic-sans]
  (futura gil-sans
    (courier "All the fonts I have loved!")))
```

you know you have a four-element list that contains a couple of symbols along with a vector and another list. But by swapping out the symbols and changing contents of the string, you can transform that data into something convincingly codelike:

```
;; Still just data -- note the quote.
'(defn print-greeting [preferred-customer]
  (if preferred-customer
    (println "Welcome back!")))
```

This last example is still just a four-element list of data—notice the quote at the front—but it's also a dead ringer for a Clojure function definition. You can, in fact, turn your data into actual code by removing the quote:

```
;; Now this is code!
(defn print-greeting [preferred-customer]
  (if preferred-customer
    (println "Welcome back!")))
```

This little journey from data to code underlines the fundamental idea of Clojure syntax: Clojure code looks like Clojure data because in Clojure code *is* data. Clojure uses the same syntax and data structures to represent both code and data. So Clojure function calls don't just look like lists; they *are* lists. The arguments to your function definitions don't get wrapped in things that look like vectors; they *are* vectors. Languages that support this sort of *code equals data* equation are said to be *homoiconic*.

Reading and Evaluating

To make all this theory a bit more real, let's dive into the machinery that Clojure uses to read data and execute code. Actually, calling it *machinery* is overstating things since we're talking about two functions, one mundane and one wonderful. The mundane function is read and it does exactly what its name suggests: it reads data. Feed read a character-producing input stream—perhaps an open file or a network connection or your terminal—and it will read and return one Clojure value. Conveniently, if you just call read without any parameters, it will read from standard input. So if you call (read) in the REPL like this:

```
user=> (read)
```

then read will sit there quietly, waiting for you to type something in. So enter 55, and read will return the number after 54. Alternatively, if you type in "hello", read will return a five-character string. And if you type in the following:

```
(defn print-greeting [preferred-customer]
  (if preferred-customer (println "Welcome back!")))
```

you will get a four-element list that looks suspiciously like a Clojure function definition but is nevertheless just some data.

Along with read, Clojure also comes equipped with read-string, a function that parses the characters in a string into a Clojure value. Thus we could get the same four-element list like this:

```clojure
;; A complicated string with some escaped quotes.

(def s
  "(defn print-greeting [preferred-customer]
     (if preferred-customer (println \"Welcome back!\")))")

;; A four-element list.

(read-string s)
```

Which brings us to the wonderful function, eval. If the read function's job is to turn characters into data structures, then it falls to eval to turn data structures into action:

```clojure
;; A three element list.
(def a-data-structure '(+ 2 2))

;; The number 4.

(eval a-data-structure)
```

The wonderful thing about eval is that it takes the data you pass in, which should look like Clojure code, and *compiles and runs it* as Clojure code:

```clojure
;; Bind some-data to a list

(def some-data
  '(defn print-greeting [preferred-customer]
    (if preferred-customer (println "Welcome back!"))))

;; At this point we have some-data defined,
;; but not the print-greeting function.
;; Now let's eval some-data...

(eval some-data)

;; And now print-greeting is defined!

(print-greeting true)
```

Essentially, eval attempts to evaluate whatever data you pass in *as Clojure code*. Sometimes that evaluation is trivial. Numbers, strings, and keywords just evaluate to themselves:

```clojure
(eval 55)      ; Returns the number after 54.
(eval :hello)  ; Returns the keyword :hello
(eval "hello") ; And a string.
```

But you can also have eval evaluate symbols or call functions:

```
(def title "For Whom the Bell Tolls")

;; Get hold of the unevaluated symbol 'title...

(def the-symbol 'title)

;; ...and evaluate it.

(eval the-symbol)

;; While a list gets evaluated as a function call.

(eval '(count title))
```

The key to understanding eval is not so much what it does—it *runs stuff as code*—as what it takes in: ordinary Clojure lists, vectors, keywords, and symbols. You can, for example, construct some code on the fly—using garden-variety Clojure functions like list and vector—and evaluate it with eval. So this is yet another way to define and then call print-greeting:

```
(def fn-name 'print-greeting)
(def args (vector 'preferred-customer))
(def the-println (list 'println "Welcome back!"))
(def body (list 'if 'preferred-customer the-println))

(eval (list 'defn fn-name args body))

(eval (list 'print-greeting true))
```

The Homoiconic Advantage

So there's our answer: Clojure's syntax is the way it is because it's amphibious, equally at home representing code and data. Having a single text format along with a single in-memory representation of both code and data is not just elegant; it also has some serious practical advantages. For example, writing Clojure code-analysis tools is very straightforward. Need to read a file full of Clojure code? No problem:

```
(ns codetool.core
  (:require [clojure.java.io :as io]))

(defn read-source [path]
  (with-open [r (java.io.PushbackReader. (io/reader path))]
    (loop [result []]
      (let [expr (read r false :eof)]
        (if (= expr :eof)
          result
          (recur (conj result expr)))))))
```

Call read-source with the path to a Clojure source file, and you will get back a sequence of all of the expressions in that file, parsed into the lists and vectors that you already know how to use.

If you look closely at read-source, you will see that at its center is a slightly more elaborate call to read: (read r false :eof). The extra arguments tell read to read from somewhere besides standard input (that's the r), and to return the keyword :eof when it hits the end of the file. But the truly remarkable thing about read-source is that most of it is devoted to the mundane tasks of opening the file and managing the results. The actual parsing of the Clojure source is all bundled up in that call to read.

Even more remarkable is that the combination of read and eval makes writing a REPL so easy that sooner or later every Clojure programmer gives it a go. Here's my shot at it:

```clojure
(defn russ-repl []
  (loop []
    (println (eval (read)))
    (recur)))
```

Just read an expression, evaluate it, print the result, and loop. Thanks mostly to eval, the REPL is the rare acronym that is nearly a program.

REPR?

Strictly speaking the loop in russ-repl is not necessary. Remove it and the recur will recursively call the function. It's there because the *L* in REPL demands it.

An Eval of Your Own

The wonderful thing about eval is that it's simultaneously a gateway to the entire Clojure programming language and a very ordinary function. That eval is just an ordinary function raises an interesting question: can we—as an intellectual exercise—implement our own version of eval?

Remarkably, we can. We've already seen that if you hand eval a string or a keyword or a number, you get the same string, keyword, or number back, unchanged. So here's a start on our own toy eval function:

```clojure
(defn reval [expr]
  (cond
    (string? expr) expr
    (keyword? expr) expr
    (number? expr) expr
    :else :completely-confused))
```

Note that the real eval throws an exception when you hand it something it doesn't understand, but to keep the example simple we'll return :completely confused.

We can make the confusion less likely by handling symbols and vectors and lists. These are all a bit more complex, so let's delegate them to separate functions:

```
(defn reval [expr]
  (cond
    (string? expr) expr
    (keyword? expr) expr
    (number? expr) expr
    (symbol? expr) (eval-symbol expr)
    (vector? expr) (eval-vector expr)
    (list? expr) (eval-list expr)
    :else :completely-confused))
```

Actually evaluating symbols isn't too difficult: just look them up in the current namespace:

```
(defn eval-symbol [expr]
  (.get (ns-resolve *ns* expr)))
```

Vectors are also straightforward. We just need to recursively evaluate the contents:

```
(defn eval-vector [expr]
  (vec (map reval expr)))
```

Things only get interesting when we evaluate lists. First we need to evaluate the contents of the list in exactly the same way that we did with vectors. Once we've done that we just need to call the function, which we do with apply:

```
(defn eval-list [expr]
  (let [evaled-items (map reval expr)
        f (first evaled-items)
        args (rest evaled-items)]
    (apply f args)))
```

We could go on, perhaps adding support for maps and if expressions and ns and so forth, but let's pause here and take stock.

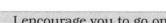

Go!

I encourage you to go on and see how much Clojure you can implement. There is nothing like building your own to get a clearer idea of how the real thing works.

The first thing to note about our excursion into programming-language implementation is that we're cheating. We're relying on all the glories that Clojure provides to implement a slow, partial subset of Clojure. What we get out of reval is not a practical programming language but *insight*—insight into how Clojure works—all courtesy of the homoiconic power of the language.

Second, it's important to keep in mind that since Clojure—real Clojure—is a compiled language, the details of the real eval are rather more complicated. Instead of saying, *Oh, this is a list. Treat it as a function call,* the real eval says, *Oh, this is a list. Generate some code to call the function and then run that code.*

Nevertheless, building toy versions of eval is so much fun and so illuminating that it has been a cottage industry among programmers using LISP-based languages for decades. Welcome to the club.

In the Wild

If you are interested in the ins and outs of implementing Clojure, you should definitely check out the MAL project.[1] MAL, short for *Make a Lisp*, defines a simple Clojure-like language and then proceeds to implement it in (as of this writing) 68 languages, everything from Ada to Visual Basic.

You can find a great example of the power of using plain old Clojure values for both code and data in metadata. Metadata is extra data that you can hang on Clojure symbols and collections, data that in some ways enhances your value without being an official part of the value.

There are two ways you can hang some metadata on a value. You can do it either explicitly with the with-meta function:

```
(def books1 (with-meta ["Emma" "1984"] {:favorite-books true}))
```

or by using the ^:keyword syntactical sugar:

```
(def books1 ^:favorite-books ["Emma" "1984"])
```

Having applied some metadata to your value, you can get it back with the meta function:

```
;; Gives you the {:favorite-books true} map.
(meta books1)
```

---

1. https://github.com/kanaka/mal

The key thing about metadata is that it is *extra* data: metadata doesn't affect the actual value. That means that two otherwise equal values are still equal even if they have different metadata:

```
;; Otherwise identical vectors with different metadata...
(def books2 (with-meta ["Emma" "1984"] {:favorite-books true}))
(def books3 (with-meta ["Emma" "1984"] {:favorite-books false}))
;; Are still equal.
(= books2 books3)    ; True!
```

If the metadata syntax looks familiar, it should. We already came across metadata when we were dealing with dynamic vars:

```
(def ^:dynamic *print-length* nil)
```

There are also less obvious uses of metadata. For example, when you define a function with a docstring, Clojure stashes the docstring of the function in the metadata of the symbol.

But don't take my word for it. Define a function with a docstring:

```
(defn add2
  "Return the sum of two numbers"
  [a b]
  (+ a b))
```

and then look at the metadata on the add2 var:

```
(meta #'add2)
```

You will see something like this:

```
{:doc "Return the sum of two numbers",
 :arglists ([a b]),
 :name add2,
 :ns #object[clojure.lang.Namespace 0xa55c011 "user"]
 :line 1
 :column 1
 ...
}
```

And there is the docstring, along with all sorts of useful information about our function, all stashed in the metadata.

Finally—and returning to the topic at hand—in exactly the same way that a function call is just a list and the parameters in a defn are just a vector, metadata is just a map. So if you pick up some metadata from a value:

```
(def md (meta books3))
```

you have a plain old map:

```
;; Do mapish things to the metadata
(count md) ; Returns 1
(vals md)  ; Returns (false)
```

Remember, Clojure code is just Clojure data, all the way down.

Staying Out of Trouble

Having introduced you to the eval function, let me now give you a critical bit of advice: *don't use it.* At least not for real, at least not now—not while you are just learning Clojure. The eval function is an incredibly useful tool to have lying around, but it's also something of a blunt instrument. Just how blunt? Think about the difference between writing this into your Clojure program:

```
(+ 1 1)
```

and this:

```
(eval '(+ 1 1))
```

The first, straightforward, bit of code adds two numbers together. If it's part of a Clojure application then it will get compiled once and it's the compiled version that will get fired off at runtime. The second rendition of the code will also get compiled once, but it's the call to eval, along with some data, that will get compiled. At runtime that call to eval will crank up the Clojure compiler *again*, this time to turn the list (+ 1 1) into something executable. And that will happen every time you want to add 1 and 1.

There are also some subtleties involved in using eval that will eventually rise up and bite you if you get too enthusiastic. To take just one example, since eval doesn't know about your local *generated by let* bindings, this:

```
(def x 1)

(let [x 10000000]
  (eval '(+ x 1)))
```

may not give you the result you are expecting.

In real life people tend to reserve eval for development tools like the REPL and for those rare moments when you need to programmatically generate and execute code. Reserve eval for those moments when you have no idea what runtime code you want to execute until some runtime data tells you. For the other 99.99 percent of the programming problems that you are likely to face, the ordinary tools of functional programming, together with macros—which we'll talk about in the next chapter—will suffice. And yes, we're now at the point where we can describe the amazing bag of tricks that is functional programming as *ordinary*.

Compared to eval, the read function is both less cool and more useful on an everyday basis. The main danger lurking inside of read is that under some circumstances it will execute arbitrary code as specified by the data you're reading. For example, try evaluating this:

```
(def s "#=(println \"All your bases...\")")
```

```
(read-string s)
```

The bottom line is that you only want to use read to read data that you trust. If you want to read some Clojure-style data from an untrusted source, use the read function from the clojure.edn namespace (the official name for the Clojure-style data format is EDN):

```
(require '[clojure.edn :as edn])
```

```
;; Read some data that I don't necessarily trust.
```

```
(def untrusted (edn/read))
```

And one final word on Clojure's syntax: as we've seen in this chapter, there is a method to the madness of Clojure's syntax. Yes, putting the function name on the inside—(rest some-seq)—looks a little strange. But at the cost of adapting to a slightly odd syntax, we get the ability to read and manipulate Clojure code as data and we get the seamless integrations of read and eval. And, as we'll see in the next chapter, we get macros.

If the Clojure syntax still bugs you, keep in mind programming-language syntax is largely a matter of taste. Nobody is born understanding what this means:

```
if (x == 0) {
  System.out.println("The number is zero");
}
```

Nor this:

```
if x == 0
  puts "The number is zero"
end
```

And certainly not this:

```
<?xml version="1.0" encoding="utf-8"?>
<books>
  <book>
    <name>Pride and Prejudice</name>
    <author>Austen</author>
  </book>
```

```
<book>
  <name>Death Comes to Pemberley</name>
  <author>James</author>
</book>
<book>
  <name>Pride and Prejudice and Zombies</name>
  <author>Grahame-Smith</author>
</book>
</books>
```

And yet we adapted. If Clojure's syntax is still giving you headaches, stick with it. It is an integral part of what makes the language go.

Wrapping Up

In this chapter we explored the ideas behind Clojure's somewhat odd but *it grows on you after a while* syntax. We saw how Clojure syntax is a bit odd because it's a compromise between being a good programming-language syntax and a good syntax for data. But that compromise pays off in a big way: by using the same syntax and data structures for code and data, we can roll the entire Clojure programming language into two simple functions: read and eval.

Now that you understand the ideas behind Clojure's syntax, it's time to turn to the final topic of this book: macros.

CHAPTER 20

Macros

We programmers both love and hate code. We love it because it's what we make. Line by painful line we labor over our keyboards, producing symbols and strings and numbers and—this being Clojure—parentheses, lots of parentheses. We hate code because the pain never stops. Every line of code needs to be debugged and tested and deployed and updated and recompiled and … well, you get it.

It's exactly because code is so painful that we try to have as little of it as we can—and why we try to keep it as concise and as expressive as we possibly can. Keeping code concise and expressive is a multilevel job. On the large scale, we struggle to find a solid design. At the medium scale, we try to pick data structures and an execution flow that make sense. And at the very smallest scale, we try to wrest the maximum coding mileage out of every expression and line.

In this chapter we're going to explore macros, a Clojure feature that can help with the smaller-scale struggles of writing expressive code. In the pages that follow we'll see how macros can automate some of your code-writing for you. We'll also explore how macros can go horribly wrong and why you should use them with more than the usual dose of caution.

There Are Three Kinds of Numbers in the World

Let's imagine we've come up with a simple rating system for books: you love a book, you hate it, or you're completely indifferent to it. To handle this, we decide to represent book ratings with integers: positive numbers for good ratings, negative numbers for bad ratings, and zero for a devastating *meh*.

Given this design, we might end up writing code that looks like this:

```
macro/examples.clj
(defn print-rating [rating]
  (cond
    (pos? rating)  (println "Good book!")
    (zero? rating) (println "Totally indifferent.")
    :else          (println "Run away!")))
```

Other than our use of pos? and zero? to pick out the numeric ranges, there is nothing very exciting going on here.

Now, if all we're talking about are a few cond expressions here and there, we're done. But what if variants of the book-rating cond started popping up throughout our system? What if you were spending a lot of time writing that same cond over and over? The thing for the astute—and fatigued—programmer to do is to factor out the common bits of that cond expression. The obvious thing to do is to write a function, which we'll call arithmetic-if:

```
(defn arithmetic-if [n pos zero neg]
  (cond
    (pos? n) pos
    (zero? n) zero
    (neg? n) neg))
```

At first blush all seems well. Have arithmetic-if return some keywords like this:

```
(arithmetic-if 0 :great :meh :boring)
```

And indeed you will get your expected :meh.

Arithmetic If

 The name *arithmetic if* is what this positive/zero/negative construct was called in FORTRAN. And if you like to think of programming as a modern activity, consider the arithmetic if first appeared in *1957*.

The trouble starts when we try something with side effects, like the println expressions we had in our original example:

```
(defn print-rating [rating]
  (arithmetic-if rating
    (println "Good book!")
    (println "Totally indifferent.")
    (println "Run away!")))

(print-rating 10)
```

Run this code and *all three* strings get printed:

```
"Good book!"
"Totally indifferent."
"Run away!"
```

Think for a second, and it makes sense: the rules of Clojure say that the first thing that happens when a function gets called is that the arguments get evaluated. *All* the arguments. That means that the second we tried to call arithmetic-if, Clojure evaluated not just the n parameter—which is fine—but also pos, zero, and neg—which is not so great. The rub is that Clojure does all this parameter evaluating *before* it evaluates the function body. This isn't just an issue with explicit side effects, either; what if one of the branches of your arithmetic-if perpetrated the very indirect side effect of taking a long time to compute?

One way to prevent all three branches of our arithmetic-if from getting evaluated is to have arithmetic-if take three *functions* as arguments—something like this:

```
(defn arithmetic-if [n pos-f zero-f neg-f]
  (cond
    (pos? n) (pos-f)
    (zero? n) (zero-f)
    (neg? n) (neg-f)))
```

With this version of arithmetic-if we would have to recast our rating-printing function to this:

```
(defn print-rating [rating]
  (arithmetic-if rating
    #(println "Good book!")
    #(println "Totally indifferent.")
    #(println "Run away!")))

(print-rating 10)
```

This would work, but it's odd—particularly if you are just trying to return some constants. What we really want is a clean version of arithmetic-if, one that doesn't require any function wrappers. Can we build that?

Macros to the Rescue

We can indeed, but to get it done we need to step back and forget about functions and argument evaluation for a second and think about what we're trying to do with arithmetic-if. What we really want to do is write something like this:

```
(arithmetic-if rating
  (println "Good book!")
  (println "Totally indifferent.")
  (println "Run away!"))
```

but execute something like this:

```
(cond
  (pos? rating)  (println "Good book!")
  (zero? rating) (println "Totally indifferent.")
  :else          (println "Run away!"))
```

Wouldn't it be great if we could somehow preprocess our Clojure code just before it gets compiled? We could take advantage of the preprocessing step to turn our arithmetic-if expression into the equivalent cond expression. And since—as we saw in the last chapter—Clojure code *is* just regular Clojure data, it should be easy to write a function to do the code transformation. In fact, here it is:

```
(defn arithmetic-if->cond [n pos zero neg]
  (list 'cond (list 'pos? n) pos
              (list 'zero? n) zero
              :else neg))
```

There's not really much to arithmetic-if->cond—it's just an ordinary function that uses some clever quoting to take its arguments and build a codelike list from them. If we feed arithmetic-if->cond the right data, making sure we quote all the symbols to prevent stray evaluation, like this:

```
(arithmetic-if->cond 'rating
  '(println "Good book!")
  '(println "Totally indifferent.")
  '(println "Run away!"))
```

we'll get back a list that looks just like the cond statement we're looking for:

```
(cond
  (pos? rating) (println "Good book!")
  (zero? rating) (println "Totally indifferent.")
  :else (println "Run away!"))
```

This is great, but it doesn't really help, because all we've done so far is to transform some codelike data into different codelike data. But it's all still just data. If only we had a way to insert arithmetic-if->cond into the Clojure compiler, so that it could transform our code just before it gets compiled, then we would be in business.

You've probably already guessed the punchline: macros let you do just that. Here is our transformation recast as a Clojure macro:

```
(defmacro arithmetic-if [n pos zero neg]
  (list 'cond (list 'pos? n) pos
              (list 'zero? n) zero
              :else neg))
```

Notice how arithmetic-if looks a lot like an ordinary function definition. In fact, as shown in the figure, macros *are* just functions, special only in that they are part of the compilation process.

So once we define the arithmetic-if macro, we can start using arithmetic-if in our code, confident that this:

```
(arithmetic-if rating :loved-it :meh :hated-it)
```

will get turned into this before it's compiled:

```
(cond (pos? rating) :loved-it (zero? rating) :meh :else :hated-it)
```

Are You a C Programmer?

If you are a C programmer, then this macro talk probably sounds familiar. Certainly Clojure's macros and C's macros are very closely related. Macros in Clojure do have the pleasant advantage that you write them in Clojure itself and, instead of dealing with program text, they work with Clojure data structures.

The thing to keep in mind about macros is that they are applied to the *code*, not to the runtime data.

For example, if we defined this simple macro:

```
(defmacro print-it [something]
  (list 'println "Something is" something))
```

and then called it like this:

```
(print-it (+ 10 20))
```

the argument passed to print-it would *not* be 30. Instead Clojure would pass the *list* (+ 10 20) to print-it, which means this is what would actually get compiled:

```
(println "Something is" (+ 10 20))
```

And *that*—when Clojure actually gets around to running it—would finally resolve to 30.

Easier Macros with Syntax Quoting

Let's return to our arithmetic-if macro:

```
(defmacro arithmetic-if [n pos zero neg]
  (list 'cond (list 'pos? n) pos
              (list 'zero? n) zero
              :else neg))
```

We're working pretty hard to produce that cond expression. After all, it's just some boilerplate code with a few custom values slotted in here and there. If this sounds like a familiar problem, it should. People who develop web applications frequently need to mix context-specific data—perhaps today's date or the current share price of Anacott Steel—into a skeleton of otherwise static HTML.

The solution in both situations is the same: use a *template*. You cook up the static bulk of your output as a sort of skeleton, which includes special markers that indicate *date here* and *share price there*. And when you have the date and share price, you jam them in the right spots and you have your finished HTML—or Clojure code.

Macro author, let me introduce you to the Clojure code templating system, *syntax quoting*. The good news is that syntax-quoted templates are just plain old Clojure data—vectors and lists and the like—with a few special tweaks. Tweak number one is that you set off syntax-quoted expressions with a backquote character, like this:

```
;; Notice the backquote character at the start.

`(:a :syntax "quoted" :list 1 2 3 4)
```

When applied to ordinary values as it is in the example, the syntax quote acts like a regular quote: it prevents the expression from being evaluated. So our first syntax-quoted expression is the same as this:

```
'(:a :syntax "quoted" :list 1 2 3 4)
```

Tweak number two is the *your value here* marker. Syntax quoting uses a ~ (tilde) character to mark the places where values should get inserted.

```
;; Set up some values.

(def n 100)
(def pos "It's positive!")
(def zero "It's zero!")
(def neg "It's negative")

;; And plug them in the cond.

`(cond
  (pos? ~n) ~pos
  (zero? ~n) ~zero
  :else ~neg)
```

Run this code, and you will get something that looks like a very respectable cond statement:

```
(cond
  (pos? 100) "It's positive!"
  (zero? 100) "It's zero!"
  :else "It's negative!")
```

Almost. One of the big issues with real-life macros is name confusion: is this pos? the one defined in the context where the macro was defined or is it the pos? defined in the context where the macro was called? To help minimize name confusion, syntax quoting outputs fully qualified symbols. So what you will really get out of the syntax-quoted expression in our example is this more verbose—but equivalent—version:

```
(clojure.core/cond
  (clojure.core/pos? 100) "It's positive!"
  (clojure.core/zero? 100) "It's zero!"
  :else "It's negative")
```

which is exactly what we need for arithmetic-if. Here's our macro redone with syntax quoting:

```
(defmacro arithmetic-if [n pos zero neg]
  `(cond
     (pos? ~n) ~pos
     (zero? ~n) ~zero
     :else ~neg))
```

It's so much clearer than the original:

```
(defmacro arithmetic-if [n pos zero neg]
  (list 'cond (list 'pos? n) pos
              (list 'zero? n) zero
              :else neg))
```

As I say, the syntax-quoted implementation produces exactly the same results as the original list-encrusted one. It's just easier to write—and read.

In the Wild

If it seems like macros might be one of those advanced programming features, something that you aren't likely to have a lot of contact with until you get really good at the language, well, no. Certainly, you can—and probably should—do a lot of Clojure programming without writing any macros. But there's no avoiding macros because much of the familiar core of Clojure is actually made of macros.

Here, for example, is a somewhat cut-down version of Clojure's own when:[1]

```clojure
(defmacro when
  [test & body]
  (list 'if test (cons 'do body)))
```

And here's the rather more complicated cond:

```clojure
(defmacro cond
  [& clauses]
    (when clauses
      (list 'if (first clauses)
            (if (next clauses)
                (second clauses)
                (throw (IllegalArgumentException.
                         "cond requires an even number of forms")))
            (cons 'clojure.core/cond (next (next clauses))))))
```

Even something as fundamental as and is implemented as a macro. Here again is a slightly simplified version:

```clojure
(defmacro and
  ([] true)
  ([x] x)
  ([x & next]
   `(let [and# ~x]
      (if and# (and ~@next) and#))))
```

Note that when and cond use our original *build the code by hand* technique, while and uses syntax quoting.

In fact, and uses a couple of features of syntax quoting we haven't seen yet. Note how the symbol bound in the let is called and#. This is another name-confusion-avoidance feature provided by syntax quoting. If you have a local symbol, perhaps a function parameter or a let bound symbol in a syntax-quoted expression, you need to add a # to the end of the symbol. The # is a signal to syntax quoting to replace your symbol with a generated, unique symbol—in and the generated symbol would be something like and__1330__auto__. Years of bitter macro-writing experience has shown that you need to watch out for local symbol name collisions.

You can spot the other syntax-quoting feature used by and in the form of the very odd-looking ~@next. To see what this is all about, let's take a shot at implementing a simplified version of defn. Our defn will take the function name, its argument vector, and any number of expressions to make up the body of the function. Here's our first cut:

---

1. https://github.com/clojure/clojure/blob/master/src/clj/clojure/core.clj

```
(defmacro our-defn [name args & body]
  `(def ~name (fn ~args ~body)))
```

It's simple, but unfortunately not quite right. The trouble is this expression:

```
(our-defn add2 [a b] (+ a b)))
```

gets expanded to something like this:

```
(def add2 (fn [a b] ((+ a b))))
```

Note the extra set of parentheses around the (+ a b). This does make sense. When we wrote ~body we asked to have the value of body—a collection—inserted right there, and that's exactly what we got, parentheses and all. But what we really want is to have the *contents* of body spliced into the expression, sans parentheses. And that's what ~@body will do. So here's our updated macro:

```
(defmacro our-defn [name args & body]
  `(def ~name (fn ~args ~@body)))
```

And now we can use it to define new functions:

```
(our-defn add2 [a b] (+ a b))

(add2 2 2)                 ; Give us 4!
```

And now we *know* that defn is just a mashup of def and fn.

Staying Out of Trouble

One thing should be clear: macros are hard to get right—much harder than plain functions. With an ordinary function you write the code and it gets executed. With a macro you write the code that writes the code that gets executed. Implicit in this two-step process is that macros make themselves felt at two distinct times. There's the moment when the macro is expanded—when it is writing the code—and then there's the moment when the generated code is executed. We can see that distinction here:

```
(defmacro mark-the-times []
  (println "This is code that runs when the macro is expanded.")
  `(println "This is the generated code."))

;; Expand the macro and you get the 1st println
;; but not the 2nd.

(defn use-the-macro []
  (mark-the-times))

;; Here we will get the second println, which is in the generated
;; code, twice.

(use-the-macro)
(use-the-macro)
```

In this example, Clojure will evaluate the first println exactly once, when the macro is expanded inside of use-the-macro. The second println—which is part of the generated code—will go off whenever you call the use-the-macro function.

While macros do make themselves felt at runtime—after all, they generate code—in a very real sense macros do not exist at all at runtime. Once it's expanded, there is only the expanded code: the macro itself fades from the scene. For example, if you wrote this pathological expression you should definitely expect to see a stack trace:

```
(arithmetic-if 1
  (/ 1 0)
  (/ 0 0)
  (/ -1 0))
```

What you should not expect to see is any mention of arithmetic-if in that stack trace. By the time the divide-by-zero exception happens, it's not arithmetic-if that is being executed, but rather the cond that arithmetic-if is expanded into. Macros are the Cheshire Cats of Clojure: all they leave behind is some code.

One handy tool in figuring out why your macro is doing what it is doing is macroexpand-1. Feed a prospective macro-containing expression into macroexpand-1 and you will get the code with the macro expanded. So do this:

```
(macroexpand-1 '(arithmetic-if 100 :pos :zero :neg))
```

and you will see something like this:

```
(cond (pos? 100) :pos (zero? 100) :zero :else :neg)
```

The macroexpand-1 function should be the first thing you reach for when your macros are misbehaving.

Another issue with macros is that, since they run at (or more accurately, just before) compile time, they form their own little world, separate from ordinary functions that execute at runtime. This means that you can't pass the name of a macro into any of those wonderful higher-order functions. Imagine, for example, you wrote a macro called describe-it, a macro that described its argument:

```
(defmacro describe-it [it]
  `(let [value# ~it]
     (cond
       (list? value#) :a-list
       (vector? value#) :a-vector
       (number? value#) :a-number
       :else :no-idea)))
```

The describe-it macro works fine when you use it directly, so that (describe-it 37) would indeed evaluate to :a-number. But if you try to use describe-it with the map function:

```
(map describe-it [10 "a string" [1 2 3]])
```

you are in for an unpleasant surprise:

```
CompilerException java.lang.RuntimeException:
Can't take value of a macro: #'user/describe-it...
```

Clojure has noticed that you are trying to use a macro—which it knows is meant to *transform code*—as an ordinary data-slinging function, and has cut you off before you hurt yourself.

The solution is simple. There is no reason why describe-it should be written as a macro:

```
(defn describe-it [it]
  (cond
    (list? it) :a-list
    (vector? it) :a-vector
    (number? it) :a-number
    :default :no-idea))
```

And this is an important lesson: if you can solve the problem concisely with ordinary functions, do that. If you find yourself—as we did with arithmetic-if—at odds with Clojure's evaluation rules or if you are writing a lot of repetitive code, then perhaps a macro is the way to go. If you find yourself in one of those excruciatingly rare situations where you need to turn data directly into code, then perhaps turn to eval.

Wrapping Up

If the power of functional programming, immutable data structures, and a concise syntax make up Clojure's first three lines of defense against spaghetti code and the maintenance horrors that go with it, then macros are the fourth. Macros give you the ability to transform your code as it gets read in but before it gets compiled. Macros mean that when you are writing Clojure you never have to spew out reams of boilerplate code. If you find yourself writing more or less the same bit of code over and over, you can roll it up in a macro.

CHAPTER 21

Conclusion

It's been a long journey from that original hello-world function through sequences and syntax, maps, atoms, and agents, to finally arrive at eval and macros. Together we've def'ed and defn'ed, recurred, reduced, and assoc'ed. We've defined protocols and record types. We've laughed and cried and written macros. And cried a little more.

Every step of the way we've seen how Clojure combines simplicity with ferocious power. We've seen how Clojure's immutable data structures keep your code—and especially your multithreaded code—from undermining its own foundation. We've explored how the functional nature of the language means that you can build programs that can attack real-world problems while remaining concise and flexible. We've seen how namespaces give you a simple way to organize your code and how sequences put a uniform face on a menagerie of collection types. And we've experienced how it's all expressed in a clean, minimalistic syntax.

As I said when we started out, I can't teach you Clojure. I can only be your guide. You have to make the journey yourself. But as you read the last chapter of this book, know that you are well on your way: you have become part of the Clojure community. So let me leave you with one final thought. Like everything technological, Clojure is an artifact, something that was built, a tool that you can learn and use. But like everything technological, Clojure is also a starting point, a place where you can begin the journey to the next thing. It's up to the community of Clojure programmers—which now includes you—to push on.

Index

Thank you!

How did you enjoy this book? Please let us know. Take a moment and email us at support@pragprog.com with your feedback. Tell us your story and you could win free ebooks. Please use the subject line "Book Feedback."

Ready for your next great Pragmatic Bookshelf book? Come on over to https://pragprog.com and use the coupon code BUYANOTHER2018 to save 30% on your next ebook.

Void where prohibited, restricted, or otherwise unwelcome. Do not use ebooks near water. If rash persists, see a doctor. Doesn't apply to *The Pragmatic Programmer* ebook because it's older than the Pragmatic Bookshelf itself. Side effects may include increased knowledge and skill, increased marketability, and deep satisfaction. Increase dosage regularly.

And thank you for your continued support,

Andy Hunt, Publisher

More on Clojure

Dig in for more on the language itself and better web development in Clojure.

Programming Clojure, Third Edition

Drowning in unnecessary complexity, unmanaged state, and tangles of spaghetti code? In the best tradition of Lisp, Clojure gets out of your way so you can focus on expressing simple solutions to hard problems. Clojure cuts through complexity by providing a set of composable tools—immutable data, functions, macros, and the interactive REPL. Written by members of the Clojure core team, this book is the essential, definitive guide to Clojure. This new edition includes information on all the newest features of Clojure, such as transducers and specs.

Alex Miller with Stuart Halloway and Aaron Bedra
(302 pages) ISBN: 9781680502466. $49.95
https://pragprog.com/book/shcloj3

Web Development with Clojure, Second Edition

Modern web applications deserve modern tools. Harness the JVM's rich infrastructure while taking advantage of the expressive power and brisk performance of a modern functional language. Exploit Clojure's unique advantages for web development. Step by step, apply the fundamentals of programming in Clojure to build real-world, professional web applications. This edition features new libraries, tools, and best practices, and focuses on developing modern single-page applications.

Dmitri Sotnikov
(306 pages) ISBN: 9781680500820. $36
https://pragprog.com/book/dswdcloj2

Better by Design

From architecture and design to deployment in the harsh realities of the real world, make your software better by design.

Design It!

Don't engineer by coincidence—design it like you mean it! Grounded by fundamentals and filled with practical design methods, this is the perfect introduction to software architecture for programmers who are ready to grow their design skills. Ask the right stakeholders the right questions, explore design options, share your design decisions, and facilitate collaborative workshops that are fast, effective, and fun. Become a better programmer, leader, and designer. Use your new skills to lead your team in implementing software with the right capabilities—and develop awesome software!

Michael Keeling
(358 pages) ISBN: 9781680502091. $41.95
https://pragprog.com/book/mkdsa

Release It! Second Edition

A single dramatic software failure can cost a company millions of dollars—but can be avoided with simple changes to design and architecture. This new edition of the best-selling industry standard shows you how to create systems that run longer, with fewer failures, and recover better when bad things happen. New coverage includes DevOps, microservices, and cloud-native architecture. Stability antipatterns have grown to include systemic problems in large-scale systems. This is a must-have pragmatic guide to engineering for production systems.

Michael Nygard
(376 pages) ISBN: 9781680502398. $47.95
https://pragprog.com/book/mnee2

Long Live the Command Line!

Use tmux and Vim for incredible mouse-free productivity.

tmux 2

Your mouse is slowing you down. The time you spend context switching between your editor and your consoles eats away at your productivity. Take control of your environment with tmux, a terminal multiplexer that you can tailor to your workflow. With this updated second edition for tmux 2.3, you'll customize, script, and leverage tmux's unique abilities to craft a productive terminal environment that lets you keep your fingers on your keyboard's home row.

Brian P. Hogan
(102 pages) ISBN: 9781680502213. $21.95
https://pragprog.com/book/bhtmux2

Modern Vim

Turn Vim into a full-blown development environment using Vim 8's new features and this sequel to the beloved bestseller *Practical Vim*. Integrate your editor with tools for building, testing, linting, indexing, and searching your codebase. Discover the future of Vim with Neovim: a fork of Vim that includes a built-in terminal emulator that will transform your workflow. Whether you choose to switch to Neovim or stick with Vim 8, you'll be a better developer.

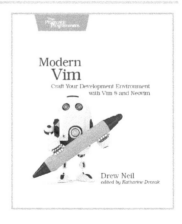

Drew Neil
(166 pages) ISBN: 9781680502626. $39.95
https://pragprog.com/book/modvim

Secure JavaScript and Web Testing

Secure your Node applications and see how to really test on the web.

Secure Your Node.js Web Application

Cyber-criminals have your web applications in their crosshairs. They search for and exploit common security mistakes in your web application to steal user data. Learn how you can secure your Node.js applications, database and web server to avoid these security holes. Discover the primary attack vectors against web applications, and implement security best practices and effective countermeasures. Coding securely will make you a stronger web developer and analyst, and you'll protect your users.

Karl Düüna
(230 pages) ISBN: 9781680500851. $36
https://pragprog.com/book/kdnodesec

The Way of the Web Tester

This book is for everyone who needs to test the web. As a tester, you'll automate your tests. As a developer, you'll build more robust solutions. And as a team, you'll gain a vocabulary and a means to coordinate how to write and organize automated tests for the web. Follow the testing pyramid and level up your skills in user interface testing, integration testing, and unit testing. Your new skills will free you up to do other, more important things while letting the computer do the one thing it's really good at: quickly running thousands of repetitive tasks.

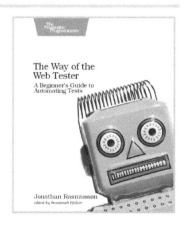

Jonathan Rasmusson
(256 pages) ISBN: 9781680501834. $29
https://pragprog.com/book/jrtest

The Pragmatic Bookshelf

The Pragmatic Bookshelf features books written by developers for developers. The titles continue the well-known Pragmatic Programmer style and continue to garner awards and rave reviews. As development gets more and more difficult, the Pragmatic Programmers will be there with more titles and products to help you stay on top of your game.

Visit Us Online

This Book's Home Page
https://pragprog.com/book/roclojure
Source code from this book, errata, and other resources. Come give us feedback, too!

Keep Up to Date
https://pragprog.com
Join our announcement mailing list (low volume) or follow us on twitter @pragprog for new titles, sales, coupons, hot tips, and more.

New and Noteworthy
https://pragprog.com/news
Check out the latest pragmatic developments, new titles and other offerings.

Save on the eBook

Save on the eBook versions of this title. Owning the paper version of this book entitles you to purchase the electronic versions at a terrific discount.

PDFs are great for carrying around on your laptop—they are hyperlinked, have color, and are fully searchable. Most titles are also available for the iPhone and iPod touch, Amazon Kindle, and other popular e-book readers.

Buy now at *https://pragprog.com/coupon*

Contact Us

Online Orders:	*https://pragprog.com/catalog*
Customer Service:	*support@pragprog.com*
International Rights:	*translations@pragprog.com*
Academic Use:	*academic@pragprog.com*
Write for Us:	*http://write-for-us.pragprog.com*
Or Call:	+1 800-699-7764

Milton Keynes UK
Ingram Content Group UK Ltd.
UKHW031133311023
431596UK00002B/16